A NEW KIND

"The War on Te

VIBS

Volume 201

Robert Ginsberg
Founding Editor

Leonidas Donskis
Executive Editor

Associate Editors

G. John M. Abbarno
George Allan
Gerhold K. Becker
Raymond Angelo Belliotti
Kenneth A. Bryson
C. Stephen Byrum
Harvey Cormier
Robert A. Delfino
Rem B. Edwards
Malcolm D. Evans
Daniel B. Gallagher
Andrew Fitz-Gibbon
Francesc Forn i Argimon
William Gay
Dane R. Gordon
J. Everet Green
Heta Aleksandra Gylling
Matti Häyry

Steven V. Hicks
Richard T. Hull
Michael Krausz
Mark Letteri
Vincent L. Luizzi
Adrianne McEvoy
Alan Milchman
Peter A. Redpath
Alan Rosenberg
Arleen L. F. Salles
John R. Shook
Eddy Souffrant
Tuija Takala
Emil Višňovský
Anne Waters
John R. Welch
Thomas Woods

a volume in
Philosophy of Peace
POP
William Gay, Editor

A NEW KIND OF CONTAINMENT
"The War on Terror," Race, and Sexuality

Edited by
Carmen R. Lugo-Lugo
and Mary K. Bloodsworth-Lugo

Amsterdam - New York, NY 2009

Cover photo: ©Dawn M. Turner

Cover Design: Studio Pollmann

The paper on which this book is printed meets the requirements of "ISO 9706:1994, Information and documentation - Paper for documents - Requirements for permanence".

ISBN: 978-90-420-2523-3
©Editions Rodopi B.V., Amsterdam - New York, NY 2009
Printed in the Netherlands

Philosophy of Peace
(POP)

William C. Gay
Editor

Other Titles in POP

Laurence F. Bove and Laura Duhan Kaplan, eds. *From the Eye of the Storm: Regional Conflicts and the Philosophy of Peace.* 1995. VIBS 29

Laura Duhan Kaplan and Laurence F. Bove, eds. *Philosophical Perspectives on Power and Domination: Theories and Practices.* 1997. VIBS 49

HPP (Hennie) Lötter. *Injustice, Violence, and Peace: The Case of South Africa.* 1997. VIBS 56

Deane Curtin and Robert Litke, eds. *Institutional Violence.* 1999. VIBS 88

Judith Presler and Sally J. Scholz, eds. *Peacemaking: Lessons from the Past, Visions for the Future.* 2000. VIBS 105

Alison Bailey and Paula J. Smithka, eds. *Community, Diversity, and Difference: Implications for Peace.* 2002. VIBS 127

Nancy Nyquist Potter, ed. *Putting Peace into Practice: Evaluating Policy on Local and Global Levels.* 2004. VIBS 164

John Kultgen and Mary Lenzi, eds. *Problems for Democracy.* 2006. VIBS 181

David Boersema and Katy Gray Brown, eds. *Spiritual and Political Dimensions of Nonviolence and Peace.* 2006. VIBS 182

Gail Presbey, ed., *Philosophical Perspectives on the "War on Terrorism.* 2007. VIBS 188

Danielle Poe and Eddy Souffrant, eds., *Parceling the Globe: Explorations in Globalization, Global Behavior, and Peace.* 2008. VIBS 194

Assistant Editor of POP
Joseph C. Kunkel

This is for the ones who stand their ground.
When the lines in the sand get deeper,
When the whole world seems to be upside down
and (the) shots being taken get cheaper.

Mary Chapin Carpenter
On with the Song

CONTENTS

PREFACE　　　　　　　　　　　　　　　　　　　　　　　　　　　xi

INTRODUCTION　　　　　　　　　　　　　　　　　　　　　　　　　1
　　　　　　　MARY K. BLOODSWORTH-LUGO AND
　　　　　　　CARMEN R. LUGO-LUGO

ONE　　　　　"The War on Terror" and Same-Sex Marriage: United
　　　　　　　States Discourse and the Shaping of Public Opinion　　9
　　　　　　　MARY K. BLOODSWORTH-LUGO AND
　　　　　　　CARMEN R. LUGO-LUGO

TWO　　　　　Political Use of the "War on Terror" to Augment Domestic
　　　　　　　and International LGBT Repression　　　　　　　　　29
　　　　　　　WILLIAM C. GAY

THREE　　　　Fear and Negation in the American Racial Imaginary: Black
　　　　　　　Masculinity in the Wars on Terror and Same-Sex Marriage　39
　　　　　　　LISA GUERRERO

FOUR　　　　　Gray Zones　　　　　　　　　　　　　　　　　　　51
　　　　　　　JOHN STREAMAS

FIVE　　　　　Defending Civilization from the Hostiles: Ward Churchill,
　　　　　　　Cultural Wars (on Terror), and the Silencing of Dissent　　65
　　　　　　　C. RICHARD KING

SIX　　　　　　United We Stay . . . Home: Reading the Racialized *Bildung*
　　　　　　　of United States' Children in Post-11 September 2001
　　　　　　　Comfort Books　　　　　　　　　　　　　　　　　75
　　　　　　　KYOO LEE

SEVEN　　　　George W. Bush's Burden: Containing the "New World
　　　　　　　(Dis)Order"　　　　　　　　　　　　　　　　　　89
　　　　　　　TRACEY NICHOLLS

EIGHT　　　　Bordering on the Absurd: National, Civilizational, and
　　　　　　　Environmental Security Discourse on Immigration　　103
　　　　　　　JESSICA LEANN URBAN

NINE	Soldiering "Green Card" Immigrants: Containing United States Citizenship JOCELYN A. PACLEB	135
TEN	The Bracero, The Wetback, and the Terrorist: Mexican Immigration, Legislation, and National Security LUZ MARÍA GORDILLO	149
WORKS CITED		167
ABOUT THE AUTHORS		185
INDEX		189

PREFACE

This collection chronicles aspects of living in the United States in the post-11 September 2001 era. The contributions provide clues about continuities and discontinuities in the historical timeline of the country, and the "mental state" of its society. Whether we continue to live embedded in this state or alter the course and seek new ways of looking at the world is contingent upon understanding the sorts of intricacies explored here.

We assembled this volume based on our interest in and concern with post-September 11 2001 modes of containment employed by the United States, especially during the George W. Bush administration. If we view containment as a process of imposing order on that which we perceive as a threat, we can see that presumed threats require imposed boundaries and that those boundaries help to define the threats themselves. Threats do not necessarily preexist modes of containing but are constructed as a result of those efforts.

The aim of this volume is to consider how acts of self-protection (or security) place boundaries around the self (or nation), thereby working to define the self in contrast to the other and to contain the other as a necessary component of self-protection.

Authors of several of the chapters originally presented versions of them at conferences and colloquia. Versions of Chapter Three and Chapter Four were presented on a panel organized by Mary Bloodsworth-Lugo and moderated by Carmen Lugo-Lugo entitled, "Brown, Gray, and Black: Color Coding a New Containment and the War on Terror," at the Pacific Northwest American Studies Association conference in Walla Walla, Washington, 2008.

Versions of Chapter One and Chapter Five were presented on a panel organized by Mary Bloodsworth-Lugo entitled, "New Forms of Containment," at the Society for Phenomenology and Existential Philosophy annual meeting in Philadelphia, Pennsylvania, 2006. A version of Chapter One was also presented for the University of Idaho and Washington State University Philosophy Colloquium at Washington State University in Pullman, Washington, 2005.

A version of Chapter Two was presented at a session of the Central Division of the American Philosophical Association conference for the Society for Lesbian and Gay Philosophy and the APA Committee on the Status of Lesbian, Gay, Bisexual, and Transgender Persons in the Profession in Chicago, Illinois, 2006.

A version of Chapter Nine was presented at the Southwest Labor Studies Association meeting at California State Polytechnic University, Pomona, California, 2008. Finally, version of Chapter Ten was presented at the History Department Faculty Colloquium at Washington State University in Pullman, Washington, 2006.

The authors wish to thank commentators and session participants for helpful remarks that contributed to revisions of these papers for inclusion in this volume.

The editors would like to thank the authors for their timely and pertinent contributions to the volume. We are also grateful to William C. Gay, Philosophy of Peace Special Series editor, and Rodopi Press for the opportunity to have this project published. Finally, we would like to acknowledge the contributions of Elizabeth D. Boepple who edited, formatted, and indexed the volume. The volume is undoubtedly a much better collection given to benefit of her expertise.

Mary K. Bloodsworth-Lugo, Assoc. Prof.
Comparative Ethnic Studies
Washington State University

Carmen R. Lugo-Lugo, Asst. Prof.
Comparative Ethnic Studies
Washington State University

INTRODUCTION

Mary K. Bloodsworth-Lugo
Carmen R. Lugo-Lugo

The motivation for the current volume is the recognition that the events of 11 September 2001 within the United States prompted new efforts at "containment." These efforts have (re)activated a set of dichotomous constructions: "us"-"them," "American"-"un-American," "safety"-"threat." Actors within the United States (state and federal governments, the George W. Bush administration, the United States military, the media, and the public) have racialized and sexualized bodies by constructing them as threats, and as un-or anti-American, and have sought to contain them. These actors have racialized "terrorists," "enemy combatants," and "illegal immigrants," presenting them as threats to the security of the nation, and put forward a variety of means by which to restrain them (for example, by placing them in prison camps or behind fences). Similarly, actors have presented same-sex couples as posing a threat to the nation and to civilization itself, and enacted amendments to state constitutions banning same-sex marriage as a means to subdue them.

Efforts at containment have occurred domestically and globally. This volume contributes to the subject of containment as it relates to interlocking discourses around the "War on Terror" as a global effort and its link to race and sexuality within the United States. Employing a transdisciplinary approach, these contributions address how containment has unfolded in racialized and sexualized ways in the context of post-11 September 2001 United States.

The authors examine these new efforts at containment in multiple arenas: state policies, military occupation, state discourse, rhetoric around the War on Terror, constructions of citizenship, articulations of homosexuality, prisoner abuse, detention, border security and control, constructions of "the other," and other national projects. While we highlight what is "new" with present forms of containment, we also analyze what historical strategies and techniques might be present within contemporary manifestations.

This collection addresses responses by the American public to the events of 11 September 2001 and examines ways in which those responses have been informed by governmental practices, including discursive efforts. The volume broadens how we might consider some common topics. For example, we usually associate the theme of containment with the Cold War era, and the War on Terror as a strictly military operation, while race and sexuality within the United States have usually been studied in isolation from events outside of the United States.

In Chapter One, "'The War on Terror' and Same-Sex Marriage: United States Discourse and the Shaping of Public Opinion," we begin a discussion of containment by presenting evidence of organized administrative efforts surrounding the War on Terror abroad and those surrounding lesbian and gay bodies at home. To do so, we examine the years 2003 and 2004, the first presidential election year after 11 September 2001. We argue that new efforts at containment are primarily aimed at firming up the categories of the American and the un-American. We relate strategies for demarcating "Americanness" to particular conceptions of terrorist bodies. We demonstrate that during 2003, we witnessed a concerted effort to protect "America" by identifying and containing "un-American" bodies.

Through this effort, actors within the United States conflated lesbian and gay bodies with terrorist bodies, and rendered lesbian and gay bodies (like other "terrorist" bodies) in need of strict containment. During 2004, this merger of issues, in addition to providing a well-administered discourse against same-sex marriage, offered Americans an agenda for action (in the form of voting).

We draw a parallel between discursive constructions of terrorism abroad and discursive constructions of same-sex marriage within the United States to demonstrate both as articulated threats to the security of the Nation. In this sense, same-sex marriage represents a threat that is discursively equivalent to the threat of international terrorism. Consequently, we are not surprised by claims that voters re-elected President Bush based on two primary concerns— the War on Terror and "moral values." Instead of viewing the War on Terror and moral values (of which same-sex marriage is a conceived part) as two separate factors, we suggest that presidential and popular discourse has broadened the definition of terrorism in the United States to place same-sex marriages on a par with international threats.

William C. Gay's, "Political Use of 'the War on Terrorism' to Augment Domestic and International LGBT Repression," Chapter Two, explores ways in which the War on Terror has included "the terror of war." Whenever war occurs, Gay points out, terror occurs. Gay argues that since 2001, the War on Terror has largely removed strong protests against human rights abuses from the United States national agenda.

One group that has become especially vulnerable in this predicament is the global lesbian, gay, bisexual, and transgender (LGBT) community. Gay attributes the unquestioned reality of the War on Terror as fostering an extensive fear and apprehension within the LGBT community about speaking against the war or "coming out" in many parts of the world. Gay contends that in its quest for allies, the United States overlooks human rights violations, considering silence on human rights abuses a small price to pay for preserving an ally. The post-11 September 2001 neglect of defending human rights has offered a chilling political discourse, which constantly invokes the threat of terrorism and offers a glimpse into some of the most violent ways of containing the "other."

Since 11 September 2001, many people, especially in the United States, have come to regard terrorism as representing the gravest security issue. Some are willing to permit the government to go to any lengths to reduce this threat. The United States government utilizes fear for political purposes—to motivate the public to accept counter terrorism measures, such as military actions and domestic surveillance (which can be cast as "self-containment"), as necessary and justified. Gay suggests that just as we are being myopic when we focus primarily on crime in the streets when confronting the problem of human violence, we are being hyperopic when we focus predominantly on the threats of global terrorism when confronting the problems of large-scale violence of war and the attendant human rights abuses.

In Chapter Three, "Fear and Negation in the American Racial Imaginary: Black Masculinity in the Wars on Terror and Same-Sex Marriage," Lisa Guerrero argues that the battles over the War on Terror and same-sex marriage in the United States have become intertwined. Simplistic and hegemonic social and political rhetoric of threat and transgression to the "American way" of life have emerged in the public sphere to create and maintain a culture of containment in a post-11 September 2001 nation. One of the ways in which the two ostensibly unrelated contemporary debates converge is in the strategic constructions of a racial imaginary that the American public can use to offset what is, in reality, an amorphous climate of fear and loathing. Guerrero indicates that "threat" is centered in the bodies of men of color and white gay men, respectively. She suggests that the inscription of threat onto these two groups of male bodies has become naturalized in the minds of the American people and the policies of American leaders since 2001.

However, Guerrero notes that we will benefit from examining this circumstance more closely to reveal what becomes of the black body—socially, politically, and ideologically—when it is reified as threat in one debate (that involving the War on Terror) and wholly erased in the other (that concerning same-sex marriage). Within the processes of reification and erasure, the black male body is contained. Guerrero examines the complex role that objectified blackness and otherness, especially the body of the black, male, other is playing in the contemporary American wars of containment being waged on terror and same-sex marriage. She connects the historical representation of the black body within the United States and its deployment within the current War on Terror to Cornel West's notion of "the niggerization of America since 9/11." It dictates 21st century racial formations, the "whitening" of representations of gayness in the United States, and the destructive denial of the black community within the United States toward black gays.

In Chapter Four, "Gray Zones," John Streamas notes that Seymour Hersh titled his 2004 *New Yorker* report on the abuses of prisoners at the Abu Ghraib prison camp in Iraq, "The Gray Zone." Streamas points out that the prisoner-abuse scandal arose not because of secret and unknowable gray zones but because of clear violations of international laws. These violations occupy a world that, even in secret intelligence parlance, interprets events as "black or white" (and in which the traditional dichotomy is reversed, with operatives regarding the "black" world as private, friendly, and containable, with the "white" as hostile, public, and in need of containment). Streamas conveys that the lexicon of politics and culture is sometimes more colored than the politics and culture. For example, in the manual for Adobe's Photoshop program is a section called "Editing a mask," which instructs users on the editing of images: "[erase] black or gray flecks . . . by painting with white." In digital imaging, "grayscale" refers to a range of shades of gray in a digital image comprised of pixels, subject to atomizing. The effect of such digital editing is to locate and flatten deviations. To locate them first is to highlight, or to render them public. To flatten is to assimilate them. Hersh's anonymous Pentagon source, referring to intelligence agents, says that these "black guys" are "vaccinated from the reality." Streamas examines this lexicon of color in the current political and cultural realms, paying particular attention to the reversal and flattening of deviation and difference. In a world of gray zones, Streamas argues, racial and sexual deviations are flattened and pushed behind "very clear red lines"— borders are constructed and policed; they act to contain. Even if the War on Terror did not originate this lexicon of politicized colors, still it has enforced it more brutally than previous political and cultural regimes had. Restoring the contours of difference may well involve redefining our colors.

In Chapter Five, "Protecting Civilization from the Hostiles: Ward Churchill, Cultural Wars (on Terror), and the Silencing of Dissent," C. Richard King illustrates that shortly after the initiation of the Second Gulf War, an open letter to the people of Iraq encouraged the formation of a Bureau of Iraqi Affairs. The letter circulated widely on the Internet and juxtaposed the invasion of Iraq with the condition of Native Americans. King indicates that military leaders quickly reiterated a preferred American imperial idiom, Indian Country, to reframe Iraq. This framing reinscribed Iraq and the insurgency in terms of the racial policing of the insecure and hostile frontiers, relying upon subdued visions of hostile "Indians."

Within the United States, King relays, public outcry emerged over a polemic, "'Some People Push Back': On the Justice of Roosting Chickens," written by activist and scholar, Ward Churchill (who claims to be of Cherokee and Creek descent). The essay, written in the immediate aftermath of the attack on the World Trade Center, originally went unnoticed and provoked little outrage. More than two years later, on the eve of Churchill's scheduled appearance at Hamilton College, an angry alumnus expressed his unhappiness to the administration and alerted the media. Almost instantaneously, Churchill became the target of charges of un-American activities. The subsequent media firestorm attacked Churchill as a radical intellectual, hostile, divisive, and dangerous. Politicians and pundits called for his firing from his tenured position in Ethnic studies at the University of Colorado and questioned the quality of his scholarship, his lack of patriotism, his claims to Indianness, and his extreme incivility in a time of national emergency. King probes the panic over Churchill and his polemic to discern the politics of containment at home by illustrating the entanglements of the War on Terror and the culture wars. He stresses the centrality of the university to both (anti)political struggles. He also traces articulations of national narratives and racial tropes to silence dissent and protect "civilization" and the state from its perceived enemies.

Kyoo Lee's Chapter Six, "United We Stay . . . Home: Interrogating the Racialized *Bildung* of American Children in Post-11 September 2001 Comfort Books," analyzes the visual and verbal rhetoric of "home" in American post-11 September 2001 books written for children and young adults. Lee focuses on signs of "racialized introversion," which she describes as running counter to American ideals of self-reliance, independence, and freedom. Lee argues that an examination of "we who share" the national trauma of 11 September 2001 reveals that the narrative centers in the recrafted entity called America remains visibly Anglo-white—scared Anglo-white. A depiction of children in need of comfort and mothering has supplanted the well-known formation of brave American children. The literalized homeland must suddenly be protected even from within, while the politics played out in the world of children's literature systematically contributed not simply to the post-11 September formation of patriotic discourse but to an exclusion or subordination of the Other, who ironically surfaces through a rhetoric of inclusion, providing a unique kind of containment. Lee suggests that we should not be surprised to learn that most post-11 September books for children and adolescents target and further reinforce the image of the child at bedtime, in need of immediate comfort and consolation, instead of a child who explores and invents. Lee asks who is left out when we see the "big, beautiful world out there" from the point of view of a cute little brown-haired person installed inside the window of a cute little suburban house.

In Chapter Seven, "George Bush's Burden: Staring Down a 'New World [Dis]Order'?," Tracey Nicholls demonstrates a marked tendency in American rhetoric to speak of 11 September 2001 as if it represents a dividing line between a secure and complacent past and an uncertain (and uncontainable) future. This notion of an abrupt moment demarcating pre- and post-11 September 2001 worlds might hold some relevance, Nicholls maintains, but it deflects our attention from dangerous continuities in America's relation to power. Emergence into empire (seen, for instance, in the assertion of itself as the world's only superpower) entails an assumption of "the white man's burden." The self-conferred white male prerogative to exercise sovereign power decides the status, and fates, of the "other(s)." The resurgent sovereignty, Nicholls claims, connects racism and the modern state through the control and preferential treatment of groups within the national population.

Taking up this notion of race as "the other," to which state power is opposed, allows us to trace some links between the old and new Americas. In both orders, the powers accruing to the executive include the power to name or classify, the power to decide limits and jurisdictions of binding agreements, and the power to oversee "security threats" and other social undesirables. These powers are, essentially, powers to contain these undesirable bodies. According to Nicholls, we can see continuities in the exercise of these powers when we consider the Bush administration's decision to create a class of "enemy combatants" (to avoid having to classify them as "prisoners of war") in the context of the racially and ideologically motivated United States' differential immigration policies applied to Cuban and Haitian refugees since the 1960s. Similarly, disregard of Geneva Convention responsibilities, of which the violations at Guantanamo and Abu Ghraib are the most obvious examples, is consistent with American reluctance to endorse the International Criminal Court (ICC) and with demands, during the William Jefferson (Bill) Clinton and George W. Bush presidencies, for an exemption from prosecution for United States citizens. Viewed through this lens, Nicholls argues that the power to contain embedded within the executive branch is a necessarily racialized project that predates the War on Terror—a root cause of it.

Jessica Leann Urban, in Chapter Eight, "Bordering on the Absurd: National, Civilizational, and Environmental Security Discourses on Immigration," discusses President Bush's 15 May 2006 announcement of the mobilization of National Guard troops on the United States-Mexico border. Although Bush and his supporters have often denied the claim that United States policies in the region constitute its militarization, Urban seeks to show that they do. This mobilization continues a legacy of militarization institutionalized by the Clinton administration's Southwest Border Strategy, the Bush administration's Secure Border Initiative and its "Vision for Comprehensive Immigration Reform," and other operations including Operation Community Shield, Operation Liberty Shield, and Operation Gatekeeper.

Urban claims that the militarization of the United States-Mexico border also encourages the rhetoric and actions of civilian paramilitary groups operating in the region, and to broader efforts at containment. Anti-immigrant positions and policies are not new; they pre-date the Southwest Border Strategy. In the United States, claims of sovereignty and fears of economic and national insecurity have long informed both, as have concerns over threats to "civilizational security"— aimed at containing "foreign" bodies in the name of national security. Urban tells us that more recently, environmental groups have targeted immigrants of color on the basis of *environmental* security concerns as well, especially in terms of the perceived threat posed by "overpopulation" in, and immigration from, "other" countries.

While national security discourse has perhaps held center stage post-11 September 2001, Urban argues that discourses of United States national, civilizational, and environmental security form a mutually supportive cluster aimed at (re)constructing both the boundaries of America and Americanness. Environmental Security discourse replays doomsday scenarios, adding an environmental twist, to anti-immigrant positions already evident in national and civilizational security discourse, thereby bolstering calls for the containment of "enemy others."

Jocelyn A. Pacleb's Chapter Nine, "Soldiering 'Green Card' Immigrants: Containing United States Citizenship," analyzes the 25 March 2006 demonstration, in which over half a million people marched in Los Angeles, against HR 4437. This bill would criminalize undocumented immigrants and those who assist individuals without proper documentation to stay in the United States. As Pacleb demonstrates, media coverage captured the sea of people wearing white shirts carrying flags and signs. One image, taken by an *L.A. Times* photographer, included a demonstrator with a large sign of the United States flag. In place of the fifty stars, the flag had a photo of a United States soldier. Written in the white stripes of the flag was: "Sons of immigrants that are in the military, pray for justice." The image of the United States soldier reveals the complex interconnection between the wars in Iraq and Afghanistan, immigration debates, United States citizenship, containment, and the War on Terror. Since the United States-led war in Iraq began in March 2003, the military service of non-United States citizens, also known as "green card soldiers," has brought to light the enlistment of immigrants in the various military branches.

President Bush has described the service of non-United States citizen soldiers as the "ultimate act of patriotism." Though military service may be an "ultimate act of patriotism," Pacleb examines how the federal government has used this discourse to construct a variation of the "model minority" immigrant in the twenty-first century. In addition to serving as the new "model minority," green card soldiers exemplify new forms of containment of "othered" bodies, as they incorporate into the fold of the United States. Pacleb suggests that the focus on the patriotism of "green card soldiers" obscures the real war on the economic, social, and political disenfranchisement of immigrant communities in the United States.

In Chapter Ten, "The Bracero, the Wetback, and the Terrorist: Mexican Immigration, Legislation, and National Security," Luz María Gordillo argues that despite the United States seeing in the first three decades of the twentieth century an average annual influx of approximately 46,000 immigrants from around the world, Mexican immigrants received the primary focus. The inception of the Bracero Program occurred during 1942 and represented one of the first official bilateral labor agreements between the United States and Mexico. Since then, Gordillo maintains, the discourse around Mexican immigration has become the property of politicians, academicians, the media, religious leaders, and political groups. Mexican immigrants, however, are conveniently "erased" or praised, depending upon the economic, political, social, and cultural atmosphere in the United States at the time.

Inasmuch as the United States has placed a historical demand on Mexican labor, it has variously manipulated the Mexican labor pool to satisfy the "appropriate" constituents. Since the 1940s, the United States has offered an inconsistent and discordant set of policies toward the importation and deportation of Mexican labor. The economic atmosphere in the United States has dictated the image and legality of the Mexican immigrant. According to Gordillo, while a constellation of agriculturalists, industrialists, and conservative politicians, who capitalize on inexpensive labor, glorify Mexicans through the image of the "good Mexican worker," social discourse demonizes Mexicans through the image of a predator, who endangers the future of the United States by threatening its political, economic, social, and cultural "integrity."

Regardless of the approach, the United States government has portrayed the Mexican as in need of containment (either as a worker or as a predator). Proposed immigration reform during the early twenty-first century catapulted the issue of Mexican immigration to the national headlines. Since the 11 September 2001 attacks on the United States, the immigration "problem" has become synonymous with Mexicans, while Mexicans have become synonymous with terrorism and drug and sex trafficking. As a response to this collective paranoia, in a recent presidential speech, President Bush proposed the deployment of the National Guard to "protect," "control," and "manage" the border between Mexico and the United States. Gordillo concludes that since 11 September 2001, immigration in general, and Mexican immigration in particular, has marked a central site of requisite containment and has encouraged what she calls severe "migraphobia" and "nativist sentiments."

One

"THE WAR ON TERROR" AND SAME-SEX MARRIAGE: UNITED STATES DISCOURSE AND THE SHAPING OF PUBLIC OPINION

Mary K. Bloodsworth-Lugo
Carmen R. Lugo-Lugo

The attacks of September the 11th showed our country that vast oceans no longer protect us from danger. Before that tragic date, we had only hints of al Qaeda's plans and designs. Today in Iraq, we see a threat whose outlines are far more clearly defined, and whose consequences could be far more deadly. Saddam Hussein's actions have put us on notice, and there is no refuge from our responsibilities. We did not ask for this present challenge, but we accept it. . . . By our resolve, we will give strength to others. By our courage, we will give hope to others. And by our actions, we will secure the peace and lead the world to a better day. May God bless America.
- George W. Bush, 2002

1. Introduction

Due to the structure of the modern world system (Wallerstein, 1998), United States capitalism has been spreading across the globe since World War II, mainly via multi- or transnational corporations and with little concept *in* the United States *of* the United States as an imperialist force. United States consumerist ideologies and practices, in addition to the development of relatively recent technologies such as the internet and mobile communications, have also contributed to this ubiquitous United States global society. Rhetoric concerning "the flow of ideas" has been circulating for decades, becoming more embellished at the end of the twentieth century with the idea that the world was at the tip of every American's fingers. The world became available "at the click of a mouse."

The now-pervasive diffusion of United States capitalist culture has revealed an interesting paradox: at the same time that United States capital(ism) became irrepressible, United States uncontainability became premised on efforts at containment (of "other" people, countries, economies). Instilled in Americans was the illusion of an open and global society—a society that contained the world. Americans began to view the world as being "within their grasp." After the events of 11 September 2001, the illusion of a global "American" nation was undermined. Responding to disillusionment, the United States government and its citizens began a speedy—and perhaps brutal—process of shutting out the world. Americans stayed at home, in their houses, and on the ground, reluctant to engage with a newly revealed *uncontained* world.

New efforts at security and containment took shape. Americans hung flags in front of the houses into which they retreated. They exchanged keyboards for remote controls as sales of home entertainment systems accelerated (Max, 2001). Americans stayed at home. Rhetoric demarcating and delimiting the boundaries of "Americanness" unfolded, and since this time, efforts to articulate what is American have been matched only by attempts to specify what is un-American. Ambiguity has been rendered not viable at a moment when Good is seen as American and Evil is depicted as un-American, and when heterosexuality (in the form of "family values") is seen as American and homosexuality (in the form of "anti-family values") is cast as un-American.

Post-11 September 2001, the mutually exclusive categories of American and un-American have been reinforced—inviting a perpetual contest between them. Within this constant exercise, what is rendered un-American is treated with suspicion and "othered." As President George W. Bush stated on 20 September 2001, "Either you are with us, or you are with the terrorists" (2001).

In the present chapter, we argue that the positions that the Bush administration has taken regarding international policies and national affairs intertwined during 2003 and 2004. "The War on Terror" and same-sex marriage came to connect in the United States public mind to render same-sex unions in need of "containment" and "the sanctity of marriage" in need of "protection." Lesbians and gay men became "domestic terrorists"—bodies in which AIDS and same-sex relations interwove, in which danger and uncontainability became one.

The general cultural view of the HIV/AIDS body has often been one of a diseased and predatory body (Mehuron, 1997) and conflated with the lesbian/gay body. The specific connection among "the War on Terror," AIDS, and same-sex marriages poses a new and unique set of concerns. The aim of the present chapter is to highlight and untangle some of these connections, and to situate the analysis within discourses of embodiment. For if, as Judith Butler (1993, p. ix) states, bodies "bleed" and resist containment despite the very efforts to define and delimit them, then what does this mean for the attempt to discredit same-sex unions? What does it mean for "the War on Terror" and its connection to lesbian/gay bodies? Lesbian/gay bodies become sites of necessary "codification," and the move to codify becomes alarmingly akin to an effort to confront and defeat a "scattered network of killers." New efforts at containment arise from within a long United States history that we will briefly address in the next section.

2. Containment, Homosexuality, and the Cold War

Six years prior to 11 September 2001, in a report prepared for the United States Air Force, Zalmay Khalilzad (1995) urged the United States to create a "grand strategy" to accommodate a post-Cold War world. According to Khalilzad, the strategy should address United States national security, economic, and foreign policy, and lead to a role of United States leadership within the international arena. Khalilzad argues that a new grand strategy would bring purpose to the United States, since "[d]uring the Cold War, the United States was relatively certain of its objective of Soviet containment, [and now] it is not [clear about its objective]" (ibid., p. vii). The lack of a post-Cold War grand strategy, he observes, "makes it more difficult to decide what is important and what is not, to determine which threats are more serious than others, and to develop coherent approaches to respond to new challenges" (ibid.).

Khalilzad extends his argument to claim that the ultimate United States goal should be to assume global leadership and preclude the rise of a rival. This technique, he argues, "would be more peaceful and more open to values of liberal democracy, free markets, and the rule of law" than would be a bi- or multi-polar system (ibid., p. viii). He encourages the United States Air Force to create a world in which the United States would be the "sole superpower" and the leader of a "democratic zone of peace and prosperity" (ibid., p. 7). He places the United States in clear opposition to what he calls "the zone of conflict," which he considers to be:

> an undemocratic zone . . . harboring dangers of major regional conflicts, attempts at regional hegemony, and proliferation of weapons of mass destruction and the means to deliver them over increasingly long distances. (Ibid., p. 11)

Even more boldly, Khalilzad maintains that given its position of power:

> in the world, the United States is in a position to shape the future . . . but it cannot succeed in shaping the post-Cold War world unless it knows what shape it wants the world to take. (Ibid.)

The argument developed by Khalilzad in his report is of particular relevance to a discussion of "containment" and the United States given the outstanding paradox that it represents. He urges the United States military to move beyond a Cold War mentality by embracing a central Cold War tenet, military and political supremacy of the United States. The paradox in/of his reasoning helps to place our present discussion of containment within a historical context, since many of the ideas embedded within President Bush's rhetoric—and that of his administration— reflect other moments in United States history.

The role of the Cold War era (especially the so-called McCarthy years) in the development of rhetoric involving un-Americanness and homosexuality is related to current events. As Peter Kuznick and James Gilbert (2001, p. 2) argue, "much of what is usually thought of as Cold War culture outlasted the Cold War itself and likely will be with us for a long time." The continuing impact of Cold War culture is evidenced by Khalilzad's desire, for instance, to move beyond the Cold War while simultaneously deploying the ideologies of supremacy developed during this era.

Kuznick and Gilbert's discussion helps to link the current administration's rhetoric to the Cold War by identifying four specific ideologies: the threat of annihilation, the replacement of direct military confrontation with surrogate and covert warfare, an opposition to a specific enemy, and the rise of the military industrial complex. The importance of these elements, Kuznick and Gilbert suggest, is that together they created the greatest and most enduring effect of the Cold War era whereby millions of Americans were persuaded to "interpret their world in terms of insidious enemies at home and abroad who threatened them with nuclear and other forms of annihilation" (ibid., p. 11).

An obvious byproduct of this "distorting lens" was a society that contemplated "threats" together. This collective "looking" occurred to such an extent that, according to Alan Brinkley (2001), the Cold War era brought the illusion of unity among Americans. The vast scholarship on the topic of a unified American culture has shown that the United States was (and has always been) far from a culturally unified society (Meyerowitz, 1994).

Given the range of social and cultural experiences as well as the considerable conflict derived from it, Brinkley points out that "the Cold War played a significant role in shaping the culture of its time" (2001, p. 62). More than an actual cohesion, he explains, this illusion of unity resulted from:

> the official and unofficial repression of political belief, the pervasive fear among intellectuals and others of being accused of radical sympathies, [and] the ideological fervor that the rivalry with the Soviet Union produced. (Ibid.)

Brinkley emphasizes that "all had a powerful effect on the way Americans thought about themselves and their culture and on what they dared to say and even think" (ibid., p. 64).

Jane De Hart (2001) contributes additional insight to discussions of consensus during the Cold War by incorporating the element of containment. She uses Elaine May's 1950s' discussion of an exaggerated domesticity and a highly politicized homophobia to argue that the rigid heterosexuality and strict adherence to traditional gender roles promoted during the Cold War years "constituted a domestic version of containment" (ibid.). In the same way that "anti-communism required the containment of Sino-Soviet expansion abroad" she claims, "gender revolution and deviant expression of sexual desire had to be effectively contained at home" (ibid., p. 125). In an eerie statement that anticipates current rhetorical techniques employed by the Bush administration, De Hart explains that during the Cold War:

> Promotion of family values, policymakers believed, would assure the stable family life necessary for personal and national security as well as supremacy over the Soviets. [D]omestic containment was part of a new Cold War-consensus about the meaning of America. (Ibid.)

Noam Chomsky refers to these efforts as "population control." He argues that after World War II, the United States controlled its domestic population via the industrial-financial-commercial sector, which was increasingly transnational in "its planning, management, and operations" (1996, p. 1). He reminds us of documents produced by the United States during the Cold War claiming a "necessity for just suppression" as a crucial part of the "democratic way," where dissent must be curbed (ibid., p. 3). He indicates that a different set of operations and strategies was used to control the population abroad, but the need for the suppression and curbing of dissent within the United States are central for the present discussion for they again highlight how the illusion of unity was constructed. The suppression of disparate views and their collapse into a unified public discourse fueled the illusion of a unified American public—a society of supposed like mind(s) and opinion(s).

A final significant connection to the notion of an illusory unity is Donald Mrozek's discussion of concerted efforts to "toughen" the American character:

> Heartened by the experience of World War II, which seemed to prove that Americans were capable of decisive action on an unparalleled scale, various figures in government, organized athletics and physical education used sport and physical training in increasingly ritualized forms to generate a tough and winning attitude in the Cold War. (1980, p. 78)

Mrozek further suggests that the desire for physical toughness became a value in and a staple of American society, where it was transformed into a ritual of painful and stressful experiences. These experiences, he argues, became the norm in sporting events, "enhancing their ritual and ceremonial importance" (ibid., p. 80). Likewise, as the image of the United States was being homogenized and "toughened up," a relentless attack against homosexuality ensued. According to John D'Emilio (1992), Republicans, led by Senator McCarthy, used the charge of homosexuality during the 1950s as a tool to exert pressure on the Democratic administration of Harry S. Truman.

Entangled with the systematic rhetoric warning Americans about threats to national security, espionage, and the spread of communism was the so-called threat of homosexuality. Homosexuality was positioned as a disease infiltrating and spreading throughout the government. When the United States Senate finally "authorized a formal inquiry into the employment of 'homosexuals and other moral perverts' in government" during June 1950, the report of the Senate Appropriations Committee portrayed homosexuality as "a contagious disease that threatened the health of anyone who came near it" (D'Emilio, 1992, p. 59).

Homosexuals were also considered susceptible to blackmail, since they were "already morally enfeebled by sexual indulgence" and "would succumb to the blandishments of the spy and betray their country rather than risk the exposure of their sexual identity" (ibid., p. 60). As a result of the Senate Appropriations Committee's report, the House Un-American Activities Committee (HUAC) incorporated "homosexuality" into its fold. Through this link, the betrayal of homosexuality was soon placed on a par with the betrayal of communism. During the Cold War era, then, homosexuality was determined to be as un-American as communist sentiment—and both were rendered in need of strict containment.

3. An Interesting Confluence of Events, or, a Political Perfect Storm

In his State of the Union Address delivered on 28 January 2003, President Bush talked ominously about "decisive days that lie ahead" and of answering "every danger and every enemy that threatens the American people" (2003). He explained that the new Department of Homeland Security was "mobilizing against the threats of a new era," while he dedicated the first few pages of the speech to domestic matters. Mid-way through his speech, President Bush shifted from "homeland topics" to international concerns, ranging from AIDS as a "plague of nature," affecting countries in Africa and the Caribbean, to "confronting and defeating the man-made evil of international terrorism." He focused the remainder of his address on "the War on Terror," which he described as a "war against a scattered network of killers."

The connections President Bush made in his speech foretold the direction he would be taking the country in the ensuing months. For instance, after discussing al Qaeda, the 11 September 2001 attacks, and Afghanistan, he swiftly steered in the direction of Iraq, explicitly relating 11 September 2001 and al Qaeda with Saddam Hussein. After discussing Iran and North Korea briefly, he refocused on Iraq and dedicated what followed in his speech to arguing the case for Iraq's imminent threat to Americans.

President Bush's conflation of 11 September 2001, terrorism, Afghanistan, and Iraq was sometimes subtle and sometimes more explicit, but it remained consistent throughout the speech. The following quote brilliantly illustrates this conflation: "Before September 11th, many in the world believed that Saddam Hussein could be contained. But chemical agents, lethal viruses, and shadowy terrorist networks are not easily contained." President Bush also directly linked 11 September 2001 to Saddam Hussein when he asked us to "[i]magine those 19 hijackers with other weapons and other plans, this time armed by Saddam Hussein." In the end, President Bush employed the terms "terrorism," "terror," and "terrorist(s)" a total of twenty times. He mentioned Iraq sixteen times, and named Saddam Hussein eighteen times in this one State of the Union address.

The State of the Union Address proved successful in rallying support for military intervention in Iraq. For instance, a poll conducted by CBS News and Knowledge Networks (28 January 2003) found that prior to the address, 67 percent of Americans supported military action to remove Saddam Hussein from power. After the address, 77 percent of respondents supported such action. More impressively, prior to the address, 54 percent of respondents believed that President Bush had the same priorities for the country as they did. After the speech, this number rose to 81 percent.

Roughly five months later, two major decisions—one outside the United States and one inside—were announced within the span of one week. On 18 June 2003, Prime Minister Jean Chretien announced that Canada would change its law to allow marriage between same-sex couples, thereby joining Belgium and the Netherlands as the only countries to recognize same-sex marriages.

By virtue of two men, Michael Lesher and Michael Stark, pressing for same-sex marriage rights in Ontario the ruling changed the language of marriage to specify "a union between two people" (instead of a union between a man and a woman) (CBS News, 2003a). In the United States, on 20 June 2003, the United States Supreme Court overturned a Texas law criminalizing sexual relations between members of the same sex. Justice Anthony M. Kennedy wrote for the majority that the two men at the center of the Texas case "are entitled to respect for their private lives. The state cannot demean their existence or control their destiny by making their private sexual conduct a crime" (CBS News, 2003b).

A month later, Cheryl Wetzstein reported in her article "U.S. Sees HIV Cases Rise among Gay, Bisexual Men," that in the United States, "[t]he number of newly diagnosed cases of HIV among gay and bisexual men rose in 2002 for the third straight year" (*The Washington Times*, 29 July 2003). The Centers for Disease Control (CDC) reported that this number represented an increase of nearly 18 percent since 1999. In response to the CDC report, Pete LaBarbera, an analyst with the Culture and Family Institute of Concerned Women for America stated:

> Maybe it's time for the CDC and federal government to research the particular health risks associated with gay sex. The federal government studies the health risks of smoking. Maybe there needs to be some public education on the risks of homosexuality. (Ibid.)

Two days later, on 30 July 2003, President Bush offered an hour-long news conference on topics ranging "from Iraq and the war to terrorism and the economy" (CBS News, 2003c). On the issue of terrorism, President Bush stated, "We will wage the war on terror against any enemy that plots against our people," and "I will never assume the restraint and good will of dangerous enemies when lives of our citizens are at work [sic]." During this news conference, President Bush also stated his views on same-sex marriage saying, "I believe a marriage is between a man and a woman. And I think we ought to codify that one way or the other. And we've got lawyers looking at the best way to do that" (Curry, 2003). On 15 May 2003—two months prior to this press conference—a Gallup poll reported "the highest level of acceptance of the legality of homosexuality measured over the 26 years Gallup has been asking [whether] homosexual relations between consenting adults should be legal" (The Gallup Organization, 2003). At that time, 60 percent of Americans responded in the affirmative. On the issue of civil unions, respondents were evenly divided, with 49 percent in favor and 49 percent opposed to granting same-sex couples "some of the legal rights of married couples" (Newport, 2003). A CBS News Poll released on 30 July 2003—the day of the Bush Press Conference—reported that 40 percent of respondents favored same-sex marriage while 55 percent opposed it (CBS News, 2003d).

A few days after President Bush's news conference, on 3 August 2003, the Episcopalian Church USA voted to approve an openly gay man, Gene Robinson, as a bishop. Despite this endorsement, Episcopalian Church leaders urged the convention not to create an official blessing for gay unions. Expressing this sentiment, retired Bishop Alden Hathaway of Pittsburgh commented that he had been told that "sanctioning gay relationships in this country could kill people in Uganda. The church teaching of celibacy outside marriage has helped slow the spread of AIDS" ("Episcopalians Wrestle with Issues of Gay Marriage, Bishop," *The Spokesman-Review*, 3 August 2003).

A series of letters in local newspapers followed. Here is one example: "Some Episcopalians have voted to sanction gay relationships. They do not speak for me. . . . I had two first cousins who were gay die of AIDS, and both were barely in their 30s. . . . I never accepted their lifestyle. . . . It's un-Godly and unnatural!" ("This Episcopalian Differs on Priest," *The Spokesman-Review*, 16 August 2003). On 14 August 2003—two weeks after the President's press conference—a Washington Post poll found "that public acceptance of same-sex unions is falling" (Alan Wolfe, "Americans Don't Have Faith in Same-Sex Marriages, Poll Finds," *The Washington Post*, 14 August 2003). The poll showed that only 37 percent of "Americans would support a law allowing gay men and lesbians to form civil unions that would provide some of the rights and legal protections of marriage." This poll represented the last published measure of United States sentiment on the issue of same-sex civil unions in 2003. By January 2004, a newly released Gallup poll showed that only 34 percent of Americans were in favor of civil unions (41 percent opposed, 25 percent reporting no opinion) (The Gallup Organization, 2004).

At the end of August 2003, CBS News conducted a poll showing that 57 percent of respondents continued to approve of the President's handling of the war in Iraq (CBS News, 2003e). More dramatically, 55 percent of respondents said that removing Saddam Hussein was worth the loss of American lives. As of 6 September 2003, a separate Washington Post poll "found that nearly 7 Americans out of 10 believe Saddam played a role in the September 11th attacks" (*USA Today*, 2003). The results of this poll came forward as the Bush administration backtracked in its discourse vis-à-vis the connection between Hussein and 11 September 2001. For instance, President Bush remarked, "We've had no evidence that Saddam Hussein was involved with the September 11th (attacks)" ("Bush Backtracks: President Says There's No Evidence Linking Saddam to 9/11 Attacks," *The Spokesman-Review*, 18 September 2003). The media coincidentally reported President Bush's statement on the same day as it reported that a same-sex couple, married in Canada, was denied entry to the United States as a family. The couple was—ironically—traveling to a human rights conference in Georgia. The men were told that the United States does not recognize same-sex marriages ("Married Gay Couple Denied U.S. Entry as Family," *The Spokesman Review*, 19 September 2003).

4. Analyzing the Perfect Storm and the Bodies in Its Wake

The figures cited above tell the story of a highly strategic and effective campaign by which President Bush used Saddam Hussein to embody the abstract notion of a terrorist. This strategy was so convincing that Americans came to believe that taking care of Saddam Hussein would mean eradicating terrorist threats in general, as shown by the *Washington Post* poll of September 2003, which culminated in 70 percent of Americans linking Saddam Hussein to the attacks of 11 September 2001 (*USA Today*, 2003).

What we can also see in the speeches and figures of this time is a comingling of issues—of terrorism, AIDS, and same-sex marriage. For instance, a coalition of conservative groups declared the week of 11 October 2003 to be Marriage Protection Week. This week followed—and offered a response to—national Gay Pride Week and was "endorsed by a proclamation from President Bush" ("Marriage Protection Week Draws Reaction from Gays," *The Spokesman Review*, 17 October 2003). Sandy Rios, a member of one of the groups in the coalition remarked:

> They really truly want to equate homosexual marriage with heterosexual marriage. The sad reality is that it's never going to be the same. The American people know marriage is not something to be messed with. (Ibid.)

Interestingly, in offering this response to gay pride week, gay pride was effectively conflated with same-sex marriage, and same-sex marriage became the rallying cry to "the American people." If, as Rios suggests, "the American people" know that marriage should not be "messed with," then lesbians, gay men, bisexuals, and even straight folks who support same-sex marriage find themselves placed outside the category "American." Many people come to define "American" as "those who think that [heterosexual] marriage should be protected." This rendering of "American" parallels the attribution of the term "American" to "those in favor of the war against terrorism," where individuals become "un-American" if they stand in opposition to such war. Consequently, to be *in favor of* same-sex marriage and to be *opposed to* war in Iraq hold their exclusion from the category "American" in common.

What the data above show is that *high* poll numbers favoring President Bush's handling of the war in Iraq are positively correlated with the *low* poll numbers favoring same-sex marriage. The two sets of numbers necessitate an inverse relationship. By highlighting the connection between United States public opinion on President Bush's handling of Iraq and United States public opinion concerning same-sex marriage, we are arguing against the prevailing view—in both the mainstream and queer presses (cf. Chris Bull, "Justice Served," *The Advocate*, 19 August 2003; *World Net Daily*, 2004; Doug Ireland, 2003). The mainstream view suggests that decline in support for same-sex marriage during the Summer of 2003 was a backlash against the 26 June 2003 United States Supreme Court decision to overturn the sodomy laws of the remaining 13 states of the United States. Our view is that the decline in support for same-sex unions must be seen from within a larger context in which the Supreme Court decision played—a context framed by historical precedents and the current discursive terrain of terror, including presidential language of "annihilating the enemy" and eradicating a "network of killers." This language, and the conflations it evokes, makes it very difficult *not* to see lesbian/gay bodies as threats. It unleashes the possibility that "married" same-sex couples will soon be moving in next door—*next door* to those *American* households with their *American* flags waving out front.

Thus, we should not see the political rhetoric unfolding in 2003 as addressing an unrelated sequence of events. Instead, during 2003 we witnessed a concerted effort aimed to protect "America" by containing the "un-American" body. The importance of this effort lies in how the discourse came together to create an overarching and distinct body of ideas that waged a literal war against three distinct groups of people: terrorists, same-sex couples, and lesbian/gay folks generally (who, in effect, were merged into one).

In addition, these strategies have influenced the United States' public perception of "the other," especially given the heightened state of patriotic fervor among Americans after 11 September 2001. Thus, these rhetorical projects must be treated as connected events which jelled together to create a story of terrorists and lesbians/gays whose sick minds (in the case of terrorists) and bodies (in the case of lesbians/gays) threaten every aspect of American life, including "the sanctity of marriage."

5. United States' State Discourse during the 2004 Election Year

The reason I keep insisting that there was a relationship between Iraq and Saddam and al-Qaeda [is] because there was a relationship between Iraq and al-Qaeda.
George W. Bush (Reichman, 2004).

I called on Congress to pass, and to send to the states for ratification, an amendment to our Constitution defining and protecting marriage as a union of a man and a woman as husband and wife. The need for that amendment is still urgent, and I repeat that call today.
George W. Bush (Bash, 2004).

Considering the 2004 election year, we press our thesis further to argue that during 2004, the presidential rhetoric of entanglement provided a well-articulated discourse against same-sex marriage and offered Americans a cleverly orchestrated agenda for action. Given connections between discursive constructions of terrorism abroad and constructions of same-sex marriage in the United States—both articulated as threats to the security of the Nation—claims by voters to have re-elected George W. Bush on the basis of two primary concerns, "the War on Terror" and "moral values," should present no surprise (ABC News, 2004). Instead of viewing the War on Terror and moral values (of which same-sex marriage is a conceived part) as two separate factors for reelection, we suggest that the definition of terrorism broadened in the United States by presidential and popular discourse to place same-sex marriages on par with international threats. Consequently, the War on Terror and moral values comprise a unified and singular set of concerns.

While we witnessed some disruptions (or interventions) to this terrorist narrative, the strength of the generally unified discourse regarding "threats" proved highly powerful and resulted in the reelection of Bush. The disruptions during 2004 came in a variety of forms: (1) same-sex marriage licenses were issued in San Francisco, Portland, and New York at the start of the year, and same-sex marriages were legally recognized in Massachusetts by May 2004; (2) the "Iraqi prisoner abuse scandal," a decline in support for the war in Iraq, a decrease in the President's overall approval ratings, and challenges to United States policies/practices involving Iraqi detainment surfaced; and (3) President Bush pushed for a United States Constitutional Amendment banning same-sex marriage, which was ultimately blocked in the House and the Senate during July 2004.

Despite these intermittent interventions, during November, in addition to the President's reelection, we saw amendments to eleven state constitutions banning same-sex marriage. While these results have been explained in different ways, we argue that the discursive link between "the War on Terror" and lesbian/gay bodies offers the greatest explanatory impact.

6. Discourse and Disruption: A Selected Survey of 2004

On 20 January 2004, President Bush delivered his annual State of the Union Address, in which he presented a consistent theme of protecting, defending, and securing America. Though heavily concentrated on terrorism abroad and on homeland defense, the address also approached domestic issues. One threat discussed that did not originate from "outside" was that against "traditional marriage." President Bush used the address to officially outline the need for a constitutional mechanism to "defend" marriage. He remarked, "[I]f judges insist on forcing their arbitrary will upon the people, the only alternative left to the people would be the constitutional process"(Bush, 2004). He concluded, "our nation must defend the sanctity of marriage."

The President's statements regarding marriage become significant when we view them in relation to similar remarks he made concerning homeland security and defense. Regarding the homeland, President Bush spoke of "protecting America" and "securing our country," urging Congress to "provide the resources for our defense," "defend[ing] the security of our country," creating a temporary worker program to "help protect the homeland," and upholding the "unseen pillars of civilization" (meaning families, schools, and religious congregations).

Using equivalent language to discuss terrorist threats and same-sex marriage, we claim, is not accidental. Instead, it represents a strategic deployment of the discourse of defense whereby terrorism, national security, and same-sex marriage are similarly categorized and by which the President is able to articulate the specter of homeland threats—including the threat of same-sex marriage.

At the time of his State of the Union Address, the media described President Bush as "stopping short of endorsing [a] constitutional amendment" (CNN, 2004a). Regardless, the public clearly received the intent of his message concerning same-sex marriage. In an ABC News/Washington Post Poll conducted prior to the address, 38 percent of respondents favored a constitutional amendment banning same-sex marriage (Morris and Langer, 2004); in a Gallup Poll conducted two weeks subsequent to the address, that number had jumped to 47 percent (Fred Bayles, "Gay Marriage Fight Nears a Peak," *USA Today*, 11 February 2004).

On 5 February 2004, a Massachusetts court determined that civil unions for same-sex couples are discriminatory. The court argued that civil unions represent a form of "separate and unequal" and that "only marriage would pass constitutional muster" (Jennifer Peter, "Massachusetts Court Backs Gay Marriage: 'Separate but Equal' Civil Unions Called Discriminatory; Same-Sex Weddings Could Start in May," *The Spokesman-Review*, 5 February 2004). We witnessed a second disruption to the discourse of marriage protection when San Francisco mayor, Gavin Newsom, began issuing same-sex marriage licenses on 12 February 2004.

Public opinion to this action was swift. In a Letter to the Editor, Rosalie Dahlvang argued, "Marriage is the foundation for a family with a mother and a father that must be protected" ("Small Group Can't Redefine Marriage," *The

Spokesman-Review, 11 February 2004). A few days later, Sandy Rios, from Concerned Women for America, claimed, "If we have homosexual marriage mainstream, I can't even describe to you what our culture will be like" (Cloud, 2004, p. 56). Significant in these two statements is the use of key ideas—"marriage is the foundation" that "must be protected," and we must take action to avert uncertainty—employed by President Bush during his State of the Union address.

During a 24 February 2004 press conference, President Bush conveyed his full support for a constitutional amendment banning same-sex marriage. He claimed that America needed such an amendment to "prevent the meaning of marriage from being changed forever" (Bush, 2004b). Re-deploying his earlier discourse, the President added, "some activist judges and local officials have made an aggressive attempt to redefine marriage," and "homosexual marriages threaten the most fundamental institution of civilization." The key statement made on this day was the following: "The amendment process has addressed many serious matters of national concern, and the preservation of marriage rises to this level of importance." The phrase "serious matters of national concern" mimics language involving national security; for example, "raising the threat level to Code Orange" and "deciding to raise the threat level for this sector."

Support for the President's proposal was strong. For instance, in another Letter to the Editor, Betty Roloff commented, "Last week I heard about a wedding in India in which a boy married his dog to ward off evil spirits. Hopefully, it was a female dog. I can't take any more gay weddings" ("Gays Want to Ruin Marriage," *The Spokesman-Review*, 26 February 2004).

On 14 May 2004, a federal judge in Massachusetts refused to halt ensuing same-sex weddings. Three days later, same-sex marriages began to take place. Interestingly, July saw heated debates involving issues of constitutional amendments and family values via same-sex marriages. Democrat Senator Frank Lautenberg asked, "Why in this election year are we debating an amendment to the constitution designed to restrict the rights of gay Americans?" (Hulse, 2004). A response came from Republican Pennsylvania Representative, Rick Santorum, who remarked, "You can say I am a hater, but I would argue I am a lover. I am a lover of traditional families and children who deserve the right to have a mother and a father" (ibid.). President Bush also used this opportunity to restate his opinion that marriage should be between a man and a woman. In his words:

> What they do in the privacy of their house, consenting adults should be able to do. This is America. It's a free society. But it doesn't mean we have to redefine traditional marriage. I believe that traditional marriage— marriage between a man and a woman—is an important part of stable families. (Stevenson, 2004)

Here, the President's use of the word "stable" resembles his use of the word "secure" in his speeches concerning terrorism and homeland security. However, during mid-July, the United States Senate defeated the proposed constitutional ban on same-sex marriages.

At the beginning of August 2004, a judge in the Superior Court of the state of Washington ruled that gay couples in that state may marry. Judge William L. Downing ruled, "denying same-sex couples the right to marry would violate their constitutional rights" (Yuxing Zheng and Virginia DeLeon, "Pastors in Region Gather to Denounce Gay Marriage," *The Spokesman-Review*, 24 August 2004). As of this writing, this decision awaits review by the State Supreme Court.

Overall, during the month of August 2004, a growing number of organized groups vocalized opposition to same-sex marriage. For instance, after the Superior Court decision in Washington, John Tusant, a representative from the Coalition for Authentic Marriage, expressed, "this is the most important issue that our nation has faced" and indicated that "children need a male figure and a female figure to enhance their own development as individuals" (Virginia DeLeon, "Judge Says Gays May Wed," *The Spokesman-Review*, 5 August, 2004).

Later in August, pastors from Eastern Washington gathered to denounce same-sex marriage, stating, "Human society will be destroyed if we lose original one-man-and-one-woman marriage" (Zheng and DeLeon, 2004). The pastors conducted a training session to "preserve authentic marriage." Significantly, a local newspaper article began to connect sentiments towards same-sex marriages and their influence on the upcoming election. It stated:

> Gay marriage has been the sleeper issue of the election year thus far, but a surprising surge of gay-marriage opponents going to the polls in Missouri on Tuesday demonstrated that an issue that went nowhere in Congress is resonating in the country. It could spread to other states planning referenda, and ultimately could help President Bush's re-election prospects (Steven Thomma, "Missouri Says No to Gay Marriage," *The Spokesman-Review*, 5 August 2004).

During October 2004, we saw a different set of actions taken in relation to same-sex marriage throughout the country. On the religious front, in mid-October, the National May Day for Marriage provided an active site of opposition to any idea of same-sex marriage. A week prior to this demonstration, a representative from Americans United to Preserve Marriage linked the issue of same-sex marriage to the upcoming presidential election using the rhetoric of "defense." In his words, "We believe it is important for the American people to know which candidates will defend traditional marriage" (Kniderbocker, 2004). Even though the United States House of Representatives defeated the Marriage Protection Amendment, defining marriage as the union of a man and a woman, House Majority Leader Tom Delay stated, "Marriage is the basic unit of society, the very DNA of civilization, and if that civilization is to endure, marriage must be protected" (Richard Simon, "House Rejects Proposal to Ban Gay Marriages,"

The Spokesman-Review, 1 October 2004). The discourse of protection invoked by Representative Delay is, not surprisingly at this point, virtually identical to the discourse developed by the Bush Administration to speak about "the War on Terror" and the idea of homeland security.

November 2004 began with the re-election of President Bush. As part of its election coverage, ABC News released the results of a poll on same-sex marriage. According to the poll, only 27 percent of respondents supported same-sex marriage and thought that same-sex couples should be allowed to legally marry, 35 percent thought that same-sex couples should be allowed to form civil unions, and 35 percent thought that same-sex couples should have no legal recognition whatsoever (2004). In eleven states, the election included ballot measures to amend state constitutions to ban same-sex marriages (Arkansas, Georgia, Kentucky, Michigan, Mississippi, Montana, North Dakota, Ohio, Oklahoma, Oregon, and Utah). All amendments passed.

In many instances, it has been noted, "the measures might prevent the extension of even very limited partnership rights to unmarried gay and straight couples" (*The Advocate*, 2004). The wording of the Michigan measure is of particular interest for it includes language of children and future generations embedded within language of security; it reads: "To secure and preserve the benefit of marriage for our society and for future generations of children, the union of one man and one woman in marriage shall be the only agreement recognized as a marriage or similar union for any purpose" (Kranish, 2004). Conservative activists reacted positively to the passage of the measures. For instance, activist, Gary Bauer, stated, "This issue does not deeply divide America. The country overwhelmingly rejects same-sex marriage" (Wire Reports, "11 States Pass Amendments Banning Same-Sex Marriage," *The Spokesman-Review*, 3 November 2004). A representative of the Christian Coalition, Sadie Fields, added, "The people of this state realized that we're talking about the future of our country here" (ibid.).

After the election, the media focused on the role of moral values (the sleeper issue) on the outcome of the election. In a not-surprising turn of events, 80 percent of those who voted for President Bush said they cared most about the moral values supported by him (Janice D'arcy, "Voters Citing 'Moral values' Win it for Bush," *The Spokesman-Review*, 4 November 2004). The election results upheld a perfect merger between voters focusing on moral values (of which same-sex marriage is a part) and "security issues" (for which "Senator John Kerry was too great a risk").

7. Same-Sex Marriage as Domestic Terrorism

While President Bush began 2004 with a job approval rating of 53 percent, his approval ratings had reached a low-point for his presidency by May 2004, with 46 percent of respondents saying that they approved of his performance as president. On the issue of the President's handling of the War in Iraq, his approval rating had reached a new low by April 2004, with only 40 percent of respondents saying that they approved of the President's handling of Iraq (while 53 percent disapproved). Regarding the War on Terrorism, respondents were evenly divided in May 2004, with 46 percent saying that the President was doing a "good" job of handling the War on Terrorism and 47 percent saying that he was doing a "bad" job. Consequently, the issue of Iraq has garnered greater overall disapproval than the more general issue of terrorism.

Interestingly, during 2004, United States public approval of same-sex marriages again tracked with the President's approval ratings in inverse fashion. A high approval rating for President Bush correlated with a low approval rating for same-sex marriage. For instance, during January 2004, when the President's approval ratings were above 50 percent, support for same-sex marriages had reached a low point. According to a Gallup Poll conducted 9–11 January 2004, only 24 percent of respondents said that they favored same-sex marriages while 53 percent said that they opposed them (23 percent registered no opinion). By late April–early May, when President Bush's approval ratings were at the lowest point of his presidency, support for same-sex marriage had increased. When asked, "Should same-sex marriages be legal with the same rights as traditional marriages?," 42 percent of respondents to a Gallup poll conducted 2–4 May 2004, said "yes"; 55 percent responded "no" (Gallup Organization, 2004).

In addition, the year 2004 introduced "children" into discussions of terrorism and homosexuality—thereby serving to link these issues. For instance, in his 2004 State of the Union Address, Bush discussed the dangers of illegal drugs for "children" and the need to expand drug testing in high schools "as a tool to save children's lives," he conveyed the importance of athletics for "children" and the poor role-modeling provided by athletes who use "performance-enhancing drugs like steroids," and he addressed the threat of sexually-transmitted diseases for "children" and promised to "double federal funding for abstinence programs." He then segued into a discussion of the importance of marriage, saying that "A strong America must . . . value the institution of marriage." The President also finished his address by responding to a letter written by Ashley Pearson, a 10-year-old girl. In her letter, Ashley asked, "Please send me a letter and tell me what I can do to save our country," to which President Bush replied, "Ashley, while you do your part, all of us here in this great chamber will do our best to keep you and the rest of America safe and free."

Thus, during 2004 we saw a concerted discursive effort to codify same-sex marriage as a sort of domestic threat—as domestic terrorism. Presidential, governmental, and religious rhetoric alike constructed this domestic threat as a top-down counter-movement to the different disruptions taking place around the nation. Invoking civilization, safety, homeland, and children, these discursive tools paralleled and were meant to create an atmosphere of fear similar to the atmosphere of fear created by discursive tools involving "the War on Terror."

Conclusion

Despite claims by the Bush Administration that "the War on Terror" is "a new kind of war" (Donald H. Rumsfeld, "A New Kind of War," *The New York Times*, 27 September 2001), given our opening remarks concerning the Cold War era and our depiction of political events unfolding during 2003 and 2004, we can now ask how "new" *is* the mindset and rhetoric behind "the War on Terror"?

The similar positioning of communists and homosexuals during the Cold War and terrorists, lesbians, and gays at the present moment in "the War on Terror," is striking. Characteristic of both cases—communists/homosexuals and terrorists/lesbians/gays—is an effort at containment and a rendering of each as un- or anti-American. As the remark by Rios implies—that "the American people" know marriage should not be "messed with"—the notion of "the American people" is constructed in a unified way.

"The American people" are thought to guard against what is "un-American" while implicitly defining the very categories "American" and "un-American" in the process. This idea of a collective lens points back to Brinkley's discussion regarding the illusion of a Cold War American unity and highlights the fact that homosexuals/lesbians/gays have been placed outside of an (illusory) American collective more than once.

Given a different sort of presidential rhetoric, events unfolding during 2003 and 2004 could have served to expand (instead of narrowing) the United States' public perception of categories such as "American," "terrorist," "marriage," and "family." The Bush Administration's rhetoric of "containment" and "annihilation of all enemies" which has accompanied "the War on Terror," together with a persistent co-mingling of same-sex marriage and AIDS issues, means that lesbian/gay bodies have been equated with terrorist bodies while neither one received renewed critical attention.

What *has* been renewed has been the so-called spirit of patriotism—a "patriotism" premised upon the reification of categories as mutually exclusive—us/them, American/un-American, family values/anti-family values— in an effort to contain what has proven uncontainable with the events of 11 September 2001.

Consequently, we maintain, despite some claims to the contrary, that the issue of war—the occupation of Iraq in particular—is "a gay issue." The entangling of issues in 2003 and 2004—terrorists, terrorism, Saddam Hussein, al Qaeda, AIDS, same-sex marriage, lesbians/gays—means that separating the War on Terror from so-called gay issues is not feasible.

As demonstrated by the results of public opinion polls cited in the discussion above, United States' public perception of the President's handling of the War on Terror and United States' public opinion regarding same-sex unions coincide. This means, we argue, that we must also expand the question of what represents "a gay issue," in light of recent political events and administrative rhetoric.

While we are aware that not all readers (especially lesbian, gay, or bisexual/queer readers) favor same-sex marriage on a variety of grounds—for example, on grounds that marriage is a mainstream, or patriarchal, or oppressive institution and thus advocating for same-sex marriage is to become complicit with this mainstream/patriarchal/oppressive structure—our aim has not been to argue for or against same-sex marriage per se.

Instead, our interest has been to highlight the restrictive and reductive framework within which recent rhetoric regarding same-sex marriage and the War on Terror has unfolded. In closing, we suggest that the years 2003 and 2004 rendered lesbian/gay bodies in need of containment or annihilation (such as by keeping legal unions out of their reach). In our view, to be so rendered is to be perceived as a threat and as trouble to "the system"—and not as complicit with it.

While a different political context and historical set of circumstances might position same-sex marriage as a conservative stance, we maintain that we have reason to pause and reflect, at this moment, on whether the recent push for same-sex marriage maintains the status quo.

We argue, to the contrary, that this push may well be an effort (conscious or otherwise) to implode an illusory, unified "American" vision. A same-sex couple living next door—even with marriage rights—is not easily assimilated as "normal." To claim that same-sex marriage is normalizing, as Michael Warner (2000) does, or mainstreaming, as Andrew Sullivan ("The Politics of Homosexuality," *New Republic*, 10 May 1993) does, is to ignore that same-sex couples will not be perceived as normal or as mainstream, regardless of their marital status.

Even if the United States government were to change the definition of marriage to allow same-sex couples to marry, and even if thousands of same-sex couples were to marry, we still would have no guarantee that the community at large would view or treat those couples as part of the norm or mainstream. We can use the example of interracial marriages to illustrate this point, for we may argue that society does not view interracial marriages as either part of the norm or as mainstream, even now, long after the repeal of anti-miscegenation laws.

The year 2004 began with the issuing of marriage licenses to same-sex couples in cities such as San Francisco and Portland by virtue of so-called activist judges and activist courts (CNN, 2004). These acts, which counter the current (marriage) system, and which have been called "acts of municipal disobedience" by President Bush (Lochhead, 2004), could demonstrate that perceived terrorist threats—even domestic ones—are neither so easily contained nor so easily mainstreamed. As Judith Butler (1993, p. ix) has remarked, bodies cannot be fixed "as simple objects." Instead, the "movement beyond their own boundaries, a movement of boundary itself, appears to be quite central to what bodies 'are.'"

During the years 2003 and 2004, the public came to view same-sex marriage as a sort of domestic terrorism. The construction of same-sex marriage as domestic terrorism is significant on two related levels: (1) the power of social construction is made evident when considering the role that the threat of same-sex marriage played in the outcome of the presidential election, and (2) the construction of same-sex marriage as domestic terrorism sheds light on state-sanctioned definitions of and responses to terrorism and terrorist threats.

Official United States documents define terrorism as "the calculated use of violence or threat of violence to attain goals that are political, religious, or ideological in nature through intimidation, coercion, or instilling fear" (Chomsky, 2003). When we say that those in power constructed same-sex marriage as a kind of domestic terrorism, we mean that they viewed same-sex marriage as a violent threat to the ideology of marriage and the family in United States society. They perceived same-sex marriage as a violent threat against the "sanctity of matrimony." In addition, given the responses to them, they viewed the disruptions witnessed by the country during the year 2004 as activist sources of intimidation and coercion—something to be feared. This was manifest in the parallel discourses denouncing same-sex marriage and international terrorism as dangers to the security of the nation and (Western) civilization.

This is not the first time that the political (and religious) leadership of the country created the image of a terrorist threat. Chomsky (2003) addresses this issue in his book, *Power and Terror: Post 9/11 Talks and Interviews*. One relevant example he provides is that of Saddam Hussein, whom, he reminds us, was regarded as an ally by the United States for decades after he became President of Iraq, including the times "when he was really dangerous" killing hundreds of thousands of Kurds in his own country" (p. 38). Yet, Chomsky continues, "[the United States] provided [Hussein] the aid and support to do it, perfectly consciously. He was a friend and ally and he remained so."

It is the ease with which the country's leadership is able to convince its people that something or someone has become a threat that interests us, for it suggests that the *perception* of a threat is as powerful as an *actual* one. In the case of same-sex marriage, an issue that was not remotely on the active agenda of the country just a couple of years ago moved from the status of non-issue to an area of extreme concern in a very short period of time. During the 2004 presidential election year, the public pressed same-sex marriage to a point of collective action, as illustrated by voter support for constitutional bans on same-sex marriage in eleven states and the re-election of President Bush.

In the end, the events and rhetoric we discussed in this chapter imply that a category like terrorism is defined to fit the interests of those defining the term. On the issue of same-sex marriage, a sophisticated discursive technique managed to turn same-sex marriage into another threat to national security without necessarily linking gays and lesbians to al-Qaeda or even using the term terrorists to reference them. We hope this paper has provided readers with sufficient evidence regarding the multiple dimensions of specific discursive projects and the impact of governmental rhetoric on its citizens.

Two

POLITICAL USE OF THE "WAR ON TERROR" TO AUGMENT DOMESTIC AND INTERNATIONAL LGBT REPRESSION

William C. Gay

1. What the 11 September 2001 Spotlight Reveals and Conceals

We hear a lot about 11 September 2001. References to the terrorist attacks on 11 September 2001 and the subsequent "war on terror" have become a justificatory refrain in United States political discourse. Shortly after the disintegration of the Soviet Union at the close of 1991, United States officials began to sing the mantra of "democracy and market economy" and continued to do so until 11 September 2001 (Gay, 2004, p. 122). This mantra meant democracy in the political sphere and non-democratic capitalism in the economic sphere. The new mantra, "9/11 and the 'war on terror'" became commonplace after 11 September 2001 and continues to the present. Politicians frequently present a policy or an action as a response to 11 September 2001; public scrutiny of such appeals to "9/11 and the 'war on terrorism'" faces the obstacle of the widely taken-for-granted view that preventing another terrorist attack justifies many measures that otherwise would require serious examination.

We can relate the prior mantra and current mantra to containment. Throughout the Cold War, the United States tried to contain the Soviet Union, preventing further Soviet territorial expansionism. Then, between 1992 and 2001, the mantra of "democracy and market economy" meant that governments were to keep out challenges to democracy and to keep out challenges to capitalism. After 11 September 2001, the mantra, "9/11 and the 'war on terrorism'" meant keeping terrorists from attacking democratic government and capitalist economic interests. The issue of containment in all these periods goes even deeper and pertains to Lesbian, Gay, Bisexual, and Transgender (LGBT) repression.

Despite the brilliance of the 11 September 2001 spotlight, much remains in the dark, especially because of the extreme narrowness of this focus. We need to examine not only what is said but also what is left unsaid. Let me give one telling example. While we hear a lot about "9/11," we do not hear much about "5/11."

We know all too well what happened on 11 September 2001. But what happened on 11 May 2001? As the After Stonewall Productions press release states about the film *Living Dangerously: Coming Out in the Developing World*:

On May 11th, 2001, 52 men in Cairo were arrested, tortured and imprisoned for simply gathering at a discothèque on the river Nile. There is no law against homosexuality in Egypt so the Egyptian Government officially accused the men of committing crimes of debauchery. The 52 were later tried, convicted, and sentenced to 3 years in prison. (Scagliotti, Hunt, Baus, and Williams, 2003)

I contend that the widespread silence about the arrests of the Cairo 52 on 11 May 2001 is connected to the United States' response to 11 September 2001. How are "5/11" and "9/11" connected? To mix metaphors, how has the spotlight of 11 September 2001 led the United States government to turn a deaf ear to 11 May 2001? In brief, the "war on terror" includes the "terror of war." Whenever war occurs, terror occurs (Holmes, 1989). In this case, fear or apprehension is quite extensive within the LGBT community about speaking out against the war or of "coming out" in many parts of the world because the United States' quest for allies in its "war on terror" has largely removed from the agenda strong protest against human rights abuses.

The United States wants to avoid erosion of support from allies. It considers silence on abuses of human rights to be a small price for maintaining an ally. From my perspective on peacemaking and social justice, advocacy for human rights and utilization of diplomacy are vital and should occur between silence and violence. I contend that silence is violence (Gay, 1994, pp. 129–132).

To remain silent about events like 11 May 2001 entails complicity in the violence of these human rights abuses. The trick is finding voice, breaking the silence, without turning to violence, without turning to the violation of the human rights of others. The United States government obviously has not learned this trick. United States officials remain largely silent regarding human rights abuses of its allies in the "war on terror" or else really mouth protest without showing any teeth—without really demanding accountability. Such responses will not do much to restrain insurgent terrorism, though we could make a case that they advance incumbent terrorism when governments are allowed to engage in demeaning actions, torture, and terrorize their own citizens with impunity. (Granted many insurgent terrorists are guilty of human rights abuses and of significant levels of killing the innocent; but their abuses and violence do not excuse governments and allow for the sanctioning of incumbent terrorism.)

The chilling effect of the post-11 September 2001 neglect of defending human rights, especially the silencing of LGBT voices, is made clear by the Audre Lorde Project's "Open Letter to LGBTST Communities Opposing the War" issued on 27 January 2003. This letter states, "This 'War on Terrorism' . . . is an umbrella term, which encompasses many unjust and dangerous strategies intended to silence dissent, while entrenching United States power throughout the world" (The Audre Lorde Project, 2003). The American Friends Service Committee LGBT Anti-War group makes a similar and more detailed statement:

The post-9/11 shockwave of hatred, fear, and violence threatens to engulf us all unless we turn to one another in a radical spirit of nonviolence, generosity, and justice to stop the devastation of civilian populations abroad and racism and repression at home. By lifting up a powerful voice of resistance and a call for authentic justice, we will encourage others to do the same.

There are risks, to be sure, in speaking out against war. In a volatile and highly charged political atmosphere, those who would try to silence dissent or convince us that our self-interest lies in promoting only narrow and timid visions of LGBT justice will always exist. But failure to speak out permits the violence to escalate. (LGBT Program, 2002)

2. Domestic and International Containment of the LGBT Community

Mary K. Bloodsworth-Lugo and Carmen R. Lugo-Lugo (2005) have cogently discussed the connection of LGBT repression in the "war on terrorism" to the United States doctrine of Containment. During the Cold War, communists and homosexuals threatened United States security. Now, in the "War on Terror," terrorists and homosexuals threaten United States security. Each of these uses of Containment renders each of these groups as un- or anti-American.

George Kennan was the architect of the Doctrine of Containment at the dawn of the Cold War. This doctrine came to involve not just military preparations but also political efforts to resist Soviet expansionism (Etzold and Gaddis, 1978). This purported threat of Soviet expansionism also served as an excuse for a variety of repressive policies, especially for domestic policy. We can understand these cases of containment through what George Lakoff calls the "fairy tale" method of presenting governmental action (Lakoff, 1991). While Lakoff applied it to the first war against Iraq, it fits the current situation as well.

We have a victim (the West), a villain (terrorists), and a hero (the United States). Just as the United States government glossed over the shortcomings of Kuwait during the first war against Iraq, it continues to gloss over human rights abuses of allies in the "war on terrorism." Throughout the nuclear age, United States policies have preserved many of these elements (Gay and Pearson, 1987).

Glossing human rights abuses of allies has been one of those elements from the Cold War to the present. Our leaders consider it a small political price to pay to retain strategic alliances. Nevertheless, then and now, real human beings have paid the personal price as governments around the world claim to be making us secure from threats that too often are more imagined than real or that are of a less violent potential than the pervasive violation by governments around the world of the bodies and liberties of "the usual suspects"—people of color, immigrants, the poor, and LGBT individuals. While this practice is common globally, it has been more intense in the United States since 11 September 2001.

In the current embodiment of containment within the United States, as Bloodsworth-Lugo and Lugo-Lugo note, "sick minds (in the case of terrorists) and bodies (in the case of lesbians/gays) threaten every aspect of American Life" (Bloodsworth-Lugo and Lugo-Lugo, 2005, p. 481). They observe:

> despite claims of the Bush Administration that the War on Terror is 'a new kind of war,' the mind-set and rhetoric behind the War on Terror lingers on from previous eras when Americans feared the past and the present. In particular, the similar positioning of communists and homosexuals during the Cold War, and terrorists and lesbians/gays at this moment in the War on Terror, is striking. Characteristic of both cases . . . is an effort at containment and a rendering of each as un- or anti-American . . . . Homosexuals/lesbians/gays have been placed outside of an (illusory) American collective more than once . . . lesbian/gay bodies have been equated with terrorist bodies while neither one has received renewed critical attention. (Ibid.)

Just as Containment in the Cold War included political practices that ignored human rights abuses of allies, even so the War on Terror includes similar practices. I began with the example of the Cairo 52. The Cairo 52 were citizens of Egypt. Egypt is an ally of the United States. After Israel, Egypt receives the most United States foreign aid. The United States wants to keep Egypt as an ally in its "war on terrorism." So, the United States kept the Cairo 52 out of the spotlight.

Other examples abound. Michelangelo Signorille's (2001) "Hate Crimes: Like the Taliban, America's Middle East Allies Tyrannize Gays and Women" provides a very compelling essay on the general attitude of the United States government toward LGBT human rights abuses. Signorille begins by citing a case prior to 11 September 2001 in which, following Taliban law, two gay men were executed on 22 March 1998 by being buried alive. He proceeds to show that in the subsequent war on the Taliban and in the war against Iraq, allies of the United States do similar violence. He notes, "many of the countries being approached to join the United States in the fight against the Taliban don't treat homosexuals, and other citizens deemed second-class, in a drastically different way." Several of these governments are dictatorial regimes and many subvert the rights of women and LGBT individuals. The general attitude in the United States toward LGBT individuals, if not also toward women, often parallels the views of some of those governments. For this reason as well, the United States government need not worry about the treatment of gays by Egypt or other allies.

The general American population does not express compassion for gays; so, the silence of the United States government to human right abuses against LGBT individuals is not going to outrage the public. In this regard, the George W. Bush administration's expression of outrage is selective, yet also revealing. Bush did express outrage about the way in which the Taliban treated women. Apparently, mistreated women garner more sympathy from Bush than mistreated homosexuals do. We must wonder whether this outrage was genuine or only a ploy used to discredit the Taliban. After all, Bush has been no champion for women's rights in the United States.

Despite its traditional claims, the United States positions itself as the bastion of human rights, one that stands against the supporters of terrorism. Signorille contends:

> George W. Bush has set the terms of the impeding battle: the good people of the world against the 'evil folks,' making it appear as if every nation in the coalition against terrorism—including the U.S.—is a bastion of human rights, while Afghanistan's Taliban and any other country that doesn't join the coalition are the planet's only torturers, murderers, and supporters of terrorism. (Ibid.)

The record speaks for itself. In the United Arab Emirates, Yemen, and Pakistan, LGBT individuals can face death as punishment for their lifestyle. In Kuwait, Bahrain, and Qatar, LGBT individuals face three to ten years in prison. In Saudi Arabia, gay men face death as punishment; in 2000, nine transvestites each received 2,600 lashes and were sentenced to several years in prison. All of these countries are United States allies or do not defy the United States in its response to those deemed as terrorists. Yet, most of those countries, though not the countries designated as the "axis of evil," are allied with one or more of them. Clearly, the violation of LGBT rights by other governments is not sufficient for being designated as evil by the Bush administration.

Egypt, beyond the Cairo 52, has shown especially strong reactions to the LGBT community. The Hosni Mubarak government has cracked down on the LGBT community, even having the police use the Internet for discovery. The State Emergency Security Court—supposedly set up to serve justice to terrorists and criminals that threaten national security—tried the Cairo 52. Largely, sweeping LGBT individuals into this net appeases the religious right, which sees the war on terrorism as an attack on Islam. Such violation of LGBT rights by governments to appease the religious right is not restricted to predominantly Islamic countries. In the United States, the war against LGBT people—by way of the war against same-sex marriage—appeases the religious right, that construes 11 September 2001 and same sex marriage as attacks on Christianity.

So, from a human rights point of view, does the religious right in Islam differ from the religious right in Christianity? We appear to have a vacuous contrast (where no real differences exist). If violation of LGBT rights is wrong, then to ignore it to appease the Islamic right or the Christian right is also wrong.

It is no coincidence, then, that while Israel receives the most United States foreign aid, Egypt is the second largest recipient of United States foreign aid. The Egyptian government is exacting a toll on the LGBT community to retain support from the Islamic right and, at the same time, continues receiving extensive foreign aid from the United States. The United States government and United States media are largely silent about the treatment of the LGBT community. This appeases the religious right and preserves United States economic support while the suffering of LGBT victims of human rights abuses continues and even increases. (Regarding the media, coverage of human rights abuses in the international media is somewhat better; BBC News, for example, has addressed how several countries are using the war on terror to cloak human rights abuses of various sorts [2002].)

Let me give just one more set of examples. On 29 November 2005, police in the United Arab Emirates (UAE), another United States ally in the War on Terror, raided a hotel and seized 26 Asian, Arab, and UAE gay men. The UAE sentenced the foreigners to time served and deported them, but the local men were given hormone treatment (induced testosterone) and each was sentenced to five years in prison (U.S. Department of State, 2007).

Although the LGBT community at home and abroad are fearful, trying to make the LBGT community fearful may be a desired result by governments that use fear, but this political use of fear is one of the problems. At issue is how to respond to this political use of fear. I turn to this task in my final section.

3. Responding to the "Fear" of Terrorists and the LGBT Community

United States politicians are fanning fear of terrorism and gay marriage to motivate letting governments restrict and even violate civil liberties and human rights both domestically and internationally. Since 11 September 2001, many people, especially in the United States, have come to regard terrorism as if it represents the most grave security issue. Some people have become so afraid that they are willing to permit the government to go to virtually any lengths to reduce this threat. The United States government is using fear to motivate the public to accept, as necessary and justified, the military actions and domestic surveillance employed to counter terrorism.

Not surprisingly, in this context, problems for LGBT individuals are increasing in these three ways. First, the LGBT community, people of color, immigrants, refugees, women, and the poor face a disproportionate burden of war-related repression. This is especially true in the use of "surveillance of domestic civic and religious organizations against whom there is no evidence of wrongdoing, and invasive information-gathering programs used by the Pentagon and other government agencies" (American Friends Service Committee, "Is Opposing the War an LGBT Issue?" n.d.).

Second, LGBT groups face the potential loss of funds from donors, foundations, and governmental agencies, and the prospect of being labeled unpatriotic. Speaking out has never been easy, but it becomes even more risky in a climate in which donors, foundations, and local, state, and federal funding sources can "blacklist" already marginalized groups when they speak out against the "war on terrorism" and can label them not only as deviant but also as unpatriotic. Third, state-sanctioned violence stands at the extreme, because it can go all the way to institutional responses that impose death as a punishment.

Regarding efforts to report on and respond to state-sanctioned violence, the International Gay and Lesbian Human Rights Commission has been especially active in many countries such as Namibia, Uganda, Argentina, Iran, Nigeria, Croatia, South Africa, and the Czech Republic. They are also active in Switzerland, Bolivia, Honduras, Thailand, Pakistan, the United Kingdom, the United States, Panama, Romania, the Russian Federation, Ghana, Korea, Cameroon, Moldova, Nepal, Israel, Chile, Palestine, St. Maarten, Bosnia-Herzegovina, Zimbabwe, Peru, Canada, Latvia, Venezuela, Brazil, Poland, Mexico, Jamaica, India, Turkey, Fiji, Sierra Leone, and Poland.

The exaggerated fears promoted by the United States government face factual, psychological, political, and moral pitfalls. First, because the claims are so extreme, they are often not credible. In many cases, arguments are made without consideration of facts. In these cases, the goal of persuasion has a higher priority than truth, especially if the fear generated through exaggeration is believed to bring about a good result. Any lapse into distortion is justified as benevolent deception, but the possibility remains that such deception may be exposed.

Are we now seeing a similar phenomenon with respect to how our government is using public fear of terrorism? LGBT and other groups that support human rights are doing little to counter governmental exaggerations about the international terrorist threat. To counter this exploitation of fear, LGBT groups and other supporters of human rights need to publicize the facts: they need to continue to challenge the deceptions and to shed light on the human rights abuses that are being pushed into the shadows. We need spotlights of our own, like the After Stonewall Productions' documentaries.

Beyond the prospect for factual rebuttal, such exaggerated fears run a psychological risk. Initially, after the events of 11 September 2001, many people were motivated to act. But many people are already beginning to suppress their fear. Suppressing negative emotions or even entering a state of denial represents the psychological risk that faces the attempt to exploit exaggerated fears. The saying that the main responses to fear are "fight or flight" is instructive. We have no way to guarantee that people who become frightened by accounts of the horrors of terrorist attacks will fight back. Many people take flight, especially when they feel disempowered in the political arena and see how limited the success of past efforts has been. These persons may suffer from psychic numbing (Lifton, 1968).

When people *suppress* fear, they *avoid* the call to action. We need to avoid the equally psychologically debilitating extremes of denial and resignation. Those who are fearful of terrorism are the most likely to be in denial that the United States government tolerates human rights abuses. Those who are most fearful of being labeled unpatriotic or a threat to security are the most likely to lapse into resignation to a presumed need to remain silent. When one has the courage to reject these extremes, action becomes relevant.

The political risk for political leaders who exploit exaggerated fears is that these concerns can get *co-opted* by the public in subsequent policy debates. How are we to fight off global terrorism? Current anti-terrorist politicians say we must rid the world of terrorists; we must wage a war against terrorism. A year after the attacks of 11 September 2001, the Bush Administration, in the new "National Security Strategy of the United States of America" (2002) declared the United States government was prepared to take pre-emptive military action. It even announced plans to have the option of using modified nuclear weapons to destroy terrorist strongholds or stashes of weapons of mass destruction or to respond to terrorist attacks that make use of biological, chemical, or nuclear weapons.

Political leaders have told the American people that governmental possession of chemical, biological, and nuclear weapons is itself one of the means of preventing evil governments or terrorist organizations from using weapons of mass destruction. Now the Bush administration claims that its proposed modified nuclear weapons that could be used in the "war on terrorism" will also function to deter terrorism.

In the past and currently, governmental leaders, by preying on public fears, achieve acquiescence to an ideology that portrays international adversaries as diabolical and untrustworthy. Under these conditions and supposedly to "save" their citizens from the "absolute evils," military and political leaders present military preparedness and military actions as the only (or best) insurance against terrorist attacks. This governmental co-opting of fear can be turned against itself by various citizen-based organizations. But to do so requires drawing attention to the real risks, namely, the real risk that our civil liberties and even our democratic government may be taken from us.

The final risk facing exaggerated fears is moral (Routley, 1984). Use of exaggerated fears is too farsighted. Farsightedness is the pathological condition in which vision is better for distant than near objects. But farsighted individuals also fail to bring nearby objects into sharp focus. Even if further terrorist attacks of the magnitude of 11 September 2001 might not be far in the future, multiple other war-like objects *are* much closer to us. They surround us.

When we devote too much of our attention to imagining the worst that could happen, we risk inflicting *moral farsightedness* on ourselves. Just as we are being myopic when we focus primarily on crime in the streets when confronting the problem of human violence, even so we are being hyperopic to focus predominantly on the threats of global terrorism when confronting the problems of the large-scale violence of war itself and the attendant human rights abuses. Exaggerated fears risk leaving us morally *shortchanged* when they lead us to fail to fight against the horrors of violence that are not distant or possible threats but everyday realities. Our leaders short change us morally and defy our Judeo-Christian-Islamic tradition which does not so sharply divide good and evil and recognizes that no one—not even our leaders—is exempt from moral shortcomings or even from potential lapses into pernicious behaviors.

A telling inadequacy of fear, whether proportionate or excessive, is that it is only negative. Anti-terrorist politicians present negative images repeatedly. Their negative images cause many people nightmares and anxiety. This negativity can get out of hand, unless coupled with a positive vision. One message of the nonviolent movements of the twentieth century is that hope serves us better than fear.

We need to seek alternative, positive images. Already, some resources are available, such as "Surviving Militarism, Racism, and Repression: An Emergency Preparedness Kit for LGBT & Queer Youth" (American Friends Service Committee, n.d.). More generally, evidence of successful nonviolent struggles abounds. For example, Ackerman and Duvall have shown how in every decade of the twentieth century and on all continents (except Antarctica) nonviolent movements have succeeded (Ackerman and Duvall, 2000).

Within the LGBT community, the American Friends Service Committee has an LGBT Peace Work project. We are at a point where LGBT groups, human rights organizations, social justice advocates, peace activists, and others need to join forces. We can build a better future.

Many of us recall the lyrics of John Lennon's "Imagine," that include the lines "all the people living life in peace" and "imagine all the people sharing all the world." He said that to imagine such is "easy if you try."

The imagining may be easy, but we need to do more than imagine. We need to engage in the arduous political work necessary to bring about such a positive vision. Kant (1983, p. 135) reminded us that since peace is possible, we have a moral duty to seek to advance it. Likewise, since the protection of human rights and the advancement of social justice are possible, we have a moral duty to advance them.

We have a moral duty to work for societies in which human emancipation, dignity, and respect are not restricted based on irrelevant factors like gender, race, or sexual orientation. One step in this journey involves exposing and overcoming the political use of the "War on Terrorism" to augment domestic and international LGBT repression.

Three

FEAR AND NEGATION IN THE AMERICAN RACIAL IMAGINARY: BLACK MASCULINITY IN THE WARS ON TERROR AND SAME-SEX MARRIAGE

Lisa Guerrero

I have stood in places
where the absence of light
allowed me to live longer,
while at the same time
it rendered me blind.

I struggle against
plagues, plots
pressure,
paranoia.
Everyone wants a price
for my living.

> Essex Hemphill
> "The Tomb of Sorrow"

1. Introduction

Essex Hemphill was a poet and an activist. He was black. He was gay. He was an American citizen. In his poem "Heavy Breathing," he writes: "I am eager to burn / this threadbare masculinity, / this perpetual black suit / I have outgrown" (1992). The "perpetual black suit" that he has "outgrown," and the "threadbare masculinity" he desires "to burn" is the hollow representation of black men in the American popular imagination that demands that black manhood be forced into an ideological procrustean bed, either to be commodified, feared, or erased.

This American tradition of the containment of the black body is the "price" that "everyone wants" for his "living." Hemphill died in 1995, five years before the first state in the United States, Vermont, would recognize the right for gays and lesbians to be joined in "civil unions." Vermont's move shook many conservatives, religious and secular, to their core over the threat that gay American people posed to family values and American traditions. It was also six years before President George W. Bush would declare a "war on terror," initiating a new era of American authoritarianism and a slow death knell for American civil liberties. Despite dying before witnessing these momentous changes to the American way of life and their consequences, Hemphill already knew what it meant to be seen as the enemy. He understood the burden of having threat and transgression inscribed on your body for the simple facts of the color of your skin and the gender of who you loved. He knew that as a black man in America, people saw him, or the images they mistook for him, virtually everywhere: on their television, in their sports arenas, in the news, around dark corners, in the prisons, in their nightmares. But his reality as a black man, and as a black, *gay* man in America was virtually invisible, marginalized within the gay community, denied within much of the black community, and feared and erased by the larger American community.

Hemphill's was a life that existed in constant material and ideological negotiation. His was a life that, like those of many black men in America, cultivated a paradoxical relationship to the persistent state of invisibility. It has become both friend and foe to black men in the United States. The state of being unseen offers a fleeting safety from the accusatory glances, fingers, opinions, and violence of those who live in fear of the threat they have created in the black man's image. As Hemphill says, "I have stood in places / where the absence of light / allowed me to live longer."

At the same time, this state of being unseen and negated has made it nearly impossible for black men in America, especially black gay men, to recognize and embolden their own identities and subjectivities, as well as those of other black men who suffer the same social paroxysm—"while at the same time / it rendered me blind." It is this representational struggle elegized by Hemphill, between disinterest, distrust, disposability, and disappearance, that the American national imaginary has foisted onto the black male body in America, and differentially onto the black, gay male body. This struggle marks the center of my interest in this essay, in particular, how this struggle plays out in service to the wedded battles in the United States over same-sex marriage and the war on terror.

These two issues predominate the social and political dialogue in America now, captivating the collective national imagination to the almost total exclusion of any other domestic or foreign issues with the substantive potential to alter the future progress and trajectory of the United States and its citizens. While focusing on this predominance, we cannot ignore the extent to which blackness, broadly construed, and black masculinity specifically, are being effectively sacrificed, rhetorically and bodily, through scapegoating, profiling, violence, unlawful imprisonment, and silencing.

In the war on terror, men of color, especially black and "Arab-looking" men, constitute the largest part of the center of suspicion. Serving as the constant locus of attention negates the reality of black male identity through precisely constructed stereotypes that maintain the fantasy of "threat" that is so central to the maintenance of the war on terror.

Alternatively, in the issue of same-sex marriage, black gay men are negated through their complete erasure from the images and voices that make up the popular understanding of the fight for gay marriage rights. In both issues, the process of the negation of black male identity is of critical importance.

In this chapter, I examine the complex role that objectified blackness and otherness, and the body of the black male other, is fulfilling in the mind of the contemporary American public as it seeks to keep itself "safe" from the "threat" of both terrorists and homosexuals. I consider the following aspects of this issue: (1) the way in which the black body has historically been defined as the locus of transgression in the United States and how that historical definition has taken on complicated nuances in service to the war on terror; (2) the question of how the phenomenon identified by Cornel West as "the niggerization of America since 9/11" (West, 2004) dictates twenty-first century racial formations and the way in which they're deployed; (3) the ways in which the popular "whitening" of representations of gayness in the United States stifles the stake of queers of color in social policy debates; and (4) the question of how the denial and heteronormativizing of the black community in the United States toward black gays contributes to the maintenance of popular rhetorics around "threat" and "containment."

I use these discrete points, and their interconnections, as a means to interrogate the *enemy* status of black identity in America as these two apparently disparate "threats have come together in the American consciousness to create an indistinguishable matrix of threat that sustains the current American culture of fear.

2. Enemy Mine

In the United States in the twenty-first century, "Americans [are] trapped within a humiliating, costly, and essentially impossible effort to secure themselves against the terrors of their own *imaginations*" (Lustick, 2006, emphasis added). The threats to the "American way of life," both imagined and real, strike a common chord of a paradoxical mix of anxiety and cocksuredness among many citizens in protecting this hallowed, (or is it *hollow*?), idealized standard of living. This, despite the popular and the political notion(s) of what the American way of life *is*, is generally accepted without ever being questioned in realistically material terms. Also, many of the citizens who play that "chord" loudly are positioned *outside* of the meaning(s) of "the American way of life" by many of their fellow citizens either because of their race, their class, their origin, their religion, or their sexual orientation.

Interestingly, in twenty-first century America, the strategic deployment of the rhetoric of "threat" is used in equal measure to unite and divide. In addition to American people wanting to feel safe in the aftermath of the attacks, they want to feel safe *from*—safe *from* a terror that has been racialized to fit into the expedient and traditional stereotypes of a black and brown menace.

The objectification of the "threat" of black men in America in the era of "the war on terror" is merely a new version of a familiar state of dislocation, disempowerment, and disservice. According to statistics presented in a special series on black men in America run by *The Washington Post* in June of 2006:

> (1) The percentage of black men graduating from college has nearly quadrupled since the passage of the 1964 Civil Rights Act, and yet more black men earn their high school equivalency diplomas in prison each year than graduate from college.
> (2) [T]he chances of a black boy serving time has nearly tripled during the last three decades.
> (3) A black man is more than six times as likely as a white man to be slain. The trend is most stark among black men 14 to 24 years old: They were implicated in a quarter of the nation's homicides and accounted for 15 percent of the homicide victims in 2002, although they were just 1.2 percent of the population, according to the Bureau of Justice Statistics.
> (4) [B]lack men are nine times as likely as white men to die from AIDS, and life expectancy for black men is 69.2 years—more than six years shorter than that of white men (Michael A. Fletcher, "At the Corner of Progress and Peril," 2 June 2006).

These statistics demonstrate the *threatened* state of black men's lives in America long before the advent of the war on terror initiated a "patriotic" justification for the diminishment of civil rights and the increase of surveillance and racial profiling, all occurrences that disproportionately affect men of color. The question becomes: Who poses the *actual* "threat"? Men of color, or an American society built on the deprivation and degradation of men of color, here and abroad?

3. Of Democracy and Demons

In his book *Democracy Matters: Winning the Fight against Imperialism*, Cornel West makes a profound characterization of the effect of the terrorist attacks on the country. He calls it "the niggerization of America":

> The ugly terrorist attacks on innocent civilians on 9/11 plunged the whole country into the blues. Never before have Americans of *all* classes, colors, regions, religions, genders, and sexual orientations felt unsafe, unprotected, subject to random violence, and hated. Yet to have been designated and treated as a nigger in America for over 350 years has been to feel unsafe, unprotected, subject to random violence, and hated . . . . Since 9/11 we have experienced the niggerization of America. (2004)

West's racialized portrayal of the United States in the aftermath of 11 September 2001 is useful in considering the transformation of America's attitudes regarding race and rights during this era of the war on terror. His comparison of America's overarching feeling of unbridled vulnerability and vilification in the face of the terrorist attacks of 11 September 2001 to the transhistorical phenomenon of daily vulnerability and vilification of African American people in the United States is disturbingly accurate. Regardless, neither the administration nor the popular media and citizens who have supported the administration's authoritarian responses to the attacks have recognized that their experience in being niggerized is a direct result of the ways in which they have made "niggers" out of their citizens of color, especially black American people. Through their privileged and paternalistic policies and the arrogant ways in which they manipulate the meaning of democracy, they have similarly niggerdized countless brown and black nations worldwide.

Ironically, the inability for many in the United States to see the ways in which the United States—its histories, policies, and attitudes—has contributed to a global "war *of* terror" has served to legitimize the increase in racial intolerance since the bombing of the twin towers. Instead of creating a solidarity among people—especially those, like African American people, who have spent lifetimes "designated and treated as a nigger" by the United States—the country and its leaders have quickly cultivated a deeper need to stratify through racial difference. They contain threat through racial profiling, racial violence, and the denial of civil rights based largely in racial suspicion.

All in the name of "protection," "prevention," and "safety," many American people have complacently accepted this American racial terrorism as a valid response. The war on terror has not decreased the visibility of "the nigger" through any post-11 September 2001 campaign of American solidarity. Instead, it has sharpened its visage with the attention given to the xenophobic hysteria around threat, and given birth to its brother, "the sand nigger." Both of these American chimeras have fortified the place of the black male body at the center of a newly conceived notion of "threat" in America. This new notion of "threat" gives no concern to the ways in which the ideology of threat in this era of the "war on terror" translates to the actual physical and material threats for men of color in the United States. Most of these people are not terrorists, conspirators, or owners of WMDs, but are just citizens who are now forced to contend with defending themselves against the indictment of America's fear-fueled imaginations. In America right now, the highest color on the terror alert is not red, but shades of black and brown.

Though this phenomenon of black male bodies defined as the ideological site of transgression and deviance is not new, in its most recent incarnation it is being deployed with a jingoistic fervor that marks a critical shift. Historically, men of color, particularly African American men, have been equated with threat and transgression through naturalistic understandings of animalistic strength and violence, hypersexuality, brute intellect, and uncivilized or primitive socialization.

They have largely been seen as a threat for whom they were thought to be, and not for what has, and had, been done to them, kept from them, and constructed around them. For most American people throughout history, the inferiority of African American people has become naturalized and their containment has become normalized.

American democracy has rarely been able to accommodate transgression. To be black and male, especially in America, is to transgress from the moment you arrive(d) in the (new) world. Within the black experience in America, this negation has been inscribed on the skin and is used as the continued justification for a compromised claim to citizenship and citizenship rights. This naturalized inscription of blackness as not just difference, but a difference that threatens, has made it possible for an ideology of fear to infiltrate the fabric of the American popular imagination with regard to black culture, black people, and especially, black men. So strong is the popular belief in the connection between blackness and threat, that it maintains a powerful ability to invoke fear, even when it is not present. In America, the "threat" may, or may not be imminent, but it is almost always black.

A case in point is the oft-mentioned case of the Oklahoma City Bomber, Timothy McVeigh. Before 11 September 2001, the bombing of the Alfred P. Murrah Federal Building in Oklahoma City, Oklahoma, stood as the largest and deadliest act of terrorism against the United States that had ever occurred within its borders. Despite the deadly way in which the act demonstrated the threat to the United States posed by anti-government citizen militias, most of which are predominantly white and Christian, no increased profiling of white men of a certain age, from certain geographies, and with certain documented interests and affiliations was forthcoming from the government.

Constitutional rights for all who were threatened were not readily dismissed to ensure the containment and punishment for the few who posed threat. Having the last name MacDonald, Kennedy, or Jones did not mean you were flagged for suspicion of terrorist connections and detained in airports or prisons. Neither did the fact that you went to church every Sunday. Though Timothy McVeigh and his conspirator, Terry Nichols, were threats, their whiteness wasn't. By comparison, in the face of 11 September 2001, blackness and brownness, including the accident of merely *looking* Arab or Muslim, have come to signify the height of "threat."

This inherent willingness for American people to trust in the reality of equating blackness with threat has made engaging in strategies founded in some of the most insidious and base racial assumptions imaginable exceedingly easy for the Bush administration. These strategies have met with little opposition from the majority of American citizens. As Michelle Alexander of the American Civil Liberties Union of Northern California has noted, "The war rhetoric is giving license to law enforcement to engage in racial profiling just as it did in the war on drugs. Both wars create a 'by any means necessary' attitude that encourages law enforcement to target people based on race" (Larry Aubry, "Racial Profiling in Spotlight after 9/11," *Los Angeles Sentinel*, 17 January 2002).

The precedent set by these tactics will invariably open—arguably already opened—a civil liberties Pandora's box, which will be impossible to contain, even after any nominal victory in the war on terror has been claimed. By then, racism as a legitimate form of domestic security will be "business as usual." As sociology professor, Abu B. Bah, has said, "While these institutional mechanisms might be seen as short-term measures intended to combat terrorism, they could easily evolve into covert draconian rules and practices that can be used against minorities" (2006). In post-11 September 2001 America, racism will never be able to compete with terrorism for the ability to mobilize the American people in the face of "threat."

4. Home/o-land Security

In considering the rhetoric of "threat" and the ways in which it links the war on terror and the virulent arguments against same-sex marriage, especially with the place of the black male body within these "wars," I am reminded of three different moments I have experienced over the past year. The first was during a classroom discussion regarding the AIDS epidemic and the catastrophic effects it is having on the African American community. I had asked why the communication about, and awareness of, the threat of AIDS is not more prevalent in African American communities. One student, a black man, said that it had to do with pride and shame and ideas of masculinity and what it meant to be a "man." Attempting to build on this student's response, another student, also a black man, said, "Yeah, I mean, the other day I was sitting out on the rock and I saw a black gay man, and I just thought to myself, 'What happened? What happened to him that *this* would happen?'" (emphasis added).

The second experience was a discussion I had with a colleague who had just returned from class. During his class, some discussion had centered around issues of black homosexuality. One of his students, a black man, interjected that he "didn't think that there really were black gay people."

Finally, I recall a moment while reading the essay "It's a White Man's World" from Dwight McBride's book, *Why I Hate Abercrombie and Fitch* in which he talks about the role of black gay men in gay culture. He relates a discussion he had with a friend, who is also a black gay man, while they were enjoying a drink in a predominantly white gay bar that was punctuated with various television screens showing black gay pornography. His friend, taking account of the surroundings, noted, "I guess virtual blackness is okay, even unremarkable for white folks ... while our presence is an entirely different story" (2005). This humorous remark led McBride to consider why black men are so desirable and abundant in gay pornography, yet so denied and invisible in wider representations of actual gay life. In the larger gay community, why are black gay men relegated to a world of virtual blackness?

> Virtual blackness, contained blackness, is always there in different forms... for the taking, the watching, the pleasuring when one wants it. But because it is contained and virtual, there is no danger of it speaking back, objecting, calling you out, making demands, or not giving you exactly what you have come to expect from it—your fetishistic fulfillment. (Ibid.)

As McBride sees it, virtual blackness, especially in the case of black gay men within the larger gay community, negates black agency and subjectivity because it denies intimacy, even fundamental interaction, replacing it instead with the constructed image of black male homosexuality that serves and pleasures white imaginations, while keeping the messiness of humanity and the threat of contamination safely contained.

Taken together, these three moments speak to the heart of a crisis surrounding black homosexual—especially male—subjectivity within the United States. The first two moments starkly illustrate the negated and transgressive position held by gay African American people in the communal imaginations of many African American people in the United States. Either others do not see them because the others in the black community truly do believe, or have willed themselves to believe, that people who are black and gay do not actually exist, or if others see them, they see them as deviant and as having an inferior racial identity. No longer are they true or authentic black men and women, but race traitors seen by others as sacrificing not only their blackness, but also the struggle(s) of the black community in favor of deviant sexual pleasure and gratification.

In part, this is a result of the larger essentializing that takes place around gay identity in the United States. Rarely do others understand the sexuality of gay African American people or the wider gay population in terms of identity. Instead, they always understand it in the reduced terms of a sex act. That reduction makes it easier for homophobic and heterosexist people to dismiss homosexuality as a choice, as chosen behavior, which they could easily "unchoose."

Especially for black gay men, whose masculinity as black men has always problematically stood as a monolith seen by the rest of black society as paramount not only to the survival of black men themselves, but also to the black community largely, this misguided notion that they have a choice to be gay doubly negates their subjectivities. They are no longer seen as men. They are also no longer seen as black, at least in the terms necessary to be counted in "the black struggle," and as part of "the black community."

The scene in the lounge illustrates that within the broader gay community, black gay men experience an invisibility and denial similar to what they experience in their racial communities. But as we can understand from McBride's discussion of "virtual blackness," the invisibility and denial to which black gay men are subjected within the gay community, has a different tone from what they experience in black communities. Inside the larger gay community, the "otherness" of black gay men is desired, is commodifiable, but most importantly, is contained, mostly in sexual arenas like the pornography talked about by McBride and his friend. The representations of black gayness within the gay community are frequently reduced to fetish. This allows for the almost literal disembdiment of black gay subjectivity from the social and political struggles facing gay communities in the United States today, most notably in this moment, the debate over same-sex marriage.

I delineate this crisis of black gay subjectivity not because I believe it is necessarily unfamiliar to many people, although it may be to some, but to provide a social genealogy for the negated position in which black gay men are being put within the debates surrounding same-sex marriage. Their almost total invisibility within these current debates has not occurred suddenly, but instead marks a kind of anti-culmination in their dislocation from the "imagined communities" to which they belong.

This phenomenon is vividly illustrated by the declaration made from the pulpit by Reverend Gregory Daniels, a black minister in Chicago, during February 2004. "If the KKK opposes gay marriage, I would ride with them" (Keith Boykin, "Whose Dream," *The Village Voice*, 28 May 2004). This is a shocking declaration of communal and moral affinity with a group, which has historically sought the degradation and destruction of all African American people, regardless of sexual orientation or position in their church. Its campaigns of violence and white supremacy against all groups seen as "deviant" (African American, immigrants, gay, lesbian, Jewish, and Muslim people) are grounded primarily in hate— its ideology and rhetoric. Daniels illustrates not just a disregard of black gays and lesbians, but a fundamental denial of their "worth" to the larger black community.

Daniels' willful misrecognition of gay rights as something other than civil rights and as a blatant threat *to* civil rights, lays bare the lengths to which larger black communities and their leaders who speak for them are willing to go to advance an ineffectual notion of the politics of respectability distanced from all forms of deviance and threat. As Essex Hemphill once noted in his essay entitled "Loyalty," black gay men are:

> emasculated in the complicity of not speaking out, rendered mute by the middle-class aspirations of a people trying hard to forget the shame and cruelties of slavery and ghettos. Through denials and abbreviated histories riddled with omissions, the middle class sets about whitewashing and fixing up the race to impress each other and the racists who don't give a damn. (1992)

These efforts at "respectability politics," employed by many in the black community, not only readily deny the lives of other black American people whose sexual orientation is somehow seen as negating their individual "black" identities, but also conveniently reimagine the domain of civil rights as exclusively about *race*, and therefore, the only front on which to fight. Many leaders within the black community are all too willing to essentialize civil rights in this way. Keith Boykin observes, "selectively target elements of white society to critique, but challenging only racism, they [black leaders] appear to accept heterosexism, homophobia, sexism, and violence" (Boykin, 1996).

Anything that appears to detract from the singular struggle in race, or appears to jeopardize it by compounding the already ingrained images of the "threat of blackness" against which all African American people must contend, is unwanted. If you are not with us, you are against us. If you are gay, you are not with us.

Neither are black gays seen as "with" the larger gay community. Amidst the sea of images of happy, middle-class, gay white men and women kissing one another on the steps of government buildings after their union ceremonies, the questions of race and class have been effectively drowned out of the debate over same-sex marriage. If the American people are to believe what they see and hear in the news regarding same-sex marriage, then the only gay people who want the right to marry are white. From there it is not too far a leap for people inside and outside of the gay community to begin to construct the notion that gay equals white. Just such a trend has characterized the mainstream explosion of gay images in the United States that began in the 1990s. Writer/activist, Kenyon Farrow notes:

> And haven't all of the popular culture gay images on TV shows like *Will & Grace*, *Queer as Folk*, etc., been exclusively white? No matter how many black divas wail over club beats in white gay clubs all over America (Mammy goes disco!) with gay men appropriating language and other black cultural norms (specifically from black women), white gay men continue to function as cultural imperialists the same way straight white boys appropriate hip-hop . . . . There has always been racial tensions in the gay community as long as there have been racial tensions in America, but in the 1990s, the white gay community went mainstream, further pushing non-hetero people of color from the movement. (2004)

These trends in American popular culture entrench the belief that gayness and whiteness are one in the same. It then follows that the mainstreaming of gayness relies on the implicit assumptions to whiteness and on the achievement of normative (read: white) institutions like marriage and family. Going further, Farrow states:

> The reason for [the schism between white gays and gays of color] is that in order to be mainstream in America, one has to be seen as white. And since white is normative, one has to interrogate what other labels or institutions are seen as normative in our society: family, marriage, and military service

to name a few. It is then no surprise that a movement that goes for "normality" would end up in a battle over a dubious institution like marriage (and hetero-normative family structures by extension). And debates over "family values," no matter how broad or narrow you look at them, always have whiteness at the center, and are almost always anti-black . . . So the fact that the white gay community continues to use white images of same-sex families is no accident, since the black family, heterosexual, same-sex or otherwise, is always portrayed as dysfunctional. (Ibid.)

So, if gay equals white, and black equals straight, what becomes of your *equality* when you are both black *and* gay?

5. The Price of the Ticket for the War on Terror

The War on Terror and the arguments against same-sex marriage have enjoyed a synergistic relationship during the last six years of the Bush administration. Each campaign has centered its focus on the defense of the American way of life, and its strategy on the creation of an "enemy" and the containment of "threat," either by military force or Constitutional manipulation. Their strategic interrelatedness reached a distressing point during the 2004 presidential election.

At that time, the debate over same-sex marriage, including George W. Bush's rhetorical support of a Constitutional amendment securing marriage as an institution between a man and a woman, renewed its center-stage status. This distracted many voters, especially and fatefully, many black voters, from the increasingly deadly, expensive, and futile imperialistic war in Iraq. This had a disturbing collateral effect on many central domestic issues including the economy, education, and unemployment, all three of which disproportionately devastate communities of color.

Baited by Bush's characterization of same-sex marriage as the end of traditional American family values, many voters, most notably working class voters and voters of color, who otherwise were not supporters of Bush's Republican platforms and policies, including the war in Iraq, carried George W. Bush into his second term. At first glance, this outcome seems counterintuitive. However, the image of safeguarding American morality from the "threat" of an enemy who is known—gays and lesbians—makes the result a bit easier to understand, if no less disturbing.

In twenty-first century America, "threat" is, for the most part, ethereal. Especially in the context of the war on terror, an indiscriminancy to the enemy makes the containment of a *real* enemy and an *actua*l threat a challenging endeavor. Though the Bush Administration has implemented "safety" measures, such as increased and unchecked racial profiling and unlawful and clandestine detention of "suspicious" people, still no definitive place exists where people can place their fear. Same-sex marriage offers an embodiment of enemy, which many people need to feel some semblance of security.

More problematically, many of the people of color who supported Bush because of his stance against same-sex marriage, did so in hopes of supplanting the enemy who is black or brown with the enemy who is gay or lesbian in the American imagination. Unfortunately, though not surprisingly, neither of these reasons would change the fact that when George W. Bush entered his second administration, he continued to deplete spending on social services, environmental issues, and education, while maintaining or increasing spending on the war, on police enforcement, and on prisons and detention centers, all of which guarantees the continued vulnerability and exploitation of poor and racialized populations in the United States. This paradoxical notion of "safety" is the true nature of threat in our country today.

6. And Justice for All

As I complete this essay during March 2007, the United States House of Representatives has just voted 218-212 for legislation H.R. 1591, which would bring the majority of American troops back from Iraq in the next year, "as part of a $124 billion emergency war spending request for military operations in Iraq and Afghanistan for the next six months" (Jeff Zeleny, "House, 218 to 212, Votes to Set Date for Iraq Pullout," *The New York Times*, 24 March 2007). At the same time, the Senate, with a vote of 50-48, defeated a Republican amendment to H.R. 643 "that would have stripped out language setting a timetable for withdrawal of troops from Iraq" (Kate Phillips, "Senate Democrats Prevail in Iraq Vote," *The New York Times,* 27 March 2007). A month earlier, on 19 February 2007, New Jersey became just the third state to allow civil unions between same-sex couples.

Both of these moments, while filled with possibility for the coming of a sea change, will likely bring about little change for black men in the contexts in which I discussed in this chapter.

Even with a possible end brought to the *actual* war in Iraq, the ideological war on terror will continue for a much longer time and may even be intensified without a "real" war through which to assuage the collective American fear, even nominally. The fear of threat will have to be served in some way and by some*one*. Men of color, black men in particular, will always be a ready, familiar, and vulnerable target. Though this is a consequence that we can almost certainly *expect*, we should not *accept* it. Threatening justice for one threatens justice for all.

As Essex Hemphill once wrote, "Let us not accept / partial justice. / If we believe our lives / are priceless / we can't be conquered" (1992, pp. 16–20). Let us hope our fear hasn't conquered us already.

Four

GRAY ZONES

John Streamas

Trash, in all its meanings, has become an obsession of powerful men and institutions. Eduardo Galeano writes that, a century after scientists advocated eradication of poor people as a solution to a perceived crime problem, "Countries of the South treat the poorest poor as if they were toxic waste. The countries of the North export their dangerous industrial waste to the South, but the South can't return the favor" (2000, p. 95). In cities of the South "leftovers" may be defined as "street kids, vagrants, beggars, prostitutes, transvestites, homosexuals, pickpockets, small-time thieves, drug addicts, drunks, squeegee kids" (ibid., p. 96).

To treat the poor as trash is not only to marginalize but also mainly—literally—to contain them. Metaphorically and geographically, marginalized peoples have no access to centers of power, but they may have some autonomy within their marginalized spaces. Still, the South's leftovers, the contained poor, while not eradicated, are buried, metaphorically and geographically, as irrecoverably as radioactive waste. The image of containment that I wish to advance here is an image of burial, far more horrible than any living death that Poe might have conjured. The South's poor become the North's trash.

Even in the New York City of the 1990s, according to Julie Sze, Mayor Rudolph Giuliani's management of garbage mirrored his management of the city's poor, clearing streets of trash and "squeegee men" (2007, pp. 9–10). In the twenty-first century streets of Iraq, according to Mike Davis, "unemployed teenage fighters of the 'Mahdi Army' in Baghdad's Sadr City—one of the world's largest slums—taunt American occupiers with the promise that their main boulevard is 'Vietnam Street'" (2006, p. 205).

Yet such a defiant linking of poverty to war fails to deter the warmongers, who in "cold-blooded lucidity," says Davis, "assert that the 'feral, failed cities' of the Third World—especially their slum outskirts—will be the distinctive battle space of the twenty-first century. Pentagon doctrine is being reshaped accordingly to support a low-intensity world war of unlimited duration against criminalized segments of the urban poor" (ibid.).

To reduce the poor to the level of trash is to extract all humanity from them. Torture does this too. In the modern political arena, the disposal of trash and the torture of prisoners are meant to produce similar results. Kristian Williams (2006, pp. 143–144) cites reports of torture in Colombia that he links to increases in United States' aid to the government's nominal anti-drug campaign.

Colombian artist Fernando Botero devoted a series of paintings to violence. He recently turned his attention to tortures at the Abu Ghraib Prison in Iraq. These new paintings and drawings represent his reimaginings of those tortures (Adler, 2006). They are stark, frightening, and brutal. In the most famously reproduced image, a meaty hand is thrust upward and a rope, dropping from the top frame, comes down into a noose wrapped twice around the wrist. Significantly, Botero's images are not renderings of the photographs made famous in 2004:

> The photographs show naked, contorted bodies arranged in a pyramid. They show hooded men masturbating while a soldier smiles and points. They show a dead body packed in ice, and smiling soldiers giving the thumbs-up. They show dogs straining at the leash, and a nude man cowering—and the same man, later, bleeding. They show a ghostly figure, hooded and draped with a blanket, standing on a narrow box, wires running from his hands (Williams, 2006, p. 1).

If his paintings and drawings refuse to reproduce the photographs even as they envision the tortures, Botero may well understand what Williams understands, that the photographs "tell us almost nothing," offering "a glimpse of horror" but failing to "explain what is happening, or why, or who benefits, or who is responsible" (ibid.). Mark Danner agrees, claiming, "the photographs . . . show nothing more than the amateur stooges of 'the process,'" and that "those who ran 'the process' and issued the orders" will surely go unpunished (2004, p. 9).

Soon after the photographs' publication, Seymour Hersh explained this process in his May 2004 articles in *The New Yorker*. I wish to focus here on his article of 24 May 2004, titled "The Gray Zone." I will argue that the world's outcasts are reduced to the level of trash through processes of torture, and that these processes are hidden under a culture and politics that are color-code pliant but seemingly inviolable borders, or zones. Such coding has much cruel irony, as people have used colors for half a millennium to construct borders between races, and racism has overlapped with poverty.

Those outcast by racism and poverty are twice trashed. This too is a kind of containment that echoes the death-in-life of burial, a secret expression of a public injustice. The trashing of prisoners at Abu Ghraib found other channels for torture also, such as religion and sex. I will examine here the color-coding and sexual abuses.

Campaigns for justice often founder on an inability to discover a language adequate to name and confront the new language of injustice. Here I will argue that the lexicon of injustice is slippery and changeable because injustice itself is fluid and flexible. Were tortures at Abu Ghraib mostly a national, a racial, a sexual, or a class injustice? The color-coded language of these tortures does not care, as long as the victims remain carefully controlled and contained. Ultimately, the tortures themselves are not new—for how many ways exist to torture a body?—but the language of containment has evolved and is purposefully impossible to pin down. Today's black may be tomorrow's white. Or, the words may change even as the things they name remain unchanged.

The word "gray" appears only once in Hersh's article, and then only in a quote attributed to an unnamed Pentagon source (identified only as "an academic"). This source argued that Congress would have to enforce a system of checks and balances by thoroughly investigating abuses: "When you live in a world of gray zones, you have to have very clear red lines" (2004, p. 44).

Yet the prisoner-abuse scandal arose not because of secret and unknowable gray zones but because of clear violations of international laws. These violations occupy a world that, even in secret intelligence parlance, interprets events as "black" and "white," in which operatives regard the white world as public and hostile, the black as private, friendly, and safe. If this construction appears to clash with a culture whose racisms privilege whiteness and demonize blackness, it is still consistent with political institutions that name a weapon a "peacemaker." Politicians hate blackness as much as ever, but they perversely envy it too, and the best place to locate this envy is in the black label they attach to their most covert and risky business.

1. Black and White

The lexicon of politics and culture is sometimes more colored than the politics and culture themselves. "Editing a Mask," a study guide for Adobe Photoshop image editing program (Adobe Creative Team, 2004), instructs users to erase "black or gray flecks . . . by painting with white." In digital imaging, "grayscale" refers to a range of shades of gray in an image reducible to pixels—subject to atomizing. The effect of such digital editing is to locate and flatten deviations. To locate them first is to highlight, or render them public. To flatten is to assimilate them. Lest this seem far-fetched when applied to the political world, Hersh's anonymous source, referring to intelligence agents, says that these "black guys" are "vaccinated from the reality" (2004, p. 44). Political-military operatives are accountable to no laws or ethical standards. They collapse the long time span of implications and consequences into the immediacy of their mission.

Differences and deviations that are reversed or flattened are subject to still further manipulation. In the human realm, they are more easily reduced to the North's trash. The phenomenon is not new, nor is it dismissible as an Orwellian trick. A decade ago, a California proposal calling itself a "civil rights initiative" opposed affirmative action.

Multiculturalism and diversity mean, in most institutional settings, not a context for innovation and resistance, but a multicolored enforcement of conformity—what critics call a "colorblind racism." In a book that wrongly minimizes the effects of racism in the United States, Walter Benn Michaels rightly insists that "the concept of diversity was introduced as a kind of end run around the historical problem of racism," and he points to studies finding that institutional diversity is "a $10-billion-a-year industry" (2006, pp. 4, 13).

In a world of gray zones, then, racial and sexual deviations are flattened and pushed behind "very clear red lines"—borders are constructed and policed. Even if the War on Terror did not invent the lexicon of politicized colors, still it has enforced it more brutally than previous political and cultural regimes. Trash is contained by being buried and the effect is so decisive that the difference between literal and metaphorical burial appears not to matter.

How, though, can a language of colors flatten differences? After all, racial categories have in the past created and enforced differences to the benefit of those at the top of the racial hierarchy. Anti-miscegenation and blood-purity laws typify past efforts to enforce clearly drawn lines, to contain differences. But the distinctions of black, brown, red, and yellow peoples have not been the main goal of these laws. Instead, the laws have intended to enforce the purity of whiteness.

Modern art and advertising provide clues to the way in which the language of colors can flatten differences and at the same time achieve the same effect—enforcement of the purity and, hence, the superiority of whiteness—that is produced by categorical borders. In a full-page advertisement in *The New Yorker* for Movado watches, black musician Wynton Marsalis holds his trumpet as if playing (*The New Yorker*, 16 October 2006, p. 11). The ad is photographed in a stark black-and-white, with a minimum of text. A block of five short lines in the lower left identifies Marsalis as a "virtuoso." It also describes the watch as having a "black dial." Marsalis is photographed in such an enveloping shadow that we cannot see whether he is wearing a Movado watch, but his being a virtuoso implies that he has enough cultural capital and wealth to own one.

We know that his black face corresponds, in this black-and-white image, to the watch's black dial. The ad's appeal is not populist. Movado constructs Marsalis differently from the ways that ads for Nike and Gatorade have constructed black athletes such as Tiger Woods and Michael Jordan.

Marsalis's appeal here reflects the class trappings that Movado associates with the jazz and classical music he plays. Yet, though he may enjoy the income of the largely white audience of this ad, his labor—his performance on the trumpet—is what we see. Movado links his labor to its audience's leisure. Is it any wonder, then, that we cannot see a watch on him?

Key to understanding the role of Marsalis's blackness is the photograph's black-and-whiteness. In his book, *Chromophobia*, art critic David Batchelor argues, "there remains a belief, often unspoken perhaps but equally often unquestioned, that seriousness in art and culture is a black-and-white issue, that depth is measured only in shades of grey" (2000, pp. 30–31).

Batchelor offers many examples of chromophobia, all exalting the black-and-white image or slight variations of it. But this creates a contradiction. For the black-and-white world harbors, the gravities of modern art and the leisure of those who listen to classical music, wear Movado watches, and look at the conceptual art which, according to Batchelor, "often made a fetish of black and white" (ibid.).

I would argue that, in this rarefied black-and-whiteness, gravity and leisure not only coexist but also are mutually dependent; and that, similarly, the color constituents, the black and the white, are mutually dependent. As I will argue later, a set of differences is flattened on one axis so that another set of differences may be enforced on another. To frame it in terms of art, the black-and-white world is often depicted in shades of gray. To frame it in terms of politics, overt emphasis on difference is flattened so that covert black operatives may contain those same differences—so that the "trash" may be buried.

Hersh defines his source's black guys as "those in the Pentagon's secret program" and the white world as the overt world (2004, pp. 44). But more than a distinction between private and public emerges. On a simple and obvious level are the photographs of torture at Abu Ghraib, which Mark Danner calls "the garish signboards of the scandal and not the scandal itself" (ibid., p. 47). Though torture is exposed, Hersh's source may rightly claim that the "black guys" remain "vaccinated from the reality."

On this level, political leaders may choose not to discuss interrogation methods. When pressed to speak, they may simply defer to claims for the uniqueness of the War on Terror. The Bush Administration, merely by labeling certain prisoners "unlawful combatants," chose to withhold protections granted by the Geneva Convention, and thus cleared a space for their torture. "And the decisions were not, at least in their broad outlines, kept secret," writes Danner. "They were known to officials of the other branches of the government and, eventually, to the public" (ibid., p. 22).

The issue within the government, then, was not whether to torture prisoners—for the uniqueness of these unlawful combatants meant that they deserved harsh punishment—but how extreme the torture should be. Torture was defined as brutalities not being committed (Danner, 2004, p. 76). If the black guys were not exactly imitating, for example, brutalities of Nazis and the Japanese Imperial Army—brutalities that most immediately sparked the sanctions of the Geneva Convention—then they could not be accused of committing real tortures.

Ironically, the black-and-white operation originated in a program called Copper Green. This was, says Hersh, the idea of United States Secretary of Defense Donald Rumsfeld "to expand a highly secret operation, which had been focused on the hunt for Al Qaeda, to the interrogation of prisoners in Iraq" (Hersh, 2004, p. 38). The Copper Green operation "encouraged physical coercion and sexual humiliation of Iraqi prisoners in an effort to generate more intelligence about the growing insurgency in Iraq" (ibid.).

According to Hersh's source, Rumsfeld's Undersecretary of Defense for Intelligence Stephen Cambone grew frustrated with a paucity of useful intelligence, so he set up a "black special-access program" and "pull[ed] the switch, and the electricity beg[a]n flowing . . . . We're getting a picture of the insurgency in

Iraq and the intelligence is flowing into the white world" (ibid., p. 41). Perhaps the surprising disclosure here is not the difference between what the black guys and the "white world" knew but that, as Danner claims, so much was publicly known.

2. The Color of Shame

The Abu Ghraib photographs are in color. To my knowledge, none of the journalists and critics has remarked on the significance of this. According to Danner (2004, p. 215), one military police officer gave another officer two compact discs containing the photographs, and eventually the discs were leaked to the media. The images are crudely made, recalling images frequently found on the Internet of drunken revelers. They further recall images of parties in which fraternity members recreate racial stereotypes—disclosure of such images has led to sanctions in some schools.

But these images are different because we see in them a sharp distinction between the powerful and the powerless. As if the torture itself were not enough to enforce that difference, taking the photographs becomes reinforcement. Yet the soldiers' vulnerability to prosecution and their scapegoating of the black men attests to their relative powerlessness in the "real" world outside the prison. Inside the prison, when Army Reserve Specialist Lynndie England leers and makes a thumbs-up gesture with her right hand while pointing to the penis of the first man in a line of naked men, she is posing not for the prisoners, who are hooded and cannot see her, but for the photographer and an as-yet unknown and unknowable audience. Most soldiers in these pictures are mugging for a camera, as they might if, at home, they were partying. They are performing.

I wish to contrast these images with the photograph of Wynton Marsalis in the Movado advertisement. For if, as Susan Sontag argues, "photographs objectify: they turn an event or a person into something that can be possessed" (2003, p. 81). If the extent of that objectification is a function of the photographer's professionalism, then we can easily agree that Marsalis exists in the thrall of his photographer and Movado.

But what can we make of the Abu Ghraib images made by soldiers? Whereas Marsalis performs for an audience that he and Movado know, the soldiers perform, apparently, only for each other. They are low-level soldiers, taking orders for all their duties, working near the far end of a chain of command.

How must we read their apparent posing for each other even as they perform their black job? Marsalis is the person who appears mostly in shadow, in a black-and-white image whose starkness enhances its appeal to leisure and luxury. The prison photographs are made mostly in garish light. The color of prisoners' flesh, often streaked in blood, casts an eerie brightness over their drab prison yard and cells.

Sontag is helpful here too: "Generally, the grievously injured bodies shown in published photographs are from Asia or Africa," she writes. "This journalistic custom inherits the centuries-old practice of exhibiting exotic—that is, colonized—human beings" (ibid.). Again, she is talking about professional photography, but the soldiers at Abu Ghraib, part of an occupying force and a colonizing mission, were mounting their prisoners, sometimes literally, in an exotic display. The prisoners were like trophies of war—or, since the soldiers were policing the prison camp and not engaging in combat, like trophies of sport. The soldiers were both models and photographers, but the prisoners were only unwilling and incapacitated models.

Four aspects of the objectification of the prisoners are particularly disturbing: the stark contrast between the prisoners' helplessness and the soldiers' lewd playfulness; the prisoners' massing together in anonymous pyramids of abject flesh; the prisoners' frequent nakedness except for hoods covering their heads; and, perhaps most terrifyingly, the soldiers' taunting of prisoners with dogs. In one photograph, a naked prisoner stands before his cell door, hands clasped behind his head, legs clenched to protect his penis, as soldiers to his left and right hold snarling and menacing dogs. He faces not the dogs but a soldier standing in front of him, pointing to the ground as if ordering him to kneel between the dogs.

Critics have condemned the soldiers' willful disrespect for prisoners' cultural and religious sense of dignity and honor, the sexual humiliations that perversely flouted Arab and Muslim codes. Quite possibly, the soldiers did not know these codes. The black mission refused to distinguish between old political differences and new, constructed differences. The mission seized a moment in which sexual difference could be constructed, Orientalized, contained, and then photographed.

If Batchelor rightly observes that black-and-whiteness is constructed to confer seriousness in art, as in the Movado ad, then these Abu Ghraib photographs suggest an opposite, garish place of menace and confinement, of flesh and bared teeth, of play and torture, all in a gray zone. The irony that surely Sontag would see is that the soldiers, when they pose with their prisoners, become prisoners themselves, captured on disc in what television once called living color.

3. The Thin Red Lines

In Botero's paintings, very clear red lines of blood streak prisoners' bodies. In one, two blindfolded prisoners, their hands tied behind their backs, press against each other. The standing man is naked, and soldiers have pushed the kneeling man between the other's legs. The kneeling man's head has been grabbed by a gloved hand coming from the left frame of the picture, presumably the hand of a soldier, grabbing as if to let his blindfolded eyes sense the presence of the man into whose crotch his face will be pushed. Small bright flecks of blood streak their bodies. Flecks that run down their cheeks could be tears.

In another photo, a blindfolded prisoner is bound by his wrists and ankles to the bars of his cell door. He wears a brassiere and panties—sexual abuses at

Abu Ghraib included forcing male prisoners to wear women's underclothes in front of their captors—and they are as bright red as the blood that stains his arms, legs, hips, and thighs. Another painting shows two blindfolded prisoners occupying a small cell, both of them naked and one positioned atop the other. Their hands are bound. The man on top has a large bloody gash in his left shoulder, and protruding from the anus of the man on bottom is the handle of a tool that has apparently been shoved deep into him. Blood pours down the backs of his thighs. In still another image, two men in blindfolds and panties are piled one atop the other, the large man on the floor spitting bright red blood (Ebony, 2006).

In introducing Botero's collection of paintings and drawings of Abu Ghraib, David Ebony argues:

> [T]he most disturbing images . . . depict instances of sexual humiliation and sexual abuse as a means to emasculate and intimidate the male prisoners. Forced homosexual behavior at Abu Ghraib was intended to shame prisoners. (Ibid., p. 16)

In Botero's paintings, colors are bright and vivid, unlike the garish but indistinct colors in the soldiers' photographs. The massive bodies do not resemble the emaciated bodies of the real prisoners at Abu Ghraib, for they fill Botero's surfaces. The bruises and bloodstains on their bright flesh are stark and confrontational, unlike the damaged flesh of the scrawny prisoners who, in the photographs, are clearly trophies of the grinning soldiers who stand above them. When prisoners' faces appear in the paintings, their mouths are usually open, not to scream but merely to gape, as if to vent the pain of the ongoing abjection and to resign the prisoners to the next.

If the black-and-white world is the place that art still honors, then the world of color represents garishness and depravity. David Batchelor lists examples of this depravity in the popular cultures of drugs and film. He quotes Salmon Rushdie's analysis of the film, *The Wizard of Oz*, for whom Dorothy is "caught up in an uprooting and displacement of colour" (2000, p. 40). Batchelor adds that metaphors of falling and leaving are closely related to metaphors of color:

> Their terminologies—of dreams, of joys, of uprootings, or undoings of self—remain more or less the same. More than that, perhaps, the descent into colour often involved lateral as well as vertical displacement. (Ibid., p. 41)

In the Abu Ghraib photographs, the soldiers, as much as the prisoners, have descended and suffered displacement. In Botero's paintings, such displacement is forced upon the prisoners. In the world of these images, color represents punishment, pain, and injustice.

The politics of color points to the significance of Batchelor's study of Le Corbusier, for whom, says Batchelor, "white is clean, clear, healthy, moral, rational, masterful.... In Le Corbusier's intoxicated rationalism, the rhetoric of order, purity and truth is inscribed in a pure, blinding white surface" (ibid., pp. 46–47). Yet the surfaces of Le Corbusier's "buildings are actually *coloured*"— which Batchelor attributes to a paradox of the politics of cultural whiteness:

> [W]e are not dealing with something as simple as white things and white surfaces, with white as an empirically verifiable fact or as a colour. Rather, we are in the realm of *whiteness*. White as myth, as an aesthetic fantasy, a fantasy so strong that it summons up negative hallucinations, so intense that it produces a blindness to colour, even when colour is literally in front of your face. (Ibid.)

If color must be contained, whiteness must contain it:

> What matters is the show of force: the rhetorical subordination of colour to the rule of line and the higher concerns of the mind. No longer intoxicating, narcotic or orgasmic, colour is learned, ordered, subordinated and tamed. Broken. (Ibid., p. 49)

Botero renders the colors of prisoners' flesh and blood bright and garish but also draws sharp boundaries between that flesh and the sites of its torture, so that he may demonstrate the role of color in the black-and-white world. Perhaps more importantly, the brightness and starkness of his colors attest, by implication and inversion, to the power of whiteness in this black-and-white world. The black guys who invent and profit from the War on Terror deploy their black operations to contain the white world of overt disclosures. The colors we see in the soldiers' photographs prove the power of whiteness, while the colors in Botero's paintings take that power and expose it—or try to expose it—to a world that resists containment.

One aspect of the abuses at Abu Ghraib was not captured in published visual images. Williams writes that forty-two women were among those imprisoned. Although none of them told the media that they were subjected to sexual violence, still:

> some information has come out: the Fay report documents incidents of sexual assault, and unreleased photographs show Iraqi women baring their breasts and being fucked by United States soldiers. (Williams, 2006, p. 14)

That such photographs exist, even if unreleased, suggests that containment was, paradoxically, widespread. By this I mean that the black realm is a compressed space; it remains black only when that space is framed or contained. The more compressed the space, the easier framing it and keeping it black becomes.

If the sexual abuse of women prisoners was photographed, and if these photographs are known to exist, even if unpublished, then the space has expanded, possibly beyond its frames and beyond a possibility of keeping it contained. The problem for the black guys is now a problem of managing information in the white world.

President George W. Bush and Secretary Rumsfeld blamed the tortures at Abu Ghraib, especially the sexual abuses, on "a handful of sadists and thugs" (ibid.). Yet, even if the soldiers were such sadists, then their deployment as prison guards suggests that responsibility for their abuses still belongs to those who deployed them. More likely, the kinds of torture they practiced, if not the acts themselves, were known to be a likely and logical outcome of the black programs.

Hersh writes that Major General Geoffrey Miller, who had headed detention and interrogation at Guantánamo Bay military prison, went to Baghdad "to 'Gitmoize' the prison system in Iraq—to make it more focused on interrogation." Miller urged "methods that could, with special approval, include sleep deprivation, exposure to extremes of cold and heat, and placing prisoners in 'stress positions' for agonizing lengths of time" (2004, p. 41).

Rumsfeld and Cambone ordered more: "The commandos were to operate in Iraq as they had in Afghanistan. The male prisoners could be treated roughly, and exposed to sexual humiliation" (ibid.). That top leadership was not unaware of the possibilities—and lurid promise—of sexual abuses is evident. Even before the invasion of Iraq, conservative officials drew from Raphael Patai's book, *The Arab Mind*, two themes of sexual humiliation: "one, that Arabs only understand force and, two, that the biggest weakness of Arabs is shame and humiliation" (ibid., p. 42). Even the prison photographs might have been orchestrated, according to Hersh's source:

> [T]here may have been a serious goal, in the beginning, behind the sexual humiliation and the posed photographs. It was thought that some prisoners would do anything—including spying on their associates—to avoid dissemination of the shameful photos to family and friends. . . . The idea was that they would be motivated by their fear of exposure, and gather information about pending insurgency action. (Ibid.)

As any glance at news reports shows, the insurgency continues and may even be gaining momentum, but the black guys who are "vaccinated from the reality" of prosecution keep working. Hersh's source argues that the program must be kept black because "the process is unpleasant" (ibid., p. 44). Yet the source also insists on very clear red lines that justify a Congressional investigation.

4. Gray Earth

I referred earlier to gray zones in which sets of differences are variously flattened or enforced. To Hersh's source, the gray zones oppose the very clear red lines that distinguish legitimate from illegitimate practices. Those red lines act as borders, leaving the gray zones amorphous and ambient. But the black world needs the approval of the white world when scandals break, as at Abu Ghraib. The Bush Administration survived the scandal and Bush won reelection a half-year after the publication of the photographs. The white world was placated and the black world survives.

Perhaps the red lines are not impermeable. Perhaps they are even interchangeable. Activists have claimed for years that, in the lexicon of the powerful, today's freedom fighters are tomorrow's terrorists, and vice versa. Soldiers plucked from the white world perform black work. The most famous of these soldiers is Lynndie England. In the war in Iraq and the War on Terror, the United States military has welcomed women as combatants and black warriors, and their assignment to, and participation in, sexualized tortures cannot be coincidental. England was discredited only when her black work leaked into the white world. Black work has conventionally been men's work, and now a red line has been crossed. But perhaps red lines are meant to be crossed. In the realm of literary and social criticism, theorists often cross red lines of their own making. In a review-essay of Terry Eagleton's *After Theory*, David Simpson notes:

> There is an obvious potential for what is called theory to function as an apologetics for global capital and American world-dominance even as most of its exponents would define themselves as resisting these exact things. (2004, p. 128).

This is not a mere question of self-contradiction. Simpson acknowledges that, by a process of "obligatory reflexivity," critics have maintained a constant self-critique. He also observes that, for Eagleton, this practice:

> is either being displaced by an affirmative mode of upbeat all-American gung-ho celebration (of difference, diversity, popular culture, one's tattoos, for example) or transforming itself into a glib relativism that accepts the partiality and impermanence of everything while believing in nothing and nobody. (Ibid.)

If Eagleton is right, then I would suggest that he is right because of the replacement of critique by celebration. To create a space for, and then to celebrate, difference is to recognize that, *because* it is difference, red lines frame and contain it. Yet celebration also absolves critics of the responsibility either to challenge that difference or to repudiate its containment. In this way, institutions create a space for "different" peoples—employees, students, clients—without working to eradicate the injustices that create the differences. The white, public world serves to condemn and, at the same time, to cover abuses committed in the black, private world. Differences are flattened along the axis of the white world and enforced along the axis of the black.

Gray zones appear, then, to facilitate and harbor the interchangeabilities of differences. They appear to be a sort of emulsion without which some processes of institutional exchange cannot happen. To the extent that they are zones, then they are also bordered, contained, and subject to manipulation. Yet perhaps because they are so numerous, or so constant and ambient, we may be mistaken in calling them zones. We may be wiser to regard them as an ambient environment, like the atmosphere or land or sea. If injustices can be facilitated and harbored in gray, then perhaps resistance and justice can be too.

According to art historian John Gage, the fifteenth-century architect Leon Battista Alberti regarded black and white as constituents and moderators of all colors. The implication of this is:

> white and black objects should be painted not with the extremes of white and black pigments, but with values of the four genera of hues, slightly darker than absolute white and lighter than absolute black. (1993, p. 118)

Gage reports that, while the Latin version of Alberti's work *On Painting* claims, "the colour of the earth is a mixture of black and white," two later Italian versions make a significantly different claim: "because the earth is the detritus . . . of all the elements, perhaps we are not wrong to say that *all* the colours are called grey . . . like the detritus of the earth" (ibid., 119). Gray, then, is of the earth and its detritus, its trash.

In a provocative essay on the politics of genocide, anthropologist Nancy Scheper-Hughes argues for what she calls a "genocide continuum." At the far end is the act of genocide itself but at the near end is everyday policy and practice "conducted in the normative social spaces of public schools, clinics, emergency rooms, hospital wards, nursing homes, court rooms, prisons, detention centers, and public morgues" (2002, p. 369). Bad nursing home care, even the result of institutional neglect, is unlikely to culminate in anything remotely like genocide. So we need not agree with her full list of sites on the near end of her continuum to grasp her sense of the whole continuum as referring to "the human capacity to reduce others to nonpersons, to monsters, or to things that gives structure, meaning, and rationale to everyday practices of violence" (ibid.).

Scheper-Hughes is not merely recognizing a capacity for violence. Instead, she sees that capacity as being institutionally encouraged: "Everyday forms of state violence—peacetime crimes—make a certain kind of domestic 'peace' possible" (2003, p. 370). Here too, differences are flattened so that differences may be enforced. To Scheper-Hughes, the racialization of the prison-industrial complex, with its ever expanding inmate population of young black and Latino men, typifies peace crimes:

> These are invisible genocides not because they are secreted away or hidden from view but quite the opposite. As [Ludwig Josef Johann] Wittgenstein observed, the things that are hardest to perceive are those that are right before our eyes and taken for granted. (Ibid.)

We are reminded that Hersh's source believed both that the black world must survive and that Congress must punish crimes in the white world. But most relevant to a study of gray zones is Scheper-Hughes's argument that, when we look at the genocide continuum, we "see the capacity and the willingness of ordinary people—society's 'practical technicians'—to enforce . . . 'genocidal'-like crimes against classes and types of people thought of as waste, as rubbish" (ibid.).

At Abu Ghraib, the role of "ordinary" soldiers on the genocide continuum was to perform sexual tortures, to reduce prisoners to trash. According to Galeano, governments of the South treat their poor as they treat trash. According to Julie Sze, during the 1990s, New York City disposed of its street poor as it disposed of its moral and material trash; and, according to Mike Davis, the Pentagon is preparing for ceaseless and ambient war in slums such as Sadr City.

So that I may not end on such dire scenarios, I offer a hopeful metaphor: The process of incineration, to which much trash is consigned, creates a flash of glowing, vivid colors. A volcanic mountain rises so high on its vertical axis before its top explodes in such fire, sending bright colors down its sides. A vertical structure remains, but brightly colored flames have pushed it down toward a leveling. Destructive distinctions cease to matter, and soon, out of gray ash, vegetation appears.

Perhaps the top-to-bottom distance between black and white worlds can grow only so far before it too erupts and the top is destroyed. The glowing colors of eruption can never be contained.

Finally, and perhaps most hopefully, we are reminded by John Gage that gray is the color not only of the earth's trash but also of the earth itself. The poor and the tortured are the fleshly realization of their own gray zone, and justice, when they have it, will be borderless and ambient—perhaps even radiantly colorful.

Five

DEFENDING CIVILIZATION FROM THE HOSTILES: WARD CHURCHILL, CULTURAL WARS (ON TERROR), AND THE SILENCING OF DISSENT

C. Richard King

1. Introduction

On 25 September 2004, Robert D. Kaplan compared the unfolding war on terror with earlier military campaigns against the native nations of North America (Kaplan, 2004). He described Iraq, Afghanistan, and other destabilized Islamic regions as Indian Country, long the preferred colloquialism for the ever-shifting space of American imperial endeavors. For Kaplan, this racialized reframing of clashes with insurgents not only highlights the nature of the struggle—civilization against savagery—but also points to unlearned lessons about war. These lessons imply that the twenty-first century United States Army must adapt to face enemies around the world who threaten the American way of life through asymmetrical operations and guerilla actions, much as American Indian warriors had to do on the western frontier in the nineteenth century. Importantly, a series of unspoken entanglements ground policy projections like Kaplan's and contribute to the many defenses of these most recent wars to defend civilization. In particular, they pivot around the blurring of here and there, past and present, and most significantly, Indianness and Islam in their effort to construct a hostile abroad that must be defeated to defend the homeland.

Six months after Kaplan's op-ed piece ran, a Weblog author writing under the name Jim Paine sought to clarify the import of the most recent front in the culture wars during a time of "war" through reference to external, alien enemies. He dubbed Ward Churchill (who claims to be Cherokee and Creek) "the Imam of Radical Indigenism," claiming that the vocal critic of federal Indian policy and United States imperialism and then Chair of Ethnic Studies at the University of Colorado shared a common goal with "anarchists, animal rights activists, *Movimiento Estudiantil Chicano de Aztlan* (MeCHA) separatists, environmental activists, black radicals," and Islamists, namely "the end of the United States" (2005). In common with Kaplan's earlier essay, Paine seeks to police individuals and organizations critical of accepted norms and practices through association with explicit, external enemies of the state. Paine sought in many ways to transform Churchill from an American citizen and rational human subject into an alien other—irrational, inhuman, abject.

Given the intensity of the neoconservative backlash over the last quarter of the twentieth century, the vitriolic attack visited upon an outspoken critic comes as little surprise. Paine's characterization of Churchill was neither isolated nor extreme. Once his essay, "Some People Push Back: On the Justice of Roosting Chickens," (2001) became the subject of intense media attention, Churchill drew the ire of neoconservatives. He became the source of a public concern. The resulting outrage worked to police critical thinking, called into question higher education and academic freedom, delineated the limits of what it means to be and be considered American, and underscored the danger of hostiles within the national body.

During the subsequent media firestorm, Churchill was attacked as a radical intellectual who was hostile, divisive, and dangerous. Politicians and pundits called for his firing from his tenured position in ethnic studies at the University of Colorado, questioning the quality and integrity of his scholarship, his lack of patriotism, his claims to Indianness, his politicization of knowledge, and his extreme uncivility (noncompliance with national official rhetoric) in a time of national emergency.

This chapter interprets the ways in which the War on Terror amplifies and intensifies the xenophobic anxieties and purifying desires central to the neoconservative movement and its persistent assault on equality, inclusion, and inquiry. It directs attention to an ideological framework hinging upon a complex rhetoric of civilization (a marker of propriety, order, development, and race), and its insurgent others (Islamic terrorists, radical academics, and un-American activists). It outlines the preoccupations and presuppositions anchoring the civilizing discourse that targeted Churchill and animates the culture wars and the war on terror more generally.

2. The Churchill Affair

The day after the New York City World Trade Center's twin towers fell, Churchill wrote the "Some People Push Back" essay, which placed the event in a global and historic context. Instead of an irrational or senseless act, he argued that we could better understand the terrorist attack as a reaction from the margins. He saw it as a weak intent to garner the attention of—if not disrupt—a global system of oppression. He asserted that those who died on 11 September 2001 were not innocent, but complicit, and as such, we should not regard them as victims. Churchill concluded his polemic by comparing those working in the Twin Towers with the bureaucrats who oversaw the Holocaust, dubbing them "little Eichmans."

Although intense, extreme, and assuredly problematic in places, his critical assessment of 11 September 2001 went almost unnoticed, languishing on obscure Internet sites, for over three years. It was not until Churchill was invited to speak at Hamilton College in Clinton, New York, as part of its Kirkland Project for fostering student engagement with social justice issues. Then the essay became an issue. In late January 2005, shortly before his scheduled lecture at the private liberal arts college, the media discovered the essay.

Fox News, a conservative cable news network in the United States that frames itselfs the proprietor of objective journalism, in particular, devoted much attention to the story, offering its usual (un)fair and (im)balanced coverage. Its self-described culture warrior, Bill O'Reilly (2005), routinely targeted Churchill and his assessment of 11 September 2001 on his nightly show. O'Reilly asserted that the ethnic studies professor was a typical liberal academic, lacking rationality, decency, and patriotism.

Quickly, the controversy entered the Weblog universe, igniting a firestorm among conservative commentators across the United States under headlines such as "Ward Churchill—Another Leftist Allowed to Promote Sedition and Treason" (Zieve, 2005), and "The Imam of Indigenism" (Paine, 2005). In post after post during the first quarter of 2005, Weblog authors repeated five key themes: Churchill as (1) an un-American figure ; (2) a supporter of terrorism; (3) a questionable scholar and guilty of academic misconduct; (4) a nonreputable source, for his credentials include only a Master's degree, not a PhD, and as someone related to a dismissible academic field (ethnic studies); and (5) someone with disputed Indianness, suggesting that his identity, like his scholarship, was fraudulent. Neoconservative talk radio show hosts, such as Bob Neuman, would not surprise us if they were to charge that Churchill's words "[have] aided terrorists by giving them recruiting assistance and boosting their morale . . . ," adding, "That's called treason" (2005). The rising torrent of invectives encouraged even elected officials, such as Governor William Forrester "Bill" Owens, to lambaste the embattled professor. In the words of Owens:

> No one wants to infringe on Mr. Churchill's right to express himself. But we are not compelled to accept his pro-terrorist views at state taxpayer subsidy . . . . If there is one lesson we hope all Coloradans take from this sad case . . . it is that civility and appropriate conduct are important. Mr. Churchill's views are not simply anti-American. They are at odds with simple decency and antagonistic to the beliefs and conduct of civilized people. (2005)

The public panic had serious consequences for Churchill and his associates. Hamilton College rescinded its invitation, the first in a series of cancellations throughout the spring. The Colorado House of Representatives went so far as to pass a resolution supporting "the victims of 9/11" and condemning Churchill, asserting that his "essay contains a number of statements and contentions that are deplorable and do not reflect the values of the people of the State of Colorado" (Text of House Resolution on Churchill, 2005).

Against a backdrop of repeated calls for his termination, Churchill resigned his position as Chair of the Ethnic Studies Department. At the same time, the controversy cost others their jobs: both the Director of Kirkland Project at Hamilton College and the President of the University of Colorado resigned. To placate critics and address formal complaints, the University of Colorado initiated an inquiry into charges of academic misconduct, later recommending his termination. Churchill subsequently appealed the decision, but his tenured position was finally terminated during the summer of 2007.

3. Forces of Containment

The Churchill affair played out during an historic moment primed to contain dissent, especially if articulated from the academy. Higher education within the United States has long been under fire for its purported liberal bias, making it a key site in the culture wars. Since 11 September 2001, academics and public intellectuals have become increasingly visible targets for reactionary forces intent on extending a neoconservative program (Giroux and Giroux, 2004).

Recent works by David Horowitz (2004) and Dinesh D'Souza (2006) clarify the ways in which the war on terror has amplified the culture wars. Whereas the first has linked radical Islam with the American left, the second has asserted that "the cultural left" bears responsibility for 11 September 2001.

Irresponsible and ungrounded at best, Horowitz and D'Souza both exemplify a cultural shift that has enabled facile and false associations between dissent and destruction, and progressivism and terrorism. Importantly, these shifts lay a foundation for policing critical thinking and silencing perspectives meant to trouble naturalized relations.

In the wake of 11 September 2001, the federal government has grown increasingly rigorous in its demands upon its citizen-subjects. The federal government passed the USA PATRIOT (Uniting and Strengthening America by Providing Appropriate Tools Required to Intercept and Obstruct Terrorism) Act (Public Law 107-56), commonly known as the Patriot Act. It grants to bureaucrats and law enforcement officials greater access to library records and financial transactions. At the same time, extra-legal programs, such as eavesdropping on telephone calls, have extended the surveillance apparatus in a previously unthinkable manner. State governments have taken equally disturbing actions. Ohio, for instance, has passed legislation requiring state employees to take a loyalty oath renouncing their involvement in or support of terrorism.

Less noticeably, a number of neoconservative political organizations have launched assaults against critical inquiry. In the wake of 11 September 2001, the American Council of Trustees and Alumni, cofounded by Lynn Cheney, former director of the National Endowment for the Humanities and spouse of Vice-president Richard Bruce (Dick) Cheney, along with former Vice-presidential candidate and Senator Joe Lieberman, authored a report identifying colleges and universities as a key problem in the war on terror. Not only did it include a list of more than 100 professors whom it described as un-American, but it also described the academy as "a fifth column," working against the interest of the United States and Western civilization.

At the same time, David Horowitz established Campus Watch and Students for Academic Freedom as a means to police faculty speech on campus. Campus Watch routinely offers superficial assessment of bias, while Students for Academic Freedom documents supposed anti-conservative bias in college classrooms. Horowitz has gone so far as to draft an Academic Bill of Rights to legislate the political affiliation and ideological positions of faculty.

At a local level, neoconservative watchdog groups have formed to scrutinize teaching and learning. The Bruin Alumni Association has created a list it dubs "The Dirty Thirty," containing the most politically problematic faculty at the University of California at Los Angeles and offered to pay students for documentation of faculty bias (Giroux, 2006).

Colleges and universities increasingly discourage critical thinking (ibid.). Corporatization in particular has worked against the democratic ideals and ideological freedoms central to the ideal of higher education in the United States. According to Beshara Doumani:

> The commercialization of education is producing a culture of conformity decidedly hostile to the university's traditional role as a haven for informed social criticism. In this larger context, academic freedom is becoming a luxury, not a condition of possibility for the pursuit of truth. (2006, p. 38)

Even Philanthropic Foundations have used terror as a rationale for restricting critical inquiry. Both the Rockefeller Foundation and the Ford Foundation have revised their granting process to include language intended to guard against the appearance of supporting terrorism. The Ford Foundation requires grantees to sign a pledge against the promotion of "violence, terrorism, bigotry or the destruction of any state" (ibid., p. 32).

Finally, reconfigurations within the media represent the most powerful force of containment. On cable television, the rise of Fox News and the ritualization of moral panics have diverted attention away from context and critical thinking and toward superficial sentiment (for example the ubiquitous patriotic ribbons on automobiles in the United States) and vacant polemic (for example, critics of war are un-American). On the radio, neoconservative talk shows crowd the airwaves, encouraging banal populism. Online, virulent Weblogs make formerly trivial stories viral, substituting personal attack and personal preference for dialogue and democracy.

In the context of post-9/11, corporate constituencies manufacture consent and undermine dissent. It challenges the principles of democracy as it silences progressive perspectives and curbs debate. It also sets narrow limits on how

Churchill might be received and what audiences might do to or with him. Finally, it allowed no other outcome than his firing from the University of Colorado.

4. Kinds of Containment

To elucidate further the content and consequences of the Churchill affair, the remainder of the chapter unpacks two online exchanges: (1) 500 electronic comments submitted to Hamilton College once news of Churchill's presentation hit the national media, and (2) nearly thirty email messages sent to the Ethnic Studies Department or its members at the University of Colorado during spring 2005. Importantly, the discourse of civilization proves central to both forums, but the tone and content associated with each displays crucial differences. Whereas forum gives voice to the struggles to assert a conservative moral order at the heart of the culture wars, the Email reiterates imperial idioms given new life by the war on terror.

A. Defending the Moral Order

The hundreds of messages sent to Hamilton College constituted a popular panic prompted by various neoconservative media outlets, particularly Fox News, talk radio, and Weblogs run by right wing pundits. Most of those who posted messages sincerely believed the brief comments they sent to administrators at the small college. Almost all of them opposed Churchill and called for his scheduled lecture to be canceled. Concerned with supposedly imperiled boundaries and the importance of their maintenance, most comments pivoted around civilization as a moral order under siege. Together, the roughly 500 notes do three things. First and most importantly, they demonize Churchill as inhuman and un-American. Second, they condemn Hamilton College for its incivility and association with evil. Third, they advance and erase the freedoms said to define American greatness.

Churchill stands at the center of the comments sent to administrators at Hamilton College. The manner in which they describe him transforms him from citizen-subject to abject other. Six motifs dominate his construction as an inhuman hostile. Perhaps most commonly, as the subsequent analysis reveals, commentators suggested that Churchill was an animal. Writers proved to be especially fond of comparisons with vermin, parasites, and predators. Others preferred more scatological language, using some version (polite or profane) of excrement to capture his true essence or portraying him as something that spews most typically vile ideas.

Many commentators questioned Churchill's mentality, classifying him as a psycho, lunatic, or simply sick. On a more political register, a number of opponents placed him on the known fringes of society, dubbing him a "pinko," a "commie," a "Nazi," and a liberal—hostile subjects all in past and present culture wars. In keeping with the spirit of the times, some felt "terrorist" better characterized the ethnic studies professor, usually for his ideological opposition to the values at the heart of Western civilization. Not surprisingly, he was also routinely rendered un-American or anti-American. In short, the notes constructed Churchill as a monster: an abject other beyond the bounds of civilization, and worse, an inhuman threat to it.

At the same time, people read Churchill's speech and thought, by extension, as fanatical, irrational, uncivil, extreme, hateful, criminal, and treasonous. The perceived impropriety of his words and work prompted many commentators to suggest that Churchill did not deserve the constitutional guarantee of free speech. When authors talked about free speech, they all endorsed it as a concept. But they questioned its applicability to Churchill. Typically, they did this by comparing the controversial dissident with groups always already understood as evil, including the Ku Klux Klan, Nazis, rapists, pedophiles, terrorists, and Muslims who behead innocent captives. Again, they implied that Churchill is so far beyond and against civilization that he does not deserve the freedoms which define it.

For its part, critics framed Hamilton College as evil. Extending an invitation to Churchill was tantamount to supporting terrorism. Given its proximity to New York City, commentators asserted that the scheduling of the lecture demonstrated the institution's lack of humanity and empathy for the victims of 11 September 2001, and threatened to re-traumatize them through the event. At the same time, the school had confirmed the liberal bias purported to dominate higher education. In allowing this bias to take precedence over the victims and the nation, some authors went so far as to assert that Hamilton College was putting the innocent, namely its students, in harm's way.

The school would not allow, some snidely commented, for a rapist or a pedophile to teach the student body how to commit sex crimes or Muslim extremists to instruct a beheading seminar, so why should they allow someone like Churchill to defile the public sphere? For all of this, many commentators indicated that Hamilton College should suffer—through declining enrollments and withering endowments. Many who submitted comments asserted that a key result of having the "true" nature of the school known to the world would be that parents and others would guide their son/daughter/niece or other relatives to another, better (more American) school.

B. Imperial Idioms

Alongside and intertwined with the neoconservative culture wars, the language of the war on terror has encouraged the reiteration of colonial clichés (Giroux, 2004; Jackson, 2006; Llorente, 2002; Puar and Rai, 2002). Not only have revitalized imperial idioms made linkages between historic and contemporary forms of United States Empire, but they have also eased practices of racialization, often in conjunction with gender and sexuality, in a purportedly raceless society. The messages sent directly to Churchill and to the ethnic studies department at the

University of Colorado bear witness to the resurgent colonial discourse at the heart of the war on terror, while enabling authors to express themselves in more overt ways at once more dehumanizing and more dependent on a notion of civilization and its enemies.

In contrast with notes sent to administrators at Hamilton College, those sent to Churchill and his colleagues were often quite vulgar and blatantly racist. Chuck McGrory, in a missive sent to Churchill's partner, Natsu Saito, rehearsed imperial assumptions about gender, language, and race:

> How squaw bitch ... tell um Chief Ward Wigwam: look like pale face who want um to be um red face is um disgraced. Why don't you BOTH come on a tour of the east coast. . . . We'd love to see both of you crazy-motherf*ckers! We're looking forward to it with no reservations. We'll go out and have some fire water. (University of Colorado Department of Ethnic Studies, 2005)

Similarly, Katy Roberts wrote, "I am working on an article about you and want to verify that your Indian name is "Colostomy Bag that Walks." An anonymous author hailed Churchill: "Dear Squanto/Crazy Horse," and continued, "GO PREACH YOUR BULLSH*T IN SAUDI ARABIA OR WHERE ELSE THERE ARE 'SAND NIGGERS' BECAUSE YOU WILL BE PUT TO DEATH . . . AND MANY PEOPLE WOULD BE HAPPY." Or as Arnold Giannetta phrased it, "ward, you suck big buffalo d*ck, you c*cksucker ingine motherf*cker."

In common with racist rhetoric and colonial discourse, more generally, many of the notes sent to Churchill relied on gender and sexuality to dehumanize and dismiss him. Tay Weinstein asserts that feminized and racialized qualities prevent Churchill from getting what he deserved: "I wouldn't expect a f*cking squaw pussy like you to understand. . . . Move to Canada." Dennis Tedder, in an email with the subject line "Commie-pinko bed-wetting left-wing long-haired faggot," opined, "Given my way, you'd be thrown into a dark cell for ten years. Then execute you after that, you homo . . ." (ibid.).

Importantly, many of these comments use an imagined liberal or leftist project to make sexing and gendering work. "WHY THE F*CK ARE YOU HERE ... WE ARE SICK OF YOU LIBERALS RUINING THIS COUNTRY . . . YOU'RE A SICK MF AND HOPE YOU FRIGIN GET ANAL CANCER FROM YOUR HOMO STUDENTS" (ibid.)

While constructing Churchill as a hostile degenerate (a criminal, a sexual deviant, a sissy), imperial projects receive great praise and celebration in the notes to him—something all but absent from the notes sent to Hamilton College. The notes have a decidedly anti-Indian tone. Consider for example, Rob Ebright's comment, "Tell Ward, my ancestors killed a lot of Indians and I'm proud of it." Or the thoughts of an anonymous author, "one, too bad you weren't in the cockpit of one of those jets. And, two ... I'm glad the Indians were wiped out" (ibid.). Others reiterated the intertwined imperial notions of white supremacy and the white man's burden. Don McCurdy exclaimed:

> Your people are a lazy bunch of scum ... a burden on society. ... I am a 52 year old son of the people that have made this miserable patch of ground called America, the greatest force of good in the world! Your sorry ancestors could not have created in their wildest dreams.... We The People Have given Freedom to all of Europe and Japan, and we are trying to bring fredon [sic] to the middle East. THESE ARE THE HISTORIC FACTS ... as a native of Colorado I will force you to become a piece of trash in the dust bin of history with the rest of your ancestors. (Ibid.)

While historic allusions to the return of the seventh cavalry should trouble readers, more disturbing is the invocation of the current occupation of Iraq. One correspondent praised his godson for his military service, noting that he "has killed over 3 ragheads, destroyed 15 tanks and 10 pickup trucks from his F-18." He continued to boast of his own exploits that resulted in "the death of over 80 Syrians" (ibid.).

Civilization, as we see in the comments sent to Hamilton College, is at once racialized and equated with its imperial exploits. The comments viciously degrade Churchill, reinscribing racist and (hetero)sexist terms to marginalize and dehumanize him. The notes to Churchill, however, hold in common with those preceding his cancelled lecture an impulse to identify him as alien, abject, and hostile, offering veiled threats against him.

5. Conclusions

This essay has had a negative tenor, written in an overly pessimistic register. In many respects, this derives from the particularities of the Churchill affair, no less than the more general forces of containment shaping everyday expression in the United States. Most significantly, my discussion highlights unique workings of the neoconservative culture wars and the neocolonial war on terror, underscoring the current dangers of their intersection within critical inquiry.

Importantly, the Churchill affair does offer one hopeful, if challenging, opening for intellectuals committed to engagement and inquiry. Isolated, elite individuals, scholars doing cultural studies, prone to jargon and uncomfortable insights, and always already suspected as standing counter to the mainstream, find themselves privileged and policed in the wake of 11 September 2001. On the margins, to speak for and about marginal peoples and perspectives places intellectuals and their efforts to interrupt history in a decidedly disempowered position.

Hope lies beyond the academy and beyond the academic individual. Change and contestation offer the greatest promise in collective mobilizations and assembled coalitions. In many ways, this dictates that cultural studies scholars not only get outside or beyond the walls of the ivory tower, but also that they actively interrogate and reinvent the models and rewards central to the maintenance of the academic life, especially its emphasis on abstract individualism, class and gender hierarchies, and the myths of dispassionate, instrumental knowledge.

Six

UNITED WE STAY... HOME: READING THE RACIALIZED *BILDUNG* OF UNITED STATES' CHILDREN IN POST-11 SEPTEMBER 2001 COMFORT BOOKS

Kyoo Lee

Now let's turn to children's book publishing. Here we find great growth, but much of it in series and packaged books. And we writers are subtly and not so subtly encouraged to write down to make our writing accessible to the widest range of reading skills and the most common sensibilities.

Compare TV news with the new breed of children's nonfiction book. We are now advised that all such books should be brief and profusely illustrated. These are the same restrictions that force TV news to be shallow. The fact is, some of the most important things we can tell children are hard or impossible to illustrate. We seem to be deciding that these things will not be said through nonfiction.

– Aaron Shepard (2001)

1. Introduction: On *Bildung*

Bildung, which can mean creation, transformation, schooling, and education, in the title of this essay, is a German word with divinized connotations cherished by the late eighteenth and nineteenth century Romantic writers of the nationalistic *Bildungsroman*— a novelistic genre that arose during the German Enlightenment—such as Johann Wolfgang Goethe and Friedrich Schiller. Authors of this genre presented the psychological, moral, and social shaping of the personality of the (generally young) protagonist. *Bildung* has been characterized as the modern bourgeois "formation (of citizens of the state) in the sense of informing submission to a discipline or curriculum" (Miller, 2000, p. 63). My thesis is that the politicized aesthetic ideal of *Bildung*, far from being dead, is now simply digitalized, more aggressively commodified, sociopolitically racialized, and imported into America—changed in form but not in spirit.

Look at the images, for instance, appearing in the "factual, tactful information" (Marsh, 2001) on 11 September 2001, which glamorizes, however crudely, the mind-numbing simplicity of "high tech" security. Such images instantly appeal to many of us, especially children who habitually use video games, and especially those accustomed to and seduced by vivid digitalized images devoid of content—precisely this "robotic" kind.

2. On Building by *Bildung*

In "An Answer to the Question: What is Enlightenment?" Immanuel Kant (1784) quipped, "it is so comfortable to be infantile." Interestingly, "infantilized" is the key word Susan Sontag used when she summarized, two weeks after the tragedy, the psychic impact of the 11 September 2001 terrorist attacks on the American public:

> The disconnect between last Tuesday's monstrous dose of reality and the self-righteous drivel and outright deceptions being peddled by public figures and TV commentators is startling, depressing. The voices licensed to follow the event seem to have joined together in a campaign to infantilize the public.
>
> Our leaders are bent on convincing us that everything is O.K. America is not afraid. Our spirit is unbroken, although this was a day that will live in infamy and America is now at war. But everything is not O.K. And this was not Pearl Harbor. We have a robotic President who assures us that America still stands tall. A wide spectrum of public figures, in and out of office, who are strongly opposed to the policies being pursued abroad by this Administration apparently feel free to say nothing more than that they stand united behind President [George W.] Bush. (2001, p.24)

One telling sign of the infantile regression of the post-11 September 2001 United States is the recurrent disconnect between the devastating reality of that day and the reality-concealing rhetoric of the United States. The mainstream media reinforces such rhetoric, which forms the concerted guardians of Kantian minorities in the nation. The nation, given that all remarks and attention have been limited to "self-congratulatory bromides" (ibid.) and self-indulgent mourning, has been "reverting to [its] childhood. Thus, we are in the same weird mood preferring fantasies and stories to reality . . . thinking 'POOR US—WE ARE ALL ALONE? POOR US—WHY DO THEY HATE US?'" (Hanson, 2004). "If the very idea of America is to have any meaning" (Mitchell, 2002, p. 571) in the post-11 September 2001 United States, we would need to be able to see, at a distance, "the robotized, infantile delusions of September 10" (Hanson, 2004). Such delusions would be revealed as composed, in essential part, of "childish persistence in self-contradiction" (ibid.), including the "unquestioning acceptance of the judgment of leadership" (Mitchell, 2002, p. 571).

In a small corner of the United States book market, we see "infantilization of the public" happening. We are seeing a glut of comfort books for children produced to help them cope with the national tragedy and trauma. With such topical urgency, I have been reading popular post-11 September 2001 books for children; that is, children's books that directly address the event itself or issues of ruptured family and community in the aftermath of the event. Some notable titles, which I will discuss shortly, are: *September 11, 2001: A Simple Account for Children* (Poffenberger and Gottesman, 2001), *September 11, 2001: The Day that Changed America* (Wheeler, 2002), and *Terrorism: The Only Way is Through a Child's Story* (Schnurr, 2002).

Mostly banal, these texts appear to provide an allegorical window into and a contemporary index of the socio-political and commercialized immaturity of the post-11 September 2001 United States. An analytic look at such therapeutic materials for traumatized "children" may elucidate factors in the national psyche that assert with robotic consistency "United We Stand." We can ask why such an automatic introversion and mechanical insistence characterizes this literature. The question that motivates my inquiry is why and how, in the wake of "9/11," that now-familiar slogan functions as a rhetorical foil for a "United We Stay . . . Home." What sort of homemaking, extension, and consolidation is happening now in the land of "Bob the Builder"—the American cartoon figure whose crew of talking machines sings, "Can we fix it? Yes, we can!"

The building at stake is founded upon racialized binarization. A closer look at the inclusive-exclusive gestures of "we who share" the national and globalized tragedy reveals that the very authorial efforts to diversify the projected members and future adult subjects of this reconstituted entity called "the United States of America" depict narrative centers and perspectives that remain visibly Anglo-white—scared Anglo-white.

White reflexivity normalizes a collective knee-jerk racism or racist discourse in the post-11 September 2001 United States. Because "white reflexivity" stems from the technical term for the ethereal effect of filmic layering seen in laminated paper, its use in the present context emphasizes the operative and layered invisibility of white-racialized, defensive emotions such as fear and hypocrisy.

White reflexivity manifests itself rapidly and collectively in the form of racialized and racially justified fear, hypocrisy, and schizophrenia towards the enemy other who is in colorful disguise. Consequently, the "enemy other" necessitates invasive and exhaustive profiling and containment. The objects of fear and suspicion are "would-be" terrorists as well as the contextually generalized enemies who would blow apart "our" wafer-thin identity, our positive and stable national identity as the global superpower—a good cop. The faith in "our" freedom becomes a thinly disguised fear of "their" free will, their own freedom.

On a deeper level, the nationalist confidence that spurred the archetypal formation of brave American children in the nineteenth century is being swiftly undermined by nationalist conservatism. Through digitalized media and imaging technology that conservatism infantilizes the potential voting public and invalidates the rest. The Constitution of the United States, historically sustained by a series of what Cornel West describes as radical "experiments with democracy," is being insidiously replaced by the racially based, codified constrictions, and constructions of "us"—the newly identified brothers and sisters of "our country under an unprecedented attack."

The "United" States of post-11 September 2001 America is a prime and recent example of how reactionary rhetoric can create a terrifyingly concrete reality. It is reconstructed rhetorically through concerted, regressive translations of mythical motherlands into the literalized homeland that suddenly must be protected from within *by* the informal and communal institution of visibly white parents, guardians, and teachers. These "bedrock" institutions that would ultimately form the moral and national "values" promise to nurture all the children, including racial and social minorities, *as long as* they show sufficient evidence of sharing the same logos, mythos, and ethos of puritan, suburban, white-fenced Anglo-America.

Under the veneer of democratic civility and bureaucratic formality, we seek to contain and detain each other in boxes of racially ready-made images, creating an allergic distance. The politics of affect and trauma played out in the current world of children's literature contributes not simply to the post-11 September 2001 construction of patriotic discourse, but more deeply to an ever more blatant subtextualization of the intra-American Other who suddenly surfaces through the bifurcated rhetoric of inclusion-exclusion. The collective reflexivity and blindness of such racialized, authorial introversion of white American values runs counter to the fundamentally American, foundational ideals, practices and promises of self-reliance, independence and freedom for each and every human being.

It is against such a background, both political and historical, that I offer here an analysis of the visual narrative and narrative sterility of post-11 September 2001 patriotic discourse that runs through even the most minor of minor literature—the massively standardized literary network television for scared little ones. I set out to analyze the visual as well as verbal rhetoric of "home building" in several post-11 September 2001 United States Children's and Young Adult books, with a critical focus on the white hetero-familial normativity that subtextually regulates and reinforces the ideological formation of super-patriotism.

3. A Scene: A White Child Reading a Book for Comfort

Imagine you are entirely new to this concept, "terrorism" or "terrorist." You might wonder: what do adults mean by terrorists, when they say we were attacked by them? Here is an answer from *Terrorism: The Only Way Is through a*

Child's Story, a book on terrorism produced and presented under the assumption that "the only way to understand it is through a child's story" (Schnurr and Strachan, 2002):

> "Dad," I said, "What's a terrorist?" The car jerked and I thought we were going off the road. Dad didn't say anything for a few minutes. He just squeezed his hands tightly on the steering wheel. Then he did a big swallow, the kind where you can see that bump in his throat going up and down. He said that a terrorist was a *very bad* person who did *very bad* things. I didn't ask any more questions because I was worried that we might go off the road or that the steering wheel would come off in his hands. (Ibid., p. 25; emphases added)

Later Dad repeats the point:

> Dad and I went out into the backyard and I kicked at things. "We're all angry," my dad said. "The only way to understand this is to know that people who are called "terrorists" do things that good people all over the world do not accept. When bad people purposefully kill other people it is called "an act of terror" or "terrorism." Do you understand?" I nodded my head. (Ibid., p. 28)

I am reminded of the definition of terrorist offered by Marsh: "a person who does bad things, usually with no warning and often against innocent people" (2001, p. 6). Interestingly, this idea of terrorism—as a mortal and *moral* threat posed by untimely contamination—often accompanies an image of differences that must at once be recognized and overcome. Consider the following five captions, from two books, each accompanied by a matching illustration:

(1) "(You are scared of) people who look different." (Carlson, 2002, p. 12)
(2) "All this scary stuff can make you want to hide under your covers and never come out." (Ibid., p. 13)
(3) "There's a Big, Beautiful World Out There" (Ibid.)
(4) "On Television we heard our President tell us everything would be all right." (H. Byron Masterson Elementary School, 2002, p. 23)
(5) "Our thought for the day became 'America United.'" (Ibid., p.10)

The first three captions portray a post-11 September 2001 home. The remaining two depict a post-11 September 2001 school. The point of all five captions, as captured by the book titles (*There's a Big, Beautiful World Out There!* and *September 12th: We Knew Everything Would Be All Right*), is that a big, beautiful world exists, and on 12 September, we knew everything would be all right. Note further how differences change from being *presumably* bad to being actually non-existent—white-washed, literally (ibid., p. 19). As the story goes, we overcome evil and become "good" by containing differences (or, our fear of them).

The book, *There's a Big, Beautiful World Out There!* allegedly "hit just the right note. . . . [because] preschoolers are sure to find the protagonist's worried but not terrified face a comforting focus on the 'scary' pages" (Sutherland, 2002). However, we might ask, what sort of face is this? In both books, the protagonists are "white"— literally in their faces and more symbolically in their representation of "America United." The "other" sorts of faces being present in the pictorial spaces is not a sufficient defense, for at issue is not the absence of multi-ethnic social awareness but the assumed, inscribed racial identity and centrality of the narrator(s).

Our focus is on "the flaming signifier," the "color of color's own subtraction and absence" (Sedgwick, 1993, p. 255) that is attempting to withdraw from and redraw the social body at once. Our issue is with the meta-color that wishes to color but not be colored. The "white lie" of multi-racial inclusivity becomes more audible, and the white reflexivity of "seeing without seeing" more apparent, when the united colors of America show the absent presence of a face—a particular set of identity markers. Visibly absent from all the pages above is one who *looks* "Arabic."

Given the seemingly exhaustive visual catalog of "scary faces" democratically united by the dated and extrapolated shock, given the caricatured racial and social markers equally distributed, it seems not accidental that the catalog does *not* include *the* face of the enemy other contextually advertised as such. Such seems a crude manifestation of the Hobbesian "racialization" (Foucault, 2003, pp. 61, 81, 87–114) of the enemy that would "permanently, ceaselessly infiltrate the social body" (ibid., p. 61), which functions as a modern political premise of justified warfare; "the specific political distinction to which political actions and motives can be reduced is that between friend and enemy" (Schmitt, 1976, p. 26).

Terrifying to the Schmittian sovereign subjects that operate on the logic of "with us or against us," pure and simple, is the possible invisibility of the enemies. One way to tackle that fear is to make sovereign subjects hypervisible by excluding them: to recruit more friends and reaffirm the absence of the enemy within the group. The facial or sartorial signifiers of "Muslim" or "Middle Eastern" have become the absent master-signifiers that silently and invisibly frame the reference of all the other signifiers appearing in the pictorial space of representation.

Here is another example that illustrates the systematic post-11 September 2001 exclusion of the emerging other: again, the picture diary book by the first-grade students of H. Byron Masterson Elementary, Missouri, *September 12th: We Knew Everything Would be All Right*, which received the Kids Are Authors Award in 2002. Given the geo-historical and demographical background of the state of Missouri, it is unsurprising that the pupils photographically represented at the beginning in the "Meet the Authors" section are black or white (with one

Hispanic boy added to one corner of the pictorial list). What remains troubling is the symbolic clue this prized model provides: the Muslim other is the new black, for blacks have been politically united with (recruited supplementarily into) whites in this time of crisis.

This point is also exemplified by Darwyn al-Sayeed (played by Michael Ealy) in the Showtime Network television drama series, *Sleeper Cell* (2005). Al-Sayeed is an undercover FBI agent, and an African-American Muslim hero, who infiltrates an Arab terrorist network that is plotting to bomb Los Angeles. Suddenly, Americans of Middle Eastern and South Asian origin/face/name find themselves terrified orphans, totally inside and outside the laws of protection.

This negatively demarcated (subtractive) national self-identity of post-11 September 2001 America is the flip side of the compulsive affirmation of extremely united "states" of America. Overnight, the people of Arab/Middle Eastern/Muslim origin or descent, exclusively and confusedly singled out, became non-people. They were transcoded into a herd of beings with evil intentions and terrorist potentials—a militarized target later piled into small pyramids of animals. "Undoubtedly a race but not human . . . in the sense of not being an image of God, the Eternal," (Fest, 1974, p. 212, quoting from Hitler's hate speech against Jewish people in May 1923, at the Krone Circus in Munich, Germany). Something akin to such an "image of the Devil" is still floating around in the subliminal consciousness of terrified America.

Immediately relevant is the fact that *There's a Big, Beautiful Out There!* was written on 12 September 2001, the author notes, which is when, while dealing with the raw emotions of shock, horror, grief and confusion, the United States affirmed that *We Knew Everything Would Be All Right*. Why and how? Because "we saw lots of flags"; "our parents still tucked us in our warm, safe beds"; "our parents said they loved us"; "the stars and moon came out and America went to sleep"; "and the next morning the sun came up again" (H. Byron Masterson Elementary School, 2002, p. 20, 24, 26–28)

How does the "we" arise so suddenly, so quickly? Here, Theodor Adorno's insight into the behavioral psychology of totalitarianism helps one understand in part the material basis of such totalized banality, the work of mortal fear:

> Totalitarian regimes . . ., seeking to protect the *status quo* from even the last traces of insubordination . . ., can conclusively convict culture and its introspection of servility. They suppress the mind, in itself already grown intolerable, and so feel themselves to be purifiers and revolutionaries. . . .The struggle against deceit works to the advantage of naked terror. "When I hear the word 'culture,' I reach for my gun," said the spokesman of Hitler's Imperial Chamber of Culture. (Adorno, 1981, p. 26)

In the reactionary immediacy with which "naked fear" converts to internalized faith in group protection, one senses the unbridled totality of freedom of a rouge state that uses a culture against culture. "Cultivated" in this case is the mob psychology of hatred that elevates mere intimidation to moral indignation. In other words, the imperial culture of conformity deprives its citizens of rational and individual *"freedom* . . ., the child that he or she has been" (Merleau-Ponty, 2003, pp. 72–74), by rewarding them with the infantile pleasures of creating and destroying enemies who they at least are not, which is a negative sign of their small privilege. Little ones who, upon reflection, knew everything would be all right, would later ensure that everything would be all right by grafting themselves onto a network of gun clubs, local and global.

To wit, post-11 September 2001 "America becomes united" by racializing morality and nationalizing the "good race"; we are a civilized, human(e) race. An interstitially abusive mobilization of logical and hypothetical connectives further reinforces the rhetorical strength of patriotism that *looks* morally fair or superior:

> We may look at a person and not know their religion. However, we often see Muslims dressed in long dresses (women) or wearing turbans and long beards (men). This is one way they express their religion. They may look different, but that is not what makes them bad or good. (Marsh, 2001, p. 17)

This passage beautifully summarizes the key points we have been building so far in this section. First, "looking different": why should it immediately invite a moral evaluation on the part of one who does the looking? Second, "bad or good" rather than the usual "good or bad": do we find this incidental reordering of moral priority accidental? Third, do "we" include readers who could be bad or good? If not, how do we recognize those who pretend but cannot be part of us? "One way they express their religion" is one way we can spot them. Consequently, "if you see something, say something" (Metropolitan Transportation Authority, 2007).

On 12 September 2001, the street rhetoric of race-based American nationalism (for example, the evasive aggression of "I am not a racist, but . . .") had been re-codified and recharged with new subtextual and transhistorical significations and resonances. The disjunctive string of binarized flashes of thoughts on the archetypical battleground of good versus evil personified into goodies versus baddies paraded as "factual, tactful information that helps us all" (Wheeler, 2002, front cover). It simultaneously confused one who *can* read the world with one who can judge without being judgmental. This analytic kid, perhaps at least one among the neatly seated sixteen kids of Booker Elementary, would be or become a "weirdo," "who sits along at the turn of the staircase, reading" (Skyes, 1996, p. 101), but who might end up becoming something weirder like a philosophy teacher.

As a matter of course, analytic demand has its share of aggressive insensitivity. But we should *feel* free to ask a question as simple as *why* "my very special" Grandma—who "lives 'on the coast'" "and is supposed to come to stay with us for a while"—is taking a bus instead of flying (Schnurr and Strachan, 2002, p. 34). Curiously, in the book, it is the child who instantly limits the possible range of questions. She imagines that the question might cause "something to happen." She doesn't ask because she has "a feeling that it had something to do with terrorists" (ibid.).

The element of magic realism to which the child naturally subscribes is sensible. To that extent, the scene of halted thought is poignantly humane and instantly relatable. What is worrisome is that the story, "the only available" story as claimed, ends right there. It shows no signs of cognitive development or epistemological adventure, negative or positive. The author does not attempt to present the world more clearly or to reconstruct the world more truthfully. Instead, the story precludes such efforts or even possibilities.

4. A Family of Color Blindness: On a "White Mom"

Even Firefighters Hug Their Moms (MacLean and Reed, 2002) is a playful allegory of masculine vulnerability. It features Big Frank, a firefighter wannabe who "every morning gets up and looks at the newspaper" (upside down) "to find out where the fires are" (ibid., p.1). An imaginative preschooler, in reality, who pretends to be busy otherwise, Big Frank eventually takes time off to hug his mom who is busy managing what appears to be a typical middle-class, white, American, heterosexual family with two children: one boy and one girl.

This story contains two messages: (1) it is perfectly fine to be and act afraid, whoever you are, even if you are the last person anyone would expect to be fearful, since (2) "we" are all hurt, bruised, confused, honest children in need of immediate comfort and consolation. This we even includes real firefighters such as *New York's Bravest*, Mose Humphreys, legendary firefighter from the 1840s, employee No. 40 (Osborne, 2002). Humphreys' story is multiplied in the narrative by post-11 September 2001 legends, "all eight feet tall and able to swim the Hudson River in two strokes" (ibid., front flap).

Lest you feel left out of the world of heroes and celebrities, a fable for ordinary folks has also been written. Such is the story that *Bravemole* (Jonell, 2002) tells. Mole's story involves his life-and-death struggle with, and eventual triumph over, a "wicked dragon with terrible teeth and terrible claws and fire inside" that "lives far away" (ibid., pp. 1–2). Originally, the dragon was a mythical creature that only the great-grandmole allegedly saw, but it suddenly became real during Mole's lifetime. Back home, "delivered from dragons" by Starmoles and Overmoles:

> Mole rocked his baby mole soft and slow, rumbling a lullaby a little off-key. His good wife came in quietly, giving his shoulders just one more squeeze, and sat beside him. It would not be easy, Mole thought, patting his wife's furry paw with his own sore one. But Overmole helping, they

would get the hard job done. Because ordinary moles were strong. And brave. And steady. There was a city of them. A country of them. A whole *world* of them. Bravemoles. (Ibid., 28–29)

Why this evocation of the localized motherland and maternal care? What kind of message is instilled in this historicized allegory of self-forgetting bravery? The question of manhood or fatherhood aside, here we would like to ask: who has access to that *über* mom that is both literal (one whom even firefighters hug and who gets to squeeze the bravemole) and metaphorical (one from whom all of New York's bravest and ordinary moles come)? Or, if there are multiple moms, as there are multiple races in the United States, which one are we to use as the shoulder, the pillow, and the womb?

In a poem entitled "Trouble, Fly," is depicted a quilt of houses where everyone is sleeping, including cats and dogs (Swanson, 2002, pp. 18–19). These are symbols of domesticated living beings. The focal point of one picture is the united nations of a nursery room (ibid., p. 19): a white mother is asleep with her arms around brown, yellow, and white children, all bundled in one bed. The sleeper series begins with the blonde mother and ends with a blond child who also had to stretch an arm vertically as if to draw a straight line, as if to bring closure to that dreamy space.

If New York City is sorted by the father, as is evidenced by the story of Mose Humphreys in *New York's Bravest*, homes are managed by the mother who will breed, feed, and multiply the next Mose Humphreys. Who else has access to that immediately and ultimately huggable *über* mom, that really tall lady from New York City, who always stands firm and holds that torch twenty four hours a day/seven days a week? None. Again, as random as the illustration accompanying this scene may appear, the visible pictorial and narrative exclusion of children of specifically Muslim, Middle Eastern or Arabic origin from the familial space, remains alarmingly intriguing.

One colorful and rather delightful, poetic exception I could locate, is *We Are All the Same Inside* (Bellavia, 2000). In this book, an extraterrestrial sage, reminiscent of Dr. Seussian characters, "comes to us, a person like *you* and *me*, but with only the *inside* we can see," with "a *goal*, . . . a *soul*, . . . with no outside *skin* (because the sage came from the "planet where we are all *kin*")" (Bellavia, 2000, pp. 6–9), and:

Sage was all alone and needed a home.
Without any fear, Sage looked far and Sage looked near. (Ibid., p. 13)

Will they think I'm Dwight when my outside is all white?
Will there be a scar due to Dasha's black and violet hair?
What about Safia's veil . . . I wonder if it will fail? (Ibid., pp. 17–19)

The insider heard some *chatter*. So you know Sage went to see what was the *matter*. (Ibid., p. 21)

An academic could specify "the matter" as follows: the implicitly sanctioned, psychosocial practices of ethno-social zoning, distancing, and outcasting, which is a function of race panic and provincial familialism as discussed earlier. *We Are All the Same Inside* is actually asking this question, again through an allegory and yet, this time, an allegory of the extraterrestrial alien. Given the color-coded boundaries of inclusion-exclusion that constitute the socio-historical ontology of America, we can ask, what kind of social justice and hope can be multilaterally envisioned, beyond and above the historicized horizon? How can we think across the social color line while acting against it? Can we even show a book of "We are all the same inside" to our "Mom and Dad, to whom the book is dedicated" (ibid., p. 38)—the Mom and Dad who do not think the alien Sage is or should be in and among us? Yes, we can, the book is trying to say and show.

5. An Open Reflection: Tomorrow, Us, and the United States

Above, I have offered a twofold—phenomenological and rhetorical—analysis of the post-11 September 2001 infantilization of American minds that racialize "the enemy." The enemy is cast as an imaginary group of hostile strangers, exactly the kind that children who read the bedtime propaganda often learn to repeat. Specifically, I have sought to draw our attention to some of the subtle and not-so-subtle ways in which the figures of the threatening other are systematically juxtaposed with those of the home or homeland and become racialized—or colorized—as one would see from the United States terror alert codification system. With this move is the reactionary formation of the discourse of nationalistic unity.

In short, I called into question the normative, sedimented whiteness of patriotic and parental discourse in post-11 September 2001 America. To this end, I have shown how, right there in the knotted, prefabricated discourses of justified infantilism and uncritical nationalism, good old white racism and raced sociality resurface and function as subtextual points of connection. The images of the housed child—innocent, vulnerable, and future adult citizens of the United States in need of parental protection and guidance—are exploited in the name of democratizing traumatic and traumatized sentiment. White *racializing* super-patriotism and, in turn, pan-*nationalizing* ("We, proud Americans") becomes a quasi-racial phantom category that remains schizophrenically incoherent and deceptively universal. On the most specific level, I focused on a shifty mechanism of the infantilization, or the infantile bipolarization of the public, by which the aesthetic hegemony of Caucasian America politicizes future subjects such as children of the nation or the nation *as* a born-again child who now returns "home."

This is an essentially white home; that is, an all-inclusive all American white mother with a reconstituted "homeland" that becomes flagged as "America" anew. On the most crudely fundamentalized binary scheme of "in versus out," "good versus bad," "white versus colored," is overlaid a relatively new, metonymic set of binary oppositions. Such oppositions include: accommodated versus drifty, and American race versus non- or anti-American race. I have concluded that analysis by introducing what I have come to see as an alternative, a future-oriented example: the open-ended and yet allegorically resonant narrative of *We Are All the Same Inside*.

Perhaps it would be unfair to say that "typical" white houses in the United States of America, as often one-dimensionally portrayed in books for 11 September 2001-trauamtized children, are joining forces with the nation's administration. Perhaps it would be unfair to say that the "white Republican middle-class soccer moms," who still form a racial and political majority of the producers and consumers of children's book, gently militarize the home by systematically hypnotizing their children with such books. Perhaps it is an exaggeration to say that most of the mainstream post-11 September 2001 books for children and adolescents "target" and further reproduce the child in bed/pajamas, in need of immediate comfort and compensatory consolation. And yet, I also find myself asking this question: is it too strange that we now rarely have the child explorers and inventors, whose patently American innocence lies in the extraordinary ability to question and discover, often outwitting the condescending adults and unveiling the ideological pretensions of the naked emperor?

So now, even an ultimately big, beautiful world out there (Cf. Carlson, 2002) has to be seen from the point of a cute little brown-haired child installed inside the window of a cute little suburban house. Who is still left out in the cold, in the city of lost children? More importantly, who will critically reconsider such an offer of accommodation? Who would start interrogating the assumed homogeneity of fears and hopes? Slowly but steadily, I have been and will continue to be nagging adults with such unpleasant questions—adults who once were children learning to see and speak the language of the world in the homes and schools.

Today, American schoolteachers, not knowing how to explain "the event," still agree on one thing. They believe that they must "emphasize the positive" (Monique Field, "Attack Anniversary Is Living History Lesson," *St. Petersburg Times* (5 September 2002). Their plan to emphasize, "how the country bonded rather than what was torn apart" (ibid.) is not simply a measure to give the nation's children a sense of vitally needed security. It is not as simple as administering psychological first aid, "a form of psychological support that teaches individuals how to care for themselves and to provide basic psychological support for family, friends and neighbors" (Jacobs, 2006, p. 69). Nor is it simply an optimistic response to or a pragmatic solution for the administrative task of "leaving no child behind." The problem arises when social cushioning furtively extends to social cocooning—a sort of self-containment.

Psychological first aid could "be developed as preparedness for disasters and terrorist attacks" (ibid., p. 68). However, such "preparedness" often manifests itself in the form of security paranoia or generalized xenophobia. The innocuous-sounding directive of "emphasizing the positive," when mindlessly repeated, brings out and blindly reactivates the political unconscious of America and will leave out many children. What is to be tightly articulated, and what I have been trying to articulate with a counterbalancing urgency, is a deeper sociopsychical impulse behind such a collective, introverted move.

Such is an ambiguous move towards an exclusive inclusion of "we Americans" engineered through a manipulation of the nation's bad faith in good terms such as cross-sectional solidarity and civic communality. At the heart of American triumphantalism, read as a case of bad faith in the Sartrean sense, is an infantile negation of (as opposed to dialectical engagement with) the politicized other. The undeniable fact is that the American ideal of freedom and patriotic solidarity historically suppressed the racial and ethnic materiality of the American body in favor of abstract autonomy, mechanical equality, and nominal independence. The post-11 September 2001 discourse of nation united by faith and hope mobilizes precisely that undercurrent through the imaginary reconstruction of the national body thus "torn apart."

This way, a collective reflex has replaced reasoned, public reflections. Now, the fear of others' freedom is overwriting faith in our freedom. Why do they hate us? This tragedy is relatively easy to understand. The more scathing riddle for us is and should be the moral ambiguity of brave new America consumed by racialized primary narcissism and capitalist individualism. The ambivalence remains structural, and its symptoms, are as old as the American history of colored crises. Forever free, America wishes to "spread freedom" all over. Forever fearful, America wishes to go home and watch television, or play video games, until sleepy with Wee Willie Winkie, hopefully dreaming of a, perhaps, kaleidoscopic society entirely composed of newborn babies:

> Racial identity will only cease to be salient when one can say of a newborn baby that his/her racial identity will have no significant impact on the kind of life he or she is likely to lead. But the conditions that would make it possible to say that cannot be brought about without a radical transformation of society of a kind that most Whites would not even contemplate. (Bernasconi, 2001, p. 284)

Seven

GEORGE W. BUSH'S BURDEN: CONTAINING THE "NEW WORLD (DIS)ORDER"

Tracey Nicholls

Among the containment efforts we are witnessing these days is the tendency to speak of 11 September 2001 as if it is a dividing line, which marks off a secure and complacent past from an uncertain future. Conservative pundits and Bush administration spokespeople tell us that this uncertain future requires a proactive approach to national security legislation and to war. As an observation of the changed psychology of (some) American citizens and the discourses they are producing, this notion may have some relevance, but it deflects our attention away from dangerous continuities in America's relation to power. The country's secure position as a modern empire (evinced, for instance, by its self-assertion as the world's only post-Cold War superpower) entails an assumption of "the white man's burden," the self-conferred white male prerogative to gather and exercise the sovereign power to decide the status, and fate, of the "Other(s)" whom he colonizes. Viewed through this lens, we can recognize the process by which the Bush administration has been containing power within the executive branch as part of a necessarily racialized project which predates—and, I argue, is a root cause of—the War on Terror.

Taking up this notion of race as determining "the Others" upon whom state power is imposed allows us to trace some now-visible links between the old United States of America and the new one which has supposedly taken its place. Race, in this sense, is not a biological fact about individuals but a social construct imposed upon them (a redefinition endorsed by scholarly research in biology and cultural studies).

In the old and new orders, the powers that accrue to (or are claimed by) the government include the power to name or classify, the power to decide limits and jurisdictions of binding agreements, and the power to oversee "security threats" and other social undesirables. We can see continuities in the exercise of these powers when we consider the current Bush administration's decision to create a class of "enemy combatants" (to avoid having to classify them as "prisoners of war"). This strategy brings to mind the racially and ideologically motivated differential immigration policies, which the United States has applied to Cuban and Haitian refugees since the 1960s.

Similarly, the violations at Guantánamo Bay and Abu Ghraib Prison appear to be obvious examples of United States' disingenuous disregard of Geneva

Convention responsibilities. This disregard is consistent with American reluctance to endorse the International Criminal Court (ICC) during both the William Jefferson (Bill) Clinton and George W. Bush presidencies, and American demands for exemption from prosecution for American citizens.

The executive branch's assertion of the right to incarcerate American citizen José Padilla without due process, which I will discuss later, is consistent with governmental action in previous cases of non-military combatants during wartime. Thus, assertions, post-11 September 2001, that we are living in a new world not only impair our ability to see the continuity in containment of power but also disguise the extent to which the War on Terror emerged in a context which was racialized from the outset.

The racialized context that I will reveal in my discussion is a field of domestic and foreign policy operations unified and made explicable only by assumption of a so-called white man's burden. Rudyard Kipling's (1899) poem of the same name introduced this phrase into political discourse, with which he urged (or "urged," in the case of some literary critics who have interpreted this work as satirical) the United States to embrace its imperial responsibility to administer the territories it had acquired during the Spanish-American War.

The essence of the burden is the civilization (which, according to many postcolonial theorists, amounts to Westernization) of foreign and subject populations, a process Kipling describes as the thankless task of serving people who are "half devil and half child." This orientation toward other cultures is necessarily hierarchical. It gives rise to an obsessive categorizing of individuals by race, a sorting of humanity into the already civilized "us" and the "them" needing to be managed, coached, and enlightened. Different races become valuable by virtue of how close they are to being fully "Western."

Emboldened by the rhetoric of a "manifest destiny," the United States embraced this burden and continues, even today, to pursue the imperial dominance that the burden justifies (Military.com, 2006). We can see evidence of this burden in the post-Cold War imperative to be the police officer of a so-called new world order. Even more recently, after 11 September 2001, we see the burden again in the War on Terror-driven imperative to be the peacemaker of what might best be termed "the new world disorder."

The entire outward focus of the War on Terror—the idea that we can contain terrorist threats by sending American military forces overseas to pacify "troubled" regions and install American-style democracy—is a logical extension of the early imperialist adventures that were undertaken by previous administrations motivated by this white man's burden.

A small but influential number of contemporary critiques of governmental ambition emphasize the process by which power, theoretically diffused among the citizens of a modern democratic state, is currently being consolidated in the hands of the executive branch or first minister, who claims a sovereign right to lead his people. In *Precarious Life: The Powers of Mourning and Violence*, Judith Butler confronts and interrogates what she calls "resurgent sovereignty," expressed in the Bush administration's claim to the prerogative of suspending law in states of emergency. The Bush administration justifies this suspension of law by appealing to the need to protect citizens from security threats. Once suspended, the rule of law is replaced by an unelected bureaucracy that functions under the direction of the executive branch (2004, pp. 51, 54).

We can see evidence of this move in President Bush's reliance on then-Assistant Attorney General Alberto Gonzales and the Department of Justice's Office of Legal Counsel to justify, in the infamous 2002 "torture memo," standards of interrogation conduct that explicitly diverge from the Geneva Conventions to which the United States is a signatory (Greenberg, 2006).

Butler directly links the mutation of sovereignty (away from law, and toward the exercise of personal authority) to Michel Foucault's notion of "governmentality" which she defines as "a mode of power concerned with the maintenance and control of bodies and persons" (2004, p. 52). Governmentality, as a mode of power, is irreducible to law, as is the resurgence of sovereignty that governmentality makes possible (ibid., p. 55). Managerial power, delegated by the executive, now determines, for instance, who will be detained as a threat to the state, under what conditions, for how long, and what judicial appeals will be permitted (ibid., pp. 54, 58). It also determines what to call them, preferring the ill-defined general label of "detainee" to "prisoner," which more clearly defines the status and rights of people so labeled (ibid., p. 64).

Those caught up under new guidelines defining who constitutes a threat to national security are distinguished by their diminished status. The people incarcerated at Camp Delta in Guantánamo Bay and the now-infamous Abu Ghraib Prison are, Butler observes, reduced to the state that Giorgio Agamben (2000) refers to in *Means without End*, as "bare life." This is a state in which a person is stripped of political rights and recourses and stripped of any "definitive prospect for a reentry into the political fabric of life" (2004, pp. 67–68).

Butler bleakly concludes that we need to recognize how the sovereignty facilitated by governmentality "manages" populations. It reduces those it deems enemies to a status below that of rights-bearing human beings through a process of "de-subjectivation" the result of which is a "subject who is no subject . . . neither fully constituted as a subject nor fully deconstituted in death" (ibid., p. 98). What is frightening here is that, using these practices, a government can deactivate the humanity of anyone at any time, by merely designating that person a threat.

Notwithstanding the us-versus-them rhetoric which runs through the Bush administration's pronouncements on the War on Terror, this augmented power to designate national security threats makes all American citizens potential candidates for de-subjectivation. In my view, this expansion of power means that citizens have no greater guarantee of civil liberties than foreign nationals. They are in the protected category of "us" only so long as this protection does not hinder the national security agenda.

While Butler's analysis of governmental power unchecked by law and electoral oversight concentrates on events occurring after 11 September 2001, Giorgio Agamben's *State of Exception* explores the history of and justifications for suspensions of law. Glossing the "state of exception" by which Carl Schmitt defines the sovereign—"he who decides on the state of exception"—as suspension of the rule of law, the book's first chapter offers a painstaking analysis of the possible roots in modern (post-French Revolution) history of the increasingly permanent state of exception we face today (2005, p. 1).

Like Butler, Agamben's overarching argument concerns challenges to the rule of law. He worries that an incident-driven disregard of cherished legal principles like habeas corpus and a resulting acceptance of the view that the sovereign, or executive, is above the law will inevitably take on the character of permanency. This "new normal" (2004) may be initially justified as a merely temporary response to a national security threat but history suggests it will result in a rollback of civil liberties.

Later in the book, Agamben takes up the Carl Schmitt-Walter Benjamin debate from the 1920s as a crucial, revelatory conflict of views on the relation that rule of law bears to power outside the law (2005). Schmitt's conservative perspective is that the sovereign is the creator of law and has, therefore, the authority to administer it and the authority to suspend it, as circumstances warrant (ibid., p. 57). His position is reminiscent of Bush's assertion that he is "the decider" who has an unchallengeable authority to say whether and when the country will enter into war, augment or draw down its military presence in other nations, and conform to or reinterpret its treaty obligations and constitutionally-guaranteed civil liberties (Henry and Starr, 2006; *USA Today*, 2006).

Benjamin, on the other hand, posits a sphere of "pure violence," outside the law (understood here as the juridical order) and capable of illuminating a vision of justice distinct from, and transformative of, law—as in a revolution which brings into being a more just legal order (Agamben, 2005, pp. 60–63). These two views, roughly corresponding to the distinction between governmentality and rule of law with which Butler is working, oppose the personal, charismatic power of the sovereign to suspend or reactivate law, which Agamben argues is fundamentally antagonistic to rule of law, to the legal power that derives its legitimacy from popular support (ibid., p. 86).

Rule of law and personal power can function together, albeit uneasily, as long as some conceptual distinction (such as a separation of powers) is made. But, Agamben warns, "when they tend to coincide in a single person, when the state of exception . . . becomes the rule, then the juridico-political system transforms itself into a killing machine" (ibid.). This consolidation and reduction of power to the whim of the sovereign (the executive branch) strips citizens of their political protections, potentially reducing us all to the "bare life" of the detainee.

The process of reducing political participants to merely-subsisting life forms is the central feature of the concentration camp in the twentieth century, prompting Agamben to say, "the camp is the space that opens up when the state of exception starts to become the rule," as he thinks it has in our contemporary political paradigm (2000, pp. 39–42). This is precisely the moral quagmire exposed in the Bush administration's decision to deny "prisoner of war" status to the so-called enemy combatants apprehended in Afghanistan and Iraq and incarcerated at Guantánamo Bay. In doing so, the administration has determined that detainees have no legal jurisdiction from which to pursue *habeas corpus* remedies (Blumner, 2007).

As Butler and Agamben each admonish, we need to read their analyses in the context of Michel Foucault's thinking on biopolitics (Butler, 2004, pp. 51–55; Agamben, 2000, pp. ix, 7; 2005, p. 63). We especially need to consider Foucault's deliberately broad account of "biopolitical" racism in the modern state, the control and preferential treatment of groups within the national population, which centrally involves determinations of "what [who] must live and what [who] must die" (2003, p. 254). The object that biopolitics seeks to manage is a statistically-measured and monitored population, a population conceived "as political problem." Thus biopolitics is very different from "discipline," the classic Foucaultian technology of power which manages and modifies individuals at the level of the body (ibid., pp. 245–246).

The subdivision, or fragmentation of a society into populations through the principle of racial differentiation is, Foucault tells us, "the first function of racism" (p. 255) and a fragmentation that we see reflected, post-11 September 2001, in the heightened suspicion and "racial" profiling of Americans of Islamic faith. Once this differentiation has been effected, identification of difference devolves into hierarchy and racism takes on the character of a social hygiene movement. Larger society deems the populations designated as inferior to constitute a threat, either internal or external (ibid., p. 256).

Racism, Foucault charges, "is the indispensable precondition that makes killing acceptable," and justifies "the murderous function of the State" (ibid.). This account of segregation, hierarchy, and state willingness to use or permit extermination as a control mechanism appears to fit the facts and social attitudes of some of the darkest days of American history: Southern slavery, Reconstruction, and the Jim Crow South. But, as an explanation of War on Terror practices such as racial profiling, suspect identification, and indefinite detention, some may well perceive it as overblown hyperbole.

So what reason would Butler and Agamben have for their interest in linking their analyses to such an exaggerated account of social control? The answer lies in Foucault's clarification of his use of the word "killing," a category in which he includes actual killings ("murder as such"). He also extends the term to include metaphorical deaths such as political marginalization and demonization, expulsion, and permanent extra-legal incarceration—exactly the kinds of treatment and concerns we are seeing today with respect to suspected terrorists and the racially- or religiously-identified populations (Arab-Americans, Muslims) thought to harbor terrorists (ibid.).

Similarly, we must understand Foucault's discussion of racism broadly. The segregated or overtly discriminatory society is racist in the Foucaultian sense. Also racist is the society that is acutely conscious of racial and ethnic difference, one that is aware of who is "us" and who is "them" even where substantive variation in the social opportunities made available to those who are us and those who are them may not (yet) exist.

Conceived this broadly, we can see the doctrine of American exceptionalism as an instance of racism. Definitions of this doctrine abound and overlap, but a post-11 September 2001 analysis of American self-assessments in *The Economist* distinguishes two ways of understanding exceptionalism. The first views the United States as an exemplar of the universal values of democracy and human rights. America is not unique, merely the most highly evolved instantiation of an ideal toward which all nations (should) strive.

The second way of grasping what exceptionalism means involves precisely the opposite claim: that America has a unique essence, which sets it apart from other nations, and its greater wealth and power are explicable through this essential difference (Parker, 2003). This second gloss is much closer to the first recorded articulation of exceptionalism, Alexis de Tocqueville's 1831 observation:

> For the last fifty years no pains have been spared to convince the inhabitants of the United States that they constitute the only religious, enlightened, and free people. They perceive that, for the present, their own democratic institutions succeed, whilst those of other countries fail; hence they conceive an overweening opinion of their superiority, and they are not very remote from believing themselves to belong to a distinct race of mankind. (Bradley, Reeve, and Bowen, 1945, pt. 7, chap. 18)

De Tocqueville's explicit linking of the feeling of exceptionalism with a perception of moral superiority is echoed in the political newsletter *CounterPunch*'s account of how exceptionalism keeps the current war in Iraq going, despite antiwar protests. The author, Ron Jacobs, understands exceptionalism as:

> the belief that, for some reason (America's system of democracy, or maybe its economic superiority), the United States system is not subject to the same contradictions and influences as those of the rest of the world. (2004)

Jacobs argues that this belief leads even those opposed to the war to think that only America can "fix" what it broke in Iraq. Acceptance of the premise that the United States functions under a different set of rules than those governing other countries leads to the conclusion ("misconception" is the term Jacobs uses) that for the government to export its own notion of democracy is appropriate (ibid.). We can coherently link exceptionalism to the view that this superior society is entitled, by virtue of its superiority, to be the arbiter of other nations' places in an international hierarchy. On this construal, it is clearly a doctrine, which meets the criteria of Foucault's expansive definition of racism and conforms to Kipling's description of the white man's burden.

In "A Nation Apart," John Parker discusses the Bush administration's commitment to American exceptionalism in its flaunting of patriotic rhetoric and ubiquitous use of flag-waving imagery (2003). He quotes Bush's description of the American mission to a Florida audience in January 2002, "We're fighting for freedom, and civilisation [sic] and universal values," and asserts that the Bush administration's preoccupation with national interests and its assumption of the right to speak as the champion of freedom embody this exceptionalism (ibid.).

To protect these national interests, the *National Security Strategy of the United States of America*, 2002, focuses on maintaining America's current military dominance as a power that cannot be equaled or even be challenged (ibid.). We can also see this doctrine underpinning the Bush administration's presumed ability to manage Iraq's "transition" to democracy, and in its presumed right to judge the legitimacy of the Palestinian Authority's election of a Hamas government in January 2006. All of this looks a lot like an exercise of the traditional prerogative that wealthy white men have accorded to themselves, to judge and rule the "Other(s)" of the world (the white man's burden).

We might view Bush's aggressive drive to contain power within the Executive Branch of government as an idiosyncratic fear-based response to the terrorist attack on the World Trade Center and the Pentagon. Alternatively, we might view it as an opportunistic attempt, capitalizing on these events, to tip the balance of power at the expense of the legislative and judicial branches of government. Americans' enthusiastic embrace of their exceptionalism and their superpower status definitely predates the War on Terror.

As an example, William Blum offers us President Lyndon Baines Johnson's assurance, during the aerial bombings, napalm attacks, and Agent Orange sprayings during the Vietnam War, "that Asians don't have the same high regard for human life as Americans do" (2005, p. 8). Blum also reiterates the terms on which Richard Milhous Nixon ended the country's failed war against the North Vietnamese: the United States promised to pay postwar reconstruction aid of $3.25 billion over five years, but reneged on this promise and instead demanded payment from Hanoi of $145 million in war debt reparations (ibid.).

Blum also quotes the 1988 comment made by then Vice President George Herbert W. Bush, speaking to Republican leaders after an American ship shot down an Iranian airplane, killing 290 passengers: "I will never apologize for the United States of America . . . I don't care what the facts are" (*Newsweek*, 1988). The arrogance of his statement predated, but nevertheless expressed, the general ethos that has guided American foreign policy since the collapse of the Soviet Union ended the Cold War.

Post-Cold War, American political discourse began to dissect the terms of a "new world order," in which America would bear the burden of maintaining peace and order. The new world order of the 1990s gave way to a rhetoric that depicts international relations as a "war of the worlds" (Latour, 2002). This is the discontinuity within an otherwise continuous tradition of presenting exceptional America as the world's natural-born leader. The response to the events of 11 September 2001 has been to construe governmental power more narrowly, to guard it more jealously in the hands of the executive branch, and deploy it within the context of a newer "world disorder" that requires the lone superpower to impose its will upon chaos.

The question raised by presenting the political attitudes of contemporary America against the backdrop of self-aggrandizing sovereign power and biopolitical racism is this: how has the drive for containment of power unfolded and refocused since 11 September 2001? In my view, examination of how American power has been exercised both before and after this fissure in the national psyche reveals a common strain of racialized exceptionalism that unifies these past and present projects. Paradoxically, we can also see a discontinuity when we consider how widely power is distributed. Previously, the point was to concentrate power in the American government—Congress, the judiciary, and the White House. Now, however, this power is being concentrated in the hands of the very few in the executive branch—the President and his inner circle of advisers.

The continuity of racialized American pre-eminence and the discontinuity of ever more concentrated power exist in the case of classifying Haitian and Cuban refugees seeking asylum and classifying so-called enemy combatants. The Immigration and Naturalization Service (INS) test for asylum requires expression of a genuine and well-founded fear of persecution. According to a Congressional Research Service Report, of the almost 23,000 Haitian refugees picked up at sea between 1981 and 1990, only eleven (less than 0.05 percent) met that criterion (Wasem, 2005, p. 3). The first five years of this period spanned the end of the bloody and brutal Duvalier dictatorship (first, François Duvalier, from 1957 until 1971, then his son Jean-Claude, until 1986). During the next four years, the tumultuous and dangerous popular democracy was emerging. To suggest that only eleven of the Haitian refugees who risked their lives in these dangerous sea voyages had such a fear stretches credulity beyond the breaking point.

Far more plausible is the explanation that United States Coast Guard and INS officials (who are not required to have translators present at interdictions) did not bother to make even the cursory inquiries that international refugee conventions require of them. They likely just rounded up the would-be refugees and returned them to the shores of Haiti at the mercy of the government they had attempted to flee (Human Rights First, 2003).

This treatment differs markedly from that given to Cuban refugees who take to the sea to flee government repression (Wasem, 2005, p. 6). Like Haitian refugees, the federal government typically returns Cuban refugees picked up at sea to their country of origin. Unlike Haitian citizens, Cuban citizens who reach American soil are allowed to stay and "adjust" to permanent residence status after one year of physical presence in the country—a policy known as the wet foot, dry foot policy (ibid.; Human Rights First, 2003).

Jan Ting, law professor at Temple University, explains this special treatment that Cuban refugees receive as "a vestige of the Cold War . . . a policy of trying to poke Castro in the eye at every opportunity" and as a political opportunity: "the Cuban American vote in Florida is the swing vote in a swing state" (PBS.org, 2002). Observers of this special treatment note that, even though both societies have documented histories of repression, "most Cuban immigrants eventually receive asylum in the U.S.; most Haitians don't" (ibid.).

Critics of American immigration policies sometimes explain this differential treatment of Cuban and Haitian refugees in terms of exactly the kind of race/color hierarchy that I discussed earlier as a central component of the white man's burden. Policy makers perceive the often lighter-skinned, Spanish-speaking Cuban refugees as having greater political value and deemed more easily assimilable than the darker, French and Creole speaking Haitian refugees.

The hierarchy here is political more than racial. Cuban refugees are fleeing communism so since 1961, the United States has designated them as political refugees. Haitian refugees, on the other hand, are fleeing the effects of the Duvalier dictatorship, which the United States tolerated as a bulwark against spreading communism in the region. The United States government therefore classified those from Haiti as "economic" refugees, seen to fall outside treaty obligations.

The "burden" of American dominance confers the power to decide the status of "Others," assigning the coveted status of political asylum to those escaping the misery caused by America's enemies and denying it to those escaping the misery caused by America's allies. This is an instance of the United States government—Congress, in its framing of immigration laws and the executive branch, in its application of policy directives—deciding to disregard international law on refugees, which mandates the same treatment for all refugees, in favor of a preferential policy intended to maintain its position of power within the region.

We can also see this sorting of people into preferred and dispensable categories in the Bush administration's derivation of a new term for people subjected to war-related detention. Instead of calling the people rounded up in Iraq and Afghanistan "prisoners of war"—which would give them status and rights under the Geneva Conventions—the Bush White House introduced the designation "enemy combatant."

Actually, Bush *reintroduced* the term. According to *SourceWatch*, the phrase was coined back in the Supreme Court ruling, *Ex parte Quirin* (317 U.S. 1, 63 S.Ct. 1, 87 L.Ed. 3 [1942]). President Franklin Delano Roosevelt defined the term as covering all persons, regardless of citizenship or country of residence, "who during time of war enter or attempt to enter the United States . . . and are charged with committing or attempting or preparing to commit sabotage, espionage, hostile or warlike acts, or violations of the law or war." (Center for Media & Democracy, 2006). The intention was to categorize spies and saboteurs in such a way that they would fall under the jurisdiction of American military tribunals instead of domestic criminal courts or the "laws of war" from which the Geneva Conventions emerged after World War II (ibid.).

The Bush administration recycled the term and used *Ex parte Quirin* to justify its policy of denying the right of *habeas corpus* to suspected terrorists and Guantánamo detainees (Vagts, 2007). However, Pentagon documents show that fewer than half (45 percent) of detainees incarcerated at the Guantánamo Bay naval base have committed hostile acts against the United States or its allies, raising the question of what justifies labeling them "combatants" (Warren Hoge, "Investigators for U.N. Urge U.S. to Close Guantánamo," *The New York Times*, 17 February 2006).

Robert Weaver, a lawyer representing two current Guantánamo inmates, considers the term to have "no satisfactory definition" despite its great usefulness in justifying the administration's claims of non-applicability of Geneva protections to people held there and at other undisclosed locations (2006, p.10).

Human Rights Watch has sharply criticized this willingness to use a category, the definition of which is deliberately developed in a vague way, to justify subjecting people arrested far from battlefields to indefinite detention based on evidence the detainees are not permitted to see or contest (2003). For example, Ali Saleh Kahlah al-Marri, a citizen of Qatar, was arrested in 2001, while studying at Bradley University in Illinois. Originally held as a material witness, he was later charged with making false statements to the FBI and to financial institutions, identity fraud, and credit card fraud. Wendy Patten, advocacy director for Human Rights Watch in the United States, charges that application of the label "enemy combatant" to al-Marri constitutes, "an end run around the criminal justice system," a military-governmental practice that "has no place in a country committed to the rule of law" (ibid.). The net effect of applying this label to al-Marri is to remove him from the jurisdiction of the criminal courts and place him in the shadowy and unsupervised space of "the camp" of which Agamben speaks, the place where no law exists except the whim of the executive.

The al-Marri case, which constitutes semantic denial of international law and national values, is not an isolated incident. Reports by the British Broadcasting Corporation (BBC, 2006a; 2006c) on the investigation of American detention practices in Afghanistan, Iraq, and Guantánamo cite accusations by rights groups that the United States is deliberately ignoring the United Nations Convention against Torture. The President has given the Central Intelligence Agency "special powers" to hold and interrogate detainees in circumstances that those who later had access to attorneys reported as violations of the Convention against Torture and the International Covenant on Civil and Political Rights, both of which the United States has ratified (Hentoff, 2006).

Congressional investigations have heard from members of the military who have testified that interrogation techniques authorized by the Bush administration do violate the Geneva Conventions (Scherer, 2006). In response, Senator Patrick Leahy notes that this destabilizes the rule of law: "We cannot credibly ask others to meet standards we are unwilling to meet ourselves," he says (ibid.).

Condoleezza Rice's 2005 "clarification" of the United States policy on torture raised the pitch of the confusion it was supposed to silence. She acknowledged that United States treaty obligations cover all American personnel regardless of where they are stationed, but she did not justify the creation of labels that put people outside of treaty protections (Reynolds, 2005). She reconciled American definitions of torture as necessarily involving "severe pain" with the much more expansive Geneva prohibitions against violence, violations to human dignity, and humiliating and degrading treatment (ibid.; Office of the United Nations High Commissioner for Human Rights, 1949).

Simone de Beauvoir's account of existentialist ethics best articulates the problem with this evasive attitude towards torture:

> A democracy which defends itself only by acts of oppression equivalent to those of authoritarian regimes, is precisely denying all these values; whatever the virtues of a civilization may be, it immediately belies them if it buys them by means of injustice and tyranny. (1948, pp. 124–125)

In these ways—the refusal to justify labels, and the disinclination to reconcile American policies on allowable interrogation techniques with an international consensus—the Bush administration skirts the limitations of humanitarian treaties it has signed and claims to respect. In so doing, it debases America's moral capital within the international community and makes the world a more dangerous place for its citizens.

A similar attitude toward international agreements is evinced in the American opposition to the ICC expressed prior to the War on Terror. The European Union was the driving force behind the ICC, hoping to create a permanent court in which issues of international justice—genocide, crimes against humanity, and war crimes—could be resolved (Human Rights Watch, 2000). Along with nations like China, Yemen, and Saddam Hussein's Iraq, the United States objected to, and refused to sign, the 1998 treaty.

In keeping with the country's exceptionalist commitments, American officials resisted the proposal of an ICC because of their concern that American nationals might face prosecution in this court. This resistance has remained consistent since the Clinton administration. During March 2000, the United States proposed an amendment that would bar ICC prosecution of persons who are citizens of non-participating states (ibid.).

This amounts to an immunity from prosecution for American citizens—a clear and unambiguous statement that Americans should be exempt from international law. We can see this position, call it "American exemptionalism," as the most extreme articulation of the doctrine of exceptionalism that has pervaded discourses within and about the United States. (Americans are so exceptional, so different from other nations, that they cannot be included in, or subject to, the rules and institutional processes of these "Others.")

Differential treatment of refugees exemplifies another such self-conferred exemption. As a party to the 1951 Refugee Convention and its 1967 Protocol, the United States has an obligation to ensure that any and all would-be refugees that it returns to a country of origin will not face persecution there (Human Rights First, 2003). While this obligation appears to be adequately respected in the case of Cuban refugees, it is deflected in the case of Haitian refugees by determinations that they are economic migrants (therefore outside the bounds of the convention) or national security risks (PBS.org, 2002; Wasem, 2005, p. 4–5).

Again, we can see the continuity of American power in the assertion of a succession of presidential administrations that America has the prerogative of unilaterally deciding whether and why the country should be exempt from international standards. In addition, we can see the discontinuity between the administrations that exercised power before 11 September 2001 and the one exercising power after that date in the extent to which these claimed exemptions are formulated by consensus across the branches of government or implemented unilaterally by the executive.

The power to decide exemptions and exceptions also translates, in the current milieu as it has historically, into the power to oversee "security threats." We see this today in the Executive Branch's initial and persistent assertion of a right to incarcerate a United States citizen, José Padilla for example, without due process or the oversight of the Supreme Court and, then, when it appeared that the Supreme Court would rule the government's action unconstitutional, the haste with which he was transferred to the civilian court system.

Padilla, also known by his Islamic name, Abdullah al-Mujahir, has been held by the government since May 2002, first in military custody until January 2006, then transferred to civilian custody and ultimately convicted, in August 2007, of providing money and support to terrorists (Aguayo, 2006; BBC, 2007). Brooklyn-born Padilla was arrested at Chicago's O'Hare airport on suspicion that he was planning to plant a "dirty bomb." Despite having no battlefield connections, he was declared an enemy combatant by President Bush (Wilson, 2005).

The Padilla case has raised a human rights controversy over the question of how long the government could hold someone in military custody without charge. This controversy is widely accepted as the motivating factor for Padilla's transfer to the civilian court system (ibid.).

Human Rights Watch has taken the position on Padilla and other American citizens designated as enemy combatants that they should have the protections of international humanitarian law (the Geneva Conventions) and the protections of American constitutional law. At minimum, they say, "[t]hese protections include the rights to be formally charged and permitted access to counsel" (2002).

Padilla has now been charged, tried, and convicted within the system designed to protect his rights as a citizen, but his civilian-court prosecution involved charges that were unrelated to those on which he was held for three and a half years as an enemy combatant (BBC, 2007). Questions about the legitimacy of the government's bait-and-switch approach to criminal indictment of Padilla are further exacerbated by psychiatric findings that the interrogations and incarceration conditions to which he was subjected during his time in military custody amounted to psychological torture, which has left him mentally broken and unfit to stand trial (Goodman, 2007).

This sobering allegation tempers any sense of satisfaction that we might feel about Padilla's civilian trial. The system has not worked to protect this citizen but has instead applied a veneer of constitutionality to the stripping of citizenship that was effectively perpetrated upon Padilla as a result of his being designated an enemy combatant.

Bush's claim of a right to incarcerate enemy combatants without civilian oversight is not without precedent. Other than Padilla's citizenship, the facts of his treatment by the Bush administration are paralleled by the facts that gave rise to *Ex parte Quirin*. This was the first instance of judicial review concerning the president's right to try wartime saboteurs in secret military tribunals. Eight German men, who had spent some time in the United States before the war, entered the country covertly in June 1942. Nazis, their mission was to fan out and destroy war industries and facilities. Two of the men foiled that plan by immediately surrendering themselves to the Federal Bureau of Investigation and, once the other six were apprehended, President Franklin Roosevelt ordered them tried by a secret military tribunal, which sentenced them to death. The two who confessed had their sentences commuted to life imprisonment but the remaining six were sent to the electric chair in August 1942—two months before the Supreme Court issued its official ruling that upheld the military tribunal's jurisdiction. The court had made its decision in July but, at the time of execution, the men's appeal was still pending (Vagts, 2007).

Quirin occurred prior to the 1949 adoption of the Geneva Conventions so no international framework against which Roosevelt's actions could be revealed as a violation existed. Only the Supreme Court played its appointed role in the balance of powers, despite the president's rush to punish. Although the international context is very different today, Bush's identification of Padilla as a security threat follows a similar script. He was arrested in May 2002 upon returning from Pakistan where intelligence officers had implicated him in an al-Qaeda plot to set off a "dirty" (radioactive) bomb somewhere in the United States (Karon, 2002).

Like al-Marri, Padilla was initially held as a material witness and has been in custody since his arrest—most of that time in military custody, incommunicado or in solitary confinement (Amnesty International, 2005). The discontinuity between the foreign agents in Quirin and Padilla, the American citizen, appears as an excess on Bush's part. This exercise of executive power exemplifies the reduction to bare life and revocation of political identity that Butler and Agamben see as paradigmatic of our "new normal," the permanent state of exception.

Throughout this discussion, I have linked the containment efforts I labeled "George Bush's burden" to a longstanding, and often implicit, commitment to national exceptionalism. I will use my concluding remarks to discuss how these adventures in imperialism might be opposed and clarify the relationship between exceptionalism and Bush's executive arrogance.

First, understand that I have labeled this burden as George W. Bush's—despite American exceptionalism predating his administration—because he is wholly responsible for the bad behavior that he has called on exceptionalism to justify. But we would be naïve to think that the end of the Bush administration will mark an end to the aggressive paternalism that characterizes America's foreign policy. Getting rid of one leader does not get rid of the underlying problem.

Written at a later point in time, I could have just as easily entitled this chapter, "John S. McCain's Burden," or, more ironically, "Barack Obama's Burden." The "burden" is the self-conferred power of being "the decider" at the helm of the world's only superpower. The doctrine of American exceptionalism is the phenomenon that makes it appear to be a power that can (and should) be deployed.

The only assurance we have that the nation will not elect another president who embarks upon wars in multiple countries, appoints subordinates who direct a rollback of civil liberties, and actively makes the world the dangerous place ripe for justification of excesses is to challenge America's leaders. Americans must relinquish cherished, albeit dangerous and disastrous, belief in their own essential difference from the people of the rest of the world.

Speaking at the London School of Economics, British Attorney General Lord Peter Henry Goldsmith said, "There should be in modern society no outlaws; no people to whom the law does not apply—and to whom therefore anything can be done" (BBC, 2006b). I agree, but would go further: I believe that no one should be above the law, claiming authority to decide whom the law protects and who it does not. If we want to end both war and terror and bring about peace, "[o]nly one thing is asked of [us]," says Bruno Latour, "that we cease to insist on a specious 'right' to dominate others and learn to negotiate with them as equals" (2002, p. 36).

The new paradigm for which we should be preparing is one in which peace, order, and good government are the collective responsibility of every member of the global political community, not the self-conferred burden of a ruling elite.

Eight

BORDERING ON THE ABSURD: NATIONAL, CIVILIZATIONAL, AND ENVIRONMENTAL SECURITY DISCOURSE ON IMMIGRATION

Jessica LeAnn Urban

1. Introduction

On 15 May 2006, the George W. Bush administration (2006a) announced the mobilization of National Guard troops to the United States-Mexico border. Although the President and his supporters insist that sending troops to the border does not constitute its militarization, I contend that the administration's border policies continue and enhance a legacy of militarization framed by Low Intensity Conflict (LIC) doctrine in the region. In addition, they contribute to a long history of punitive immigration control policies and practices more generally, although neither the category of "illegal immigrant" nor border control existed prior to the Chinese Exclusion Act of 1882 (Zinn, 2007, p. 14). It was not until 1924 that the Border Patrol was created and the concept of "illegal alien" targeting Mexican people gained widespread appeal (Fernandes, 2007, p. 56). I use scare quotes for "illegal alien" and similar phrases to elucidate and problematize the dehumanization that such phrases engender. By contrast, I use "undocumented immigrant," which I believe is a less dehumanizing term that better captures the reality of what I am discussing in this chapter. As the popular immigrant rights slogan suggests, "no one is illegal."

For nearly a century, claims of sovereignty and fears of economic, political, social, and national *in*security have informed dominant state, academic, and public responses to issues of undocumented immigration, as have concerns over "civilizational security" (Persaud, 2002, p. 56). Here, American national identity is socially constructed, represented, and idealized as homogenously white, middle class, and masculine (all of which are problematic social constructions backed by institutional power), as well as individualistic, modern, Western, and strong. Based on characteristics such as these, dominant state and academic security discourse and public opinion often equate American national identity with civilization itself, which we must preserve as a matter of national security.

On the other hand, this discourse often links social constructions and representations of "threat" to external anarchy, illegality, and conflict. Threat is further constructed and represented as non-white, feminine, poverty-stricken, and inferior (also problematic social constructions backed by institutional power), and the concept of threat is predominantly equated with the so-called Third World or less pejoratively stated, the Global South. Undocumented immigration into the United States from the Global South, according to dominant state and academic security discourse and much public opinion, is one of the primary means by which this threat is internalized. Each often represents undocumented immigration across the United States-Mexico border as an alien virus threatening the otherwise healthy body politic and security of the American nation. These representations focus especially on female immigrants of color who, as reproductive agents, will presumably reproduce future communities of color and therefore dilute and/or pollute national ("white") identity. These fears are not new. Andrea Smith draws attention to the mass sterilization campaigns against indigenous women in the United States during the colonial conquest. These campaigns were based on the perception of Native women as a disease polluting the American nation (2002, p. 124).

More recently, what I call "mainstream Environmental Security (ES) discourse" in the United States has targeted immigrants of color based on *environmental* security concerns. A key focus of mainstream ES discourse is the presumed threat that "overpopulation" in, and "mass illegal immigration" from, "Other" (meaning inferior, subhuman, backward, uncivilized, dangerous, exotic, Third World) countries poses to the carrying capacity and security of the United States. Neo-Malthusian theory, whose proponents contend that population growth especially in the Global South is a primary cause of global environmental destruction and often offer apocalyptic predictions of the earth's environmental demise, lies at the heart of mainstream ES discourse today. Mainstream ES discourse replays Neo-Malthusian doomsday scenarios and adds an environmental twist to anti-immigration positions already evident in dominant state and academic discourse of national and civilizational security. Mainstream ES discourse in the United States also engages in what Betsy Hartmann (2004) calls the "greening of hate," whereby environmental degradation is blamed on poor populations of color on the basis of highly xenophobic, classist, racist, and sexist assumptions about uncontrolled fertility, immorality, criminality, selfishness, and danger. Together, all three discourses bolster calls for the deterrence and containment of "enemy Others" (Urban, 2004; 2008).

Concerns over environmental security in the United States have not supplanted the security concerns characteristic of traditional International Relations (IR) or state security discourse in either the post-Cold War or post-11 September 2001 era. Instead, discourses of national, civilizational, and environmental security form a mutually supportive discursive cluster that (re)constructs and (re)enforces the boundaries of "America" and "Americanness." In this post-11 September 2001 era, the Bush administration presents an interesting blend of "old" and "new" modes of (and justifications for) containment and deterrence in its approach to addressing the United States-Mexico border. As Zilla Eisenstein (2004, p. 4) explains, "so much is said to be new, when most everything is almost always also old." This includes, I argue, the border's militarization, the "enemy-creation process" underlying its militarization, and the myriad ways in which United States foreign and domestic economic policy simultaneously encourages and pushes people to cross the United States-Mexico border and then criminalizes and persecutes them for doing so.

In this chapter, I examine the interlocking cluster of national, environmental, and civilizational security discourses in relation to undocumented immigration and the material consequences of these discourses. I pay special attention to the United States-Mexico border, to the policies of the Clinton administration, and to some of the post-11 September 2001 rhetoric and policies of the George W. Bush administration. I draw heavily on my other writings (Urban, 2004; 2007) and I elaborate on the arguments I present in this chapter in much greater depth in *Nation, Immigration, and Environmental Security* (Urban, 2008). I also draw on data from that publication for this chapter.

I use the analytical and activist framework of Intersectional Feminism throughout this chapter. In its most basic terms it focuses on, and helps scholar-activists interrogate and work to dismantle, interlocking ideologies and systems of power, privilege, and oppression. These include, but are not limited to, sexism, racism, and classism, and their intersections with xenophobia, colonization, militarization and neo-liberal globalization, or what bell hooks calls "white supremacist capitalist patriarchy" (Jhally, 1997; hooks, 2000). Neo-liberalism is an economic theory and set of policies that privilege the rule of the market, privatization, deregulation, cutting social services, and reducing social welfare spending (including spending on healthcare and education). The United States pursues neo-liberal policies domestically (for example, so-called Welfare Reform) and internationally with the International Monetary Fund (IMF), the World Trade Organization (WTO), and the World Bank. Neo-liberal policies are directed primarily at countries of the Global South and according to critics, exacerbate inequality between nations of the Global North and the Global South (See Martinez and García [2006] for more explanation).

Neo-liberal globalization is grounded in legacies of colonialism; I often associate neo-liberal globalization with neo-colonialism when discussing the United States' relationship with Mexico and Latin America today. Colonial and neo-colonial relationships refer to the process whereby the United States benefits from the expropriation of resources from countries of the Global South including raw materials and agricultural products, and benefits from the exploitation of cheap and coerced labor (Aviva Chomsky, 2007, pp. 56–57). This dynamic allows the United States to industrialize and, for those with class privilege, allows United States citizens to enjoy a comfortable lifestyle (ibid.). Under neo-liberal globalization, or neo-colonialism, resources and labor continue to be expropriated and exploited in the service of American hegemony and empire. As Aviva

Chomsky explains, "[a]lthough the United States does not directly govern their countries, it exerts economic, political, and military control through indirect means" (ibid., p. 126).

Speaking again of Intersectional Feminism, I agree with Seager's contention:

> Only an integrated approach ... can bring us to a holistic understanding in which racial justice, gender justice, environmental justice, economic justice, and universal human rights are understood as an indispensable foundation for a peaceful and sustainable future for our world. (2003, p. 5)

I use the integrated and holistic framework of Intersectional Feminism to examine the enemy-creation process underlying punitive, militarized efforts at stemming undocumented immigration across the United States-Mexico border. In so doing, I examine the production and mobilization of racialized, xenophobic, and gendered images of enemy Others as national, civilizational, and environmental security threats. Interrogating this enemy-creation process within the framework of Intersectional Feminism is critical given that interlocking national, environmental, and civilizational security discourses, alongside ideologies supporting systems of inequality, helps provide ideological "justification" for the militarization of the United States-Mexico border. This includes "justification" for the pattern of human rights violation, violence, repression, and death among targeted populations in the region.

Jennifer Milliken defines discourse as "an ordering of terms, meanings, and practices that form the background presuppositions and taken-for-granted understandings that enable people's actions and interpretations" (1999, p. 92). Edward Said similarly defines discourse as "a regulated system of producing knowledge within certain constraints whereby certain rules have to be observed" (Jhally, 2002). On the basis of these definitions, I define "mainstream ES discourse" in the United States as the dominant assumptions, meanings, categories, theories, and knowledge produced by privileged actors within institutions such as academia, the mainstream news media, the state, and environmental non-governmental organizations (NGOs). I also examine the knowledge produced by anti-immigration groups in the United States such as Ranch Rescue, the Minutemen groups, and American Patrol in this context. Overall, mainstream ES discourse in the United States is (re)produced in security documents, speeches, press releases, research projects, journals, newspaper and online articles, other Internet materials, and university textbooks (Urban, 2008).

2. National and Civilizational (In)Security

During his 11 September 2006 address to the nation, President George W. Bush explained that the struggle against terrorism "has been called a clash of civilizations. In truth, it is a struggle for civilization. We are fighting to maintain the way of life enjoyed by free nations" (2006b). The *National Strategy for Homeland Security* (NSHS) similarly contends, "The responsibility of our government extends beyond the physical well-being of the American people. We must also safeguard our way of life . . . ." (Office of Homeland Security, 2002, p. 8) with "our way of life" presented as the epitome of civilization itself. Border security and immigration policy are key elements of homeland security and have always been a cornerstone of national security policy.

Not all people equally share safety, security, and freedom across the United States. Within dominant security discourse and immigration policy, the state defines the "our" in "our way of live" in narrow terms and limits it to those more "genuine" citizens; meaning those privileged by and within interlocking systems of power, privilege, and oppression. Anannya Bhattacharjee argues, "the figure of the immigrant is a reminder of the oppressive system of exclusion by which some are more citizen-like than others" (1997, p. 325).

Post-11 September 2001 immigration policies have had horrendous consequences for immigrants of color across the United States, in violation of international standards of human rights. In the name of "keeping the homeland safe," the United States government initiated a series of policies targeting immigrants of color for arbitrary detention, interrogation, and in some cases, deportation (American Civil Liberties Union, 2004; Fernandes, 2007). These policies and the sentiments behind them reflect and reinforce the sentiments of many in the public, as immigrants were (and still are) targeted for hostility, hate speech, and violence nationwide.

Dominant security discourse and much public opinion in the United States, alongside post-11 September 2001 immigration rhetoric and policies, helped normalize already popular constructions of immigration as synonymous with terrorism, and terrorism as synonymous with Islam. As a result, the state targeted Arab or South Asian men, nearly all of whom are Muslim (American Civil Liberties Union, 2004, p. 1). This does not mean that anti-immigrant hostility and repression against Mexican and Central American people crossing the United States-Mexico border disappeared after 11 September 2001. As the American Civil Liberties Union (ACLU) notes, "immigrants have become scapegoats of the generalized fear-mongering that is prevalent in today's post-9/11 America" (2006b, p. 8). This includes undocumented workers (and those assumed to be undocumented), and people of color residing in (especially but not exclusively) border communities of the southwest United States.

Dominant national security discourse relies on the continual maintenance and containment of borders, literally (as in the boundary between the United States and Mexico) and figuratively (as in the construction of American identity). Each of which is grounded in the understandings of civilizational security. Security discourse and the processes by which the state forms and enforces geographical boundaries in the name of security rely on representations elucidating the ideological boundaries between self/Other, citizen/alien, superior/inferior, white/non-white, masculine/feminine, rational/irrational, us/them, civilized/backwards, and security/danger. Racialized and gendered constructions of the "alien" (undocumented or not) are central to the construction of national boundaries (and vice versa), and are vital to the representation of American whiteness, masculinity, and genuine citizenship within those boundaries. "Us" is constructed against "them" leading to state control and containment of "them." Likewise, in attempting to ensure the neatness of its sovereign borders through constructions of the "genuine" citizen versus the "illegal," threatening interloper, the state perpetuates constructions of its own identity and that of the "American nation." The "self" is always constructed, differentiated from, and revalued against the Other.

The continual process by which identity is reproduced is central to the construction of the nation and the identification and interpretation of threats to the security of the state and nation, within which "citizen" is most often equated with the rhetoric of national defense, and "alien" with that of danger and threat. "Citizenry" in the United States is defined by state immigration policy in very limited terms. "Real citizens" are ideally middle and upper class male consumers (as social groups), and the fullness of citizenship rights has historically been reserved for these more genuine citizens as a matter of policy.

The Naturalization Act of 1790 is a key example. As America's first immigration law, it limited naturalization to "free white persons" who had resided in the United States for two years; it was not repealed until 1952 (Kirk and Okazawa-Rey, 2007, p. 69). White European immigrants were heavily favored by early immigration laws in the United States, while people of color were often denied citizenship and entry, with the Chinese Exclusion Act of 1882 and the Immigration Acts of 1921 and 1924 as examples (Aviva Chomsky, 2007, pp. 53–55). The story is much different for those who were forced to come to the United States via the slavery system and for those who were internally colonized within the current borders of United States. This includes Mexican (after the 1848 Treaty of Guadalupe Hidalgo) and Indigenous peoples, who were forcibly incorporated and internally colonized through state policies of Manifest Destiny, war, and conquest (ibid., pp. 54, 91).

Critics such as Aviva Chomsky (ibid., p. 52) argue that immigration laws are arbitrary, discriminatory, and based not on humanitarianism or justice, but on racism and politics. Many of the immigrants that come to the United States today do so from countries in which the United States has been deeply involved for the past 100 years or more, including (but not limited to) Mexico, El Salvador and Guatemala (ibid., pp. 56–57). This involvement has been social, economic, political, and military. Aviva Chomsky explains,

> The United States has the highest standard of living in the world, and it maintains it by using its laws, and its military, to enforce the extraction of resources and labor from its modern version of colonies, with little

compensation for the populations. It is no wonder that people from these countries want to follow their resources to the place where they are being enjoyed (ibid, p. 56).

Despite popular myths about the ease with which people can obtain legal immigration documents, for the majority of people of color from countries of the Global South such as Mexico, obtaining permission to migrate to the United States is severely limited. Although immediate family members of those who have citizenship or permanent residency in the United States are given priority, applicants may have to wait up to twenty years to obtain permission to enter (ibid, p. 57). Those without family members who have United States citizenship or permanent residency are excluded (ibid.). By restricting immigration among peoples of color, historically and today, "immigration and naturalization law created, in the words of Aristide Zolberg, 'a nation by design'" (ibid, p. 54).

Constructions of national ("white") identity and concerns over civilizational security play a key role in rationalizing anti-immigration stances. Advocates of strict immigration control policies often view immigration-induced and fertility-induced population growth among non-white communities as a threat to "the core connection between whiteness and "American"-ness that comprises the mythology of a homogenous American national identity, a prospect that has put many white United States residents on edge" (Lindsley, 2000).

Population growth is a core preoccupation of mainstream ES discourse in the United States. Staying with civilizational and national security for another moment however, racialized, xenophobic, and gendered constructions of the "Other as threat" are required to rationalize the preservation of American identity and national and civilizational security through increasingly restrictive immigration policies and practices post 11 September 2001. The state has sought to protect America's civilizational security through immigration policies that exclude people of color from the Global South from citizenship rights. Immigrants of color are depicted as criminals who ostensibly exploit the good nature of "genuine" citizens, and simultaneously breed poverty, economic downturn, and decreased availability of social and political resources for genuine citizens. Framing national and civilizational security in these terms provides a perfect opening for the introduction of mainstream ES discourse and its attendant constructions of immigrants of color, especially undocumented Latina immigrants, as threats to environmental security.

3. Environmental (*In*)Security

Mainstream IR scholarship and security discourse are concerned with innumerable security dangers. Environmental degradation is among the more recently identified security dangers. ES scholars and activists such as Lester Brown, Paul and Anne Ehrlich, and Thomas Homer-Dixon, and politicians such as Albert

Arnold "Al" Gore, along with mainstream environmental organizations such as the Sierra Club and anti-immigration/environmental groups such as Population-Environment Balance have all demonstrated a growing interest in redefining national security to include resource and environmental threats. Environmental concerns have also found a place in the realm of "high politics" within the IR sub-field of ES, whose proponents argue that environmental degradation can cause or at least exacerbate conflict, which can threaten United States interests and national security (Urban, 2008).

Although some IR scholars and NGOs have been expressing deep concern over environmental destruction since the 1970s, it was not until the 1990s that environmental security foci were institutionalized in the state, academia, and other arenas. Former Vice-President Al Gore played a key role in popularizing ES foci and promoting institutional change, which included the creation of the Strategic Environmental Research and Development Program (SERDP) within the Department of Defense in 1990 (Thomas, 1997). Gore also supported the creation of the Woodrow Wilson Center's Environmental Change and Security Program (Butts, 1999, p. 117). These and numerous other institutional changes led to a "rapidly growing enterprise that involves the United States Departments of State and Defense, the Central Intelligence Agency (CIA), academic research institutes, private foundations, and nongovernmental organizations" replacing the military-industrial complex with a "military-environmental-security complex" (Ronald Deibert in Hartmann, 1999, pp. 1–2).

Concerns about the connections between ecological destruction and conflict have also come to be incorporated in governmental National Security Strategy (NSS) documents, required of all presidential administrations by the Goldwater Nichols Act of 1986. According to this Act, the NSS must articulate "U.S. interests, such as regional stability, free market economies, and democracy, that must be maintained if America is to survive" (Butts, 1999). With regard to environmental security, the Clinton administration's 1997 NSS claims, "environmental threats do not heed national borders and can pose long-term dangers to our security and wellbeing. Natural resource scarcities often trigger and exacerbate conflict" (National Security Council, 1997).

Thomas Homer-Dixon bluntly argues that environmental scarcity "contributes to social breakdown and violence" (1999, p. 4). With Homer-Dixon, many environmental security advocates identify population issues, especially "overpopulation" and "mass immigration," as key, if not root causes of hunger, ecological harm, and violent conflict, in strongly Neo-Malthusian terms (Ehrlich, 1968; Ehrlich et. al., 1993; Homer-Dixon, 1998; 1999). By contrast, I concur with Intersectional Feminist scholar-activists such as Betsy Hartmann (2006) who argue, "The root causes of poverty, environmental degradation, and political instability lie in unjust and inequitable social and economic systems—not in women's fertility" or migration. Hartmann further explains:

The modern-day proponents of population control have reinterpreted Malthusian logic, selectively applying it only to the poor majority in the Third World and, in some cases, to ethnic minorities in the West. (1995, p. 15)

Scapegoating poor populations of color (the greening of hate) has resulted in coercive and violent population control programs within the United States and around the world, often at the behest of the United States (Hartmann, 1995; Roberts, 1998; Silliman and King, 1999), and violent immigration control policies on the United States-Mexico border (Allen, 2003; Urban, 2004, 2008).

Based on my research (2004; 2008), I contend that mainstream ES discourse in the United States (including that articulated in academia, mainstream news media, environmental organizations, and anti-immigration groups) provides little in-depth factual analysis of the link between undocumented immigration and environmental destruction. Instead, people within these arenas often utilize a series of strategies to justify the claim that undocumented immigration causes environmental destruction.

One common strategy is to define population growth as a core cause of environmental destruction in heavily Neo-Malthusian terms, and then define undocumented immigration itself as a population issue. On a similarly Neo-Malthusian basis, mainstream proponents of environmental security blame immigration-induced population growth in the United States for the depletion of resources, which I have called "resource depletor" representation (Urban, in Lindsley, 2002). Proponents of this position provide little analysis of how immigrants actually impinge on social/public services and provide little analysis of state failure to provide equitably for basic social services across lines of gender, class and race. Few address the state's failure to privilege spending on social services over military spending, which actually accounts for a much larger portion of the United States federal budget than social services.

"Litany statements" and the "footpaths arguments" are also common strategies by which ES scholars and activists attempt to link undocumented immigration to environmental degradation, scarcity, and conflict. In litany statements, authors list undocumented immigration among a litany of environmental and social problems and imply connections between them without providing clear or compelling evidence of their connection. With respect to footpaths arguments, proponents of immigration control claim that undocumented migrants destroy the desert environment by walking across it.

I further contend that the work of Neo-Malthusian theorist Garrett Hardin lies at the center of mainstream ES discourse on population and immigration. Deep racism and sexism (given the historical and contemporary focus of eugenics theory and practice on the bodies of women of color and working class women) underlie Hardin's population and immigration-control positions. His serving as Vice President of the American Eugenics Society (Sferios, 1998) evinces Hardin's commitment to eugenics philosophy. He was also an honorary chair and advisory board member for Population-Environment Balance (ibid.; Hardin, 2003) and received awards from Federation for American Immigration Reform for his work (Hardin, 2003). Both organizations hold virulently anti-immigration positions and, like Hardin, engage directly in the greening of hate.

Southern Poverty Law Center lists the Federation as a hate group (2007). Hardin also had significant links to The Pioneer Fund, a white supremacist organization that seeks to advance eugenics "science" inside and outside academia. The Southern Poverty Law Center has also labeled the Pioneer Fund a hate group (2006). Hardin earned grant monies from the Pioneer Fund between 1988 and 1992 (Lynn, 2003), and Hardin thanks the Pioneer Fund and the Federation for American Immigration Reform for supporting his work in the Acknowledgements section of the 1998 edition of *The Ostrich Factor*.

Through an Intersectional Feminist lens, Syd Lindsley deconstructs the Hardinian constructions and representations of female immigrants of color (especially Latinas) popular during the 1990s (2002, p. 176). Proponents of immigration control, including ES scholars and activists, frequently represent Latina immigrants as lawless, lazy, promiscuous "resource depletors" (ibid.) who, as reproductive agents, ostensibly threaten to increase population, weaken national identity, and deplete social, economic, and natural resources for America's "real citizens." America's "real citizens" are (by contrast) constructed as self-organized, responsible, hard working, educated, trustworthy, and white. These assumptions underlie the 1996 Illegal Immigration Reform and Immigrant Responsibility Act (IIRIRA), provisions of the 1996 Personal Responsibility and Work Opportunity Reconciliation Act (so-called Welfare Reform), and policies like California's Proposition 187 and Arizona's Proposition 200.

These policies violate the rights of immigrants to care and provide for their families, and immigrant women to reproduce (ibid.). IIRIRA gives states the right to deny undocumented workers income-based federal nutrition programs like food stamps as well as health care services (Hayes, 2001, p. 2). Welfare Reform places limits on food stamps and Supplemental Security Income (SSI) for legal immigrants; Clinton later restored access to food stamps for many, but not SSI (ibid., p. 8). Welfare Reform also prohibits non-refugee immigrants from receiving "federal means-tested public benefits" like Medicaid, Temporary Assistance for Needy Families (TANF, which replaced AFDC), and the Children's Health Insurance program for their first five years in the United States (Lindsley, 2002, p. 185).

Undocumented immigrants are barred from thirty-one different Health and those that provide services for the disabled. California's Proposition 187 (1994) denied local and state social services, education, welfare, and non-emergency health care (including prenatal care) to anyone unable to prove United States citizenship or legal entry (Lindsley, 2002, p. 185). Lindsley (2000) contends:

Proposition 187 proponents placed little value on the reproductive health of undocumented women and their children. Proposition 187's proposed ban on public education funds for undocumented children was also an attempt to permanently exclude these children from integration into U.S. society.

Arizona's Proposition 200 (passed in 2000) mirror images Proposition 187. Unlike Proposition 187, Prop 200 has not yet been overturned on constitutional grounds.

These modes of representation and legislation suggest that female immigrants of color are targeted for immigration and population control and containment through punitive state policies, based on stereotypes about uncontrolled fertility, irresponsibility, laziness, selfishness and significantly, their representation as dangerous security enemies.

I agree with Cornel West who argues, "[h]ow we set up the terms for discussing racial issues shapes our perception and response to these issues" (2004, p. 120). In sum, just as the state and other social institutions represent immigrant women of color as social and economic resource depletors, so, too, do they represent women of color as depletors of environmental resources. In its engagement with the greening of hate, mainstream ES discourse scapegoats poor populations of color as a primary cause for environmental degradation and obfuscates the core causes of ecological devastation and insecurity. In so doing, mainstream ES discourse, especially in its intersection with national and civilizational discourse, also reinforces the racialized and gendered boundaries of American identity and nationhood, and discursively "justifies" the policing, punishment, and containment of those constructed as enemies. Given its focus on "women's fertility [as] the cause and solution to global environmental problems" (Rutherford, 2005, p. 20), mainstream ES discourse renders women's bodies (especially women of color) key battlegrounds in defense of a "civilized" and secure American nation.

These are not merely abstract, academic issues. Concrete, material consequences result from discourse and the politics of representation. As such, a genuine need exists for Intersectional Feminist analysis and activism around the politics of representation and the larger processes by which knowledge and policy are produced in the service of United States hegemony and empire.

4. Discourse of (In)Security and the Militarization of the United States-Mexico Border

From the conquest and colonization of land once a part of Mexico and policies aimed at keeping Communism "out of our backyard," to contemporary policies of neo-liberal globalization such as NAFTA, the United States' relationship with Mexico is a long and complicated one. Issues of immigration often take center stage in the relationship between the United States and Mexico and this relationship is marked by patterns of violence, exploitation, and repression, exemplified in part by the militarization of the United States-Mexico border. The United States-Mexico border region is "perhaps the key locus of militarization of law enforcement in the U.S." and "the site of the longest-running manifestation of such efforts . . . and the home of the deepest institutional ties between the military and police bodies" (Dunn, 2001, p. 7). The militarization of the United States-Mexico border is part of a larger strategy of Low Intensity Warfare guided by LIC doctrine.

The border's militarization is (re)produced not only by actors within traditional institutions such as the state, but also by groups such as Ranch Rescue, Minuteman, and American Patrol who are part of one of the most organized anti-immigration movements in the nation. Minuteman divided over allegations of financial wrongdoing on the part of Jim Gilchrist (Sonya Geis, "Minuteman Project in Turmoil Over Financial Allegations," *Washington Post*, 13 March 2007). In addition to the 2007 financial controversy, Sonya Geis explains that "the Minuteman Civil Defense Corps has operated separately from the Minuteman Project since December 2005, after a bitter internal dispute over funding." There are now two wings of Minuteman: Jim Gilchrist's Minuteman Project and Chris Simcox's Minuteman Civil Defense Corps. Both share virulent anti-immigration positions, and I label both wings (along with Ranch Rescue and American Patrol) paramilitary groups, the reasons for which I explain in the next section.

At its foundation, "militarization" refers to the use of military rhetoric, ideology, tactics, strategies, technology, equipment, and armed forces (Dunn in Martinez, 1996). It can be further described as a "warlike situation in which troops, weapons and other military hardware are amassed in a particular area—either as a show of force, or in preparation of war" (Border Action Network, 2002), as is the case with the United States-Mexico border region. The Clinton administration's Southwest Border Strategy (formally initiated in 1994), played a major role in militarizing the border. This multi-year border enforcement policy aims to strengthen existing immigration laws, disrupt popular crossing routes into the United States, and reduce undocumented immigration across the southwest border through its cornerstone policy referred to as the "program of deterrence."

LIC doctrine—designed to quell civil insurgencies in Latin America and impose "social control over targeted civilian populations" (Dunn, in Martinez, 1996)—frames the program of deterrence and the overall militarization of the border region. The government utilized LIC doctrine during the United States-driven proxy wars (also referred to as the "dirty wars") in Central and Latin America during the 1980s. LIC doctrine continues to represent a "particularly insidious strategy of militarization . . . designed to deteriorate the quality of life in areas where it is used" by creating "a climate of fear, wherein people subjected to LIC are too afraid of the repressive government apparatus to resist it" (Border Action Network, 2004b). Sandia Laboratories in New Mexico and the Pentagon's Center for the Study of Low Intensity Conflict designed LIC strategies for the border (Phares, 2000; Dunn, 2001). The Immigration and Naturalization Service (now United States Bureau of Citizenship and Immigration Services [USCIS] under the Department of Homeland Security) also worked with the Pentagon's LIC Center to create strategies for enhancing immigration enforcement (Palafox, 1996).

The program of deterrence under Clinton's Southwest Border Strategy and continued under the Bush administration's Secure Border Initiative (SBI, initiated in 2005) both reflect LIC doctrine. With greater infrastructure (walls, fences, sensors, stadium lights), increased funding and personnel, plus working relationships between local law enforcement, Border Patrol officials, state and federal politicians, and the military (such as the Marine's Joint Task Force-Six/JTF-6), the program of deterrence aims to close the most popular migration routes into the United States. It attempts to do so by consciously shifting:

> traffic to areas that are more remote and difficult to cross illegally, where INS has the tactical advantage. . . . The overarching goal of the strategy is to make it so difficult and so costly to enter this country illegally that fewer individuals even try. (Department of Justice/Immigration and Naturalization Service, 1996)

The Southwest Border Strategy further emphasizes deterrence by treating the nearly 2,000-mile border between the United States and Mexico "as a single, seamless entity" (United States Immigration and Naturalization Service, 1999). This is effected through operations such as Gatekeeper in California, Operation Hold the Line in Texas, Operation Rio Grande, which began in Texas and expanded into New Mexico, and Operation Safeguard in Arizona. Former United States Immigration Commissioner Doris Meissner explains to Tessie Borden that proponents of Operation Safeguard thought:

> the sheer harshness of the Arizona desert would discourage would-be border crossers from attempting the journey . . . . [believing that] geography would be an ally to us. . . . It was our sense that the number of people crossing the border through Arizona would go down to a trickle once people realized what [it is] like. ("INS: Border Policy Failed," *Arizona Republic*, 10 August 2000)

Proponents are quite wrong in this assumption as demonstrated by the over 4,000 recorded deaths (ACLU, 2006a, 2006b) in the region since the inception of the Southwest Border Strategy in the 1990s. Deaths primarily result from exposure, drowning, and dehydration after the deterrence program pressures crossers into more perilous areas of the desert. Given the harsh and remote conditions that characterize many parts of the southwest border, not to mention difficulties in identifying bodies; some estimates put the number of deaths as high as 5,000 since 1994 (Hammer-Tomizuka, 2008).

In *Accepting the Immigration Challenge*, which initiated the Southwest Border Strategy, Clinton (1994) explains the rationales behind the Strategy, but does not directly draw connections between undocumented immigration and environmental security. The connection between environmental insecurity and undocumented immigration does figure prominently in other Clinton administration documents however, and is explained in ways that reflect the larger mainstream ES discourse on immigration into the United States. The 1997 NSS claims for instance:

> Our strategy focused on the security implications for both present and long-term American policy raised by transnational problems that once seemed quite distant—such as resource depletion, rapid population growth, environmental degradation and refugee migration. (National Security Council, 1997)

This serves as an example of a litany statement, whereby proponents of environmental security list migration as one of many different environmental and security concerns facing the United States. This approach allows politicians, scholars, and activists to imply connections between immigration and environmental damage without having to meaningfully explore, explain, or necessarily substantiate those connections. Like other components of mainstream ES discourse on undocumented immigration, I find little in depth analysis of this linkage, even though proponents of environmental security mention it quite frequently.

The resource depletor representation finds expression in the introduction to the Clinton administration's President's Council on Sustainable Development report, *Sustainable America*:

> Growing populations demand more food, goods, services, and space. Where there is scarcity, population increase aggravates it. Where there is conflict, rising demand for land and natural resources exacerbates it. (1996)

The Council further explains, "We also support the creation of policies that recognize both the nation's historic acceptance of immigrants as well as the need to limit population growth" (ibid., chap. 6). Broadly speaking, the resource depletor representation is grounded in Hardin's call for population control in "The Tragedy of the Commons" (1968) and his classic anti-immigration treatise "Lifeboat Ethics" (1974), which continues to serve as a powerful population control and immigration control metaphor today. For Hardin, communities, which overrun their own carrying capacities via overpopulation, will migrate to other lifeboats for sanctuary and will sink them (ibid.). According to him, we must deny immigrants access to the United States lifeboat. Both of Hardin's essays ground the popular position that immigration-induced and fertility-induced population growth is to blame for strains on the social, political, economic, and environmental resources that belong to "real" United States citizens. Hardin, and mainstream ES discourse in the United States more broadly, define women (especially women of color) not only as resource depletors, but also as enemies of civilizational, national, and environmental security.

Though not absent from the pre-11 September 2001 agenda, the Bush administration greatly enhanced the militarization of the United States-Mexico border since that time, as reflected in the *NSHS* (Office of Homeland Security, 2002). It provides the "strategic vision" for the Department of Homeland Security (DHS). The establishment of DHS is extremely significant, as it exemplifies one of the biggest institutional re-organizations since the 1947 National Security Act. The ideas behind DHS are not as new or original to the Bush administration as proponents suggest. The United States Commission on National Security/21st Century (USCNS/21) advanced recommendations for such a department before the 11 September 2001 attacks. It sought to provide the most comprehensive security analysis of the last fifty years. This resulted in a three-part report examining current and future security concerns as well as recommendations for ensuring national security. Among them is the Commission's call for the creation of a National Homeland Security Agency based upon their concern over a potential act of "mass-casualty terrorism directed against the U.S. homeland" (2001, p. vi). Like DHS, the agency proposed by USCNS/21 was to "consolidate and refine the missions of the nearly two dozen disparate departments and agencies that have a role in U.S. homeland security today" (ibid.). The idea to create the DHS has been, to the best of my knowledge, wholly attributed to the George W. Bush administration.

Today, the DHS has brought together twenty-two agencies and emphasizes:

> three national security priorities: preventing terrorist attacks within the United States; reducing America's vulnerability to terrorism; and minimizing the damage and facilitating the recovery from attacks that do occur. (Bush, 2006c, p. 43)

Immigration quickly became a central element of national security policy as reflected in the transfer of immigration responsibilities to DHS and away from the Department of Justice (Hyunhye Cho, 2003, pp. 19–20). The Whitehouse, in its estimation, fulfilled its "National Vision" for border and transportation security in the *NSHS* by having created a:

> single entity in the Department of Homeland Security [that] will manage who and what enters our homeland in order to prevent the entry of terrorists and the instruments of terror while facilitating the legal flow of people,

goods, and services on which our economy depends. (Office of Homeland Security, 2002, p. 22)

The *NSHS* prioritizes border security as part of protecting the "homeland," given its general contention: "Our enemies seek to remain invisible, lurking in the shadows" (ibid., p. vii). In the "Border and Transportation Security" section of the *NSHS*, the White House highlights six major initiatives including the development of "smart borders" and the reform of immigration services as part of its overriding goal of securing America's borders (ibid., p. viii) by containing the enemy Others supposedly lurking in the shadows. "Smart borders" will comprise the "border of the future" and:

> provide greater security through better intelligence, coordinated national efforts, and unprecedented international cooperation against the threats posed by terrorists, the implements of terrorism, international organized crime, illegal drugs, illegal migrants, cyber crime, and the destruction or theft of natural resources. (Ibid., p. 22)

This last sentence is consistent with the linkages between immigration and environmental destruction advanced by the Clinton administration and is an example of a litany statement. It also reflects mainstream ES discourse more generally in its concern over the threat posed by "Third World Others" to the resource base of the United States. In doing so, the *NSHS* rationalizes the enhanced militarization of the border and new/old modes of motivated containment of gendered and racialized enemy Others on the United States border with Mexico.

The *NSHS* calls for close collaboration "with Canada and Mexico to increase the security of our shared borders while facilitating commerce within the North American Free Trade Agreement (NAFTA) area" (ibid., 22). The 2006 NSS, which refers to relations in the Western hemisphere as "the frontline of defense of American national security," further illustrates the special relationship between the United States and Mexico (Bush, 2006c, p. 37). In addition to smart borders, SBI enhances the militarization of the border with more Border Patrol agents, greater infrastructure support (roads, stadium lighting, fencing and barriers, cameras, and Unmanned Aerial Vehicles), and stronger immigration enforcement measures within the interior of the United States (Basham, 2006).

The Bush administration presents an interesting blend of old and new forms of containment, deterrence, and security discourse in its approach to addressing the United States-Mexico border in this post-11 September 2001 era. Although the Clinton Administration heavily militarized the border, the Bush administration intensified the militarization of the United States-Mexico border, especially with the program of deterrence. A heightened sense of urgency characterizes its rhetoric in support of a more fortified border. The assumption that we must protect the "homeland" from terrorists trying to cross the United States-Mexico border underlines this urgency. Although not original to the Bush administration, its policies enhance modes of deterrence and containment that negatively impact immigrants of color, border communities, and indigenous nations in the southwestern United States, in addition to communities of color throughout the United States.

Bush administration policies mirror the interconnection of discourses of national, civilizational, and environmental security aimed at (re)constructing and (re)enforcing the boundaries of America and Americanness by simultaneously (re)constructing and (re)enforcing the construction of enemy Others in its conflation of terrorism, "illegal immigrants," and environmental destruction as threats to the security of the American nation. Consequently, extreme levels of death, injury, and human rights violation by state policies such as the program of deterrence, in addition to state agents and vigilante (or what I identify as paramilitary) groups typify the militarization of the border under the Clinton and Bush administrations. Speaking of state agents, critics have alleged that human rights abuses along the United States-Mexico border have included intimidation, excessive use of force, and sexual violence during both administrations (Border Action Network, 2003. See also Urban, 2008; Allen, 2003). This is not to say that every Border Patrol or other state agent engages in human rights violation, or that there are not individuals with the best of intentions working on the border to feed their families and put roofs over their heads. It is to say however, that there is a demonstrable *pattern* of human rights violation in the region by agents of the state.

The shooting death of Ezequiel Hernandez by a member of JTF-6 in 1997 dramatically illustrated the grave human rights situation. A Marine erroneously identified Hernandez as a drug smuggler and killed him in Redford, Texas during a covert military operation. Today, under the Bush administration:

> [t]he policing of the already heavily militarized U.S.-Mexico border has intensified, placing severe strains and hardship on border crossers and border communities. Human rights abuses are commonplace. (AFSC and NYAC, 2003, p. 36)

Given the post-11 September 2001 climate of anti-immigrant hysteria and motivated containment, I am not surprised that policies like SBI have exacerbated the violence and repression connected to the border's militarization under LIC doctrine. The ACLU shares the United Nations Human Rights Committee's "grave concerns over the United States' human rights record," including increased militarization on the border and the enforcement of immigration laws by agents lacking adequate training on immigration issues (ACLU, 2006a). Importantly, not only are "illegal immigrants" targeted for surveillance and human rights violation, but so too is anyone who happens to appear Mexican, as dominant constructions and representations of "illegal immigration" rest heavily upon and even conflate "illegal immigration" with "Mexicanness," regardless of actual ethnicity much less country of birth or citizenship status. As the ACLU further explains, the "militarization of the border creates a low-intensity conflict zone where anybody with brown skin becomes a potential victim" (ACLU, 2006b).

Research undertaken by members of Border Action Network, a grassroots environmental justice and immigrant rights organization in southern Arizona, exposes a pervasive pattern of state violence on the United States-Mexico border. In its report, *Justice on the Line*, members interviewed over 300 primarily Latina/o families in Nogales, Douglas, Pirtleville, and Naco, Arizona about the impacts of Border Patrol on daily life in the region (Allen, 2003). They found an institutionalized pattern of racial profiling, abuse of power, harassment, intimidation, and corruption among Border Patrol agents. They heard allegations of excessive use of force, assault, and sexual violence. These findings are consistent with those of the ACLU (ACLU, 2006a).

The intent of Border Action Network's report is to document:

> these experiences so that they are heard by decision-makers and policy makers.... to break the isolation of the many residents we spoke with who expressed tremendous fear of retribution for speaking out and skepticism that the Border Patrol or the federal government would be doing anything to end the harassment and intimidation they endure. (Allen, 2003, p. 1)

The 2003 report and many others like it expose and interrupt the foundations of militarization and importantly, its grounding in LIC doctrine. Border Action Network members also provide a number of recommendations including a call for Border Patrol to end racial profiling, provide training in de-escalation tactics, and allow outside civilian monitoring (ibid., p. 14).

According to the ACLU, the number of deaths on the United States-Mexico border increased during 2005, even though over twice as many agents worked on the border as compared with 1995 (ACLU, 2006b, p. 60). Given the Bush administration's enhanced program of deterrence under SBI, Border Patrol is becoming:

> the nation's largest law enforcement entity as President Bush aims to have over 18,000 Border Patrol agents by the end of his term. Undoubtedly, the number of deaths will continue to rise exponentially with the number of Border Patrol agents, as migrants will be forced to cross in increasingly remote areas. (Ibid.)

Ironically, enhanced militarization has not reduced the level of migration across the southwest border. It has enhanced the climate of Low Intensity Warfare in the region. This climate is a result of the actions of some state agents and the program of deterrence itself, which has resulted in the death of thousands of border crossers.

The environmental, national, and civilizational security discourse employed by the Bush administration post-11 September 2001 represents a blend of old and new modes of (and justifications for) deterrence and containment. Turning again to environmental security, the 2006 NSS continues Clinton-era ES discourse by implying connections between illicit trade (drugs and human beings), environmental destruction (man made and natural), disease, and pandemics (Bush, 2006c, p. 47). Mainstream ES (and national and civilizational security) discourse is also reflected in the *NSHS*, which connects terrorism, crime, drugs, undocumented immigration and the "destruction or theft of natural resources" (Office of Homeland Security, 2002, p. 22).

I have also seen some new and noteworthy security shifts. Among them, the call to "permanent war" stands out. As the Bush administration contends, the "threat of terrorism is an inescapable reality of life in the 21st century. It is a *permanent condition* to which America and the entire world must adjust" (Bush, 2002b, p. 2, emphasis added). It also reasons:

> The need for homeland security, therefore, is not tied to any specific terrorist threat. Instead, the need for homeland security is tied to the underlying vulnerability of American society and the fact that we can never be sure when or where the next terrorist conspiracy against us will emerge. (Ibid., p. 2)

This call for permanent war represents a significant shift in national security policy.

John Gaddis (2002) holds that Cold War definitions of containment and deterrence will not work with enemies who are not easily identifiable or, as Bush contends, lurk in the shadows. Because "our enemies" now supposedly seek weapons of mass destruction, preemption must also be added to permanent war, containment, and deterrence (another significant shift in national security policy illustrated in the 2002 NSS), and preemption requires hegemony (ibid.). The maintenance of that hegemony requires natural resources (as does preemption, permanent war, deterrence, and containment), which point to another area in which old and new modes of (and justifications for) containment and deterrence are blended.

Jon Barnett (2001) raises an interesting point that sheds light on the blend of "old" and "new" with respect to national security and the Bush administration's regard for the environment. Although he does not focus explicitly on the Bush administration in this context, Barnett notes that a frustrating element of environmental security literature is the frequent conflation of "resources" with the "environment" (ibid., p. 51). A long tradition of this is evinced in mainstream IR security discourse (especially Realist theory), within which environmental issues are typically ignored, except for the recognition that power and survival depend in large part on the natural resources states may own, acquire, and manipulate. I believe the Bush administration conflates "resources" with the "environment" and regards them as valuable only insofar as they can support or be sacrificed in the promotion of national security, preemption, and permanent war, or rather, United States hegemony and empire building.

Although I do not think that this dynamic was wholly absent during the Clinton administration, I do believe that Clinton-era policies did reflect concern for the environment on its own terms, at least rhetorically. I am ambivalent about the degree to which Clinton administration policies actually regarded the environment as valuable in its own right, especially given the lack of a meaningful enforcement structure within the environmental side agreement of NAFTA. By contrast, I do not believe Bush administration policies reflect concern for the environment in its own right rhetorically or otherwise.

The 2002 NSS provides support for my argument in its claim that rogue states "brutalize their own people and *squander their national resources for the personal gain of the rulers*" (Bush, 2002a, p. 14, emphasis added). This perhaps operates as one rationale for engaging rogue states and "properly" using their natural resources to support the "gains" associated with United States hegemony. The 2005 National Defense Strategy similarly argues:

> Problem states will continue to undermine regional stability and threaten United States interests. These states are hostile to United States principles. *They commonly squander their resources to benefit ruling elites, their armed forces, or extremist clients.* (United States Department of Defense, 2005, p. 4, emphasis added)

Instead of seeing the environment as valuable in its own right, both documents define and value the natural environment in utilitarian terms and in terms of its ability to provide resources with which to support the needs of the United States-led "war on terror" and maintain United States empire and hegemony. Both documents also highlight the colonialist assumption that the United States government can and should own and control the resources of so-called rogue states.

Border fencing in southern California provides another instructive example of my argument. During the Clinton administration (mid-1990s), the government attempted to supplement the fencing separating Tijuana, Mexico, from the Imperial Beach area of California. The double and in some areas triple fencing project runs approximately fourteen miles from the Pacific Ocean to the Otay Mountains. Fencing projects like this were especially important to the program of deterrence under the Clinton administration and its goal of keeping immigrants from gaining assess to heavily populated areas like San Diego.

A diverse collection of government leaders, environmental organizations, and activists, along with members of the California Coastal Commission responded to the completion of the last 3.5 miles of fencing with litigation and protest. Among many objections, those made on environmental grounds argue against the provision that a canyon called "Smuggler's Gulch" be filled in with approximately 2.2 million to 5.7 million cubic yards of soil. The soil was to be bulldozed from nearby hills, whose tops will be shaved off to build access roads (John Broder, "With Congress's Blessing, a Border Fence May Finally Push

Through to the Sea," *New York Times*, 4 July 2005; Chris Moran, "Make Friends not Fences," *San Diego Union-Tribune*, 3 April 2005). The project could destroy the tidal estuary near the Pacific Ocean into which the canyon drains. Broder further explains that filling the canyon with dirt would increase silt buildup and destroy a federally protected wetland and wildlife refuge.

Proponents of the fencing project support their position with the footpaths argument, which constructs immigrants as threats to the environmental security of the United States by virtue of damage their border crossing (walking) causes. This strategy provides little in the way of in depth analysis of the factors pushing and pulling immigration, such as legacies of colonialism and myriad consequences of policies of neo-liberal globalization. Instead, obfuscation of structural inequalities in tandem with Neo-Malthusian doomsday scenarios harkening global environmental destruction function to "substantiate" the threat posed by immigrants to the environmental and national security of the United States. The "us versus them" orientation upon which the footpaths argument (and mainstream ES discourse more broadly) is based, reproduces the assumption that gendered and racialized enemies from the Global South threaten the carrying capacity, stability, and security of the United States. The state brings together national, environmental, and civilizational security to justify particularly destructive policies.

With regard to the southern California fence project, proponents use the footpaths argument to claim that additional fencing will help preserve the environment by deterring foot traffic. Homeland Security Secretary Michael Chertoff reasons:

Illegal migrants really degrade the environment. I've seen pictures of human waste, garbage, discarded bottles and other human artifacts in pristine areas. . . . And believe me, that is the worst thing you can do to the environment. (Sullivan, 2007)

Opponents argue that the fencing provisions for Smuggler's Gulch will irreparably harm the environment. In addition, Border Action Network's 2004 report, *Environmental Protection on the Line* profoundly illustrates the deep flaws in the footpaths argument (Border Action Network, 2004a). Among other things, the report points to the irreparable damage caused by the militarization of the border itself and finds that the environmental consequences of militarization far outweigh the impacts of people walking across the desert.

The Bush administration has gone so far as to shut down all compromise and all litigation by invoking 11 September 2001 as a platform upon which to push through the completion of the fencing project on homeland security grounds, with the explicit claim that terrorists are using the border to access the United States. No evidence has ever been provided to support this claim. Even so, Michael Chertoff was granted authority to finish the fence and "almost total authority to sidestep environmental and labor laws in the process," as Kimberly Edds notes in "U.S. Calls Entry Point in San Diego a Possible Security Risk"

(*Washington Post*, 10 March 2005). Chertoff also used his authority to quash litigation, flout environmental regulations, and avoid public comment on fencing projects in Cochise County, Arizona, claiming that any delay would pose "unacceptable risks to our nation's security" (quoted Howard Fischer, "Chertoff Exempts Fence: National Security Trumps Environmental Concern for San Pedro River," *Sierra Vista Herald*, 23 October 2007).

Chertoff used this same strategy to complete another project near the Barry M. Goldwater Range in southwestern Arizona (Fischer, 2007). In addition to using 11 September 2001 as a key justification, Chertoff reasons that people crossing the border (not militarization), is to blame for environmental destruction. Once again, immigrants of color from the Global South are constructed as environmental and national security threats, as is consistent with the greening of hate.

These moves exemplify the Bush administration's regard for the environment. I argue that the Bush administration values natural resources only insofar as they can serve the needs of the United States so-called war on terror, hegemony, and empire. Although apparently contradictory, the examples of Chertoff's positions on the fencing projects and the ways in which the environment is addressed within Bush administration security documents, demonstrate that for the Bush administration, "environmental protection" means the protection of natural resources in the service of empire. These examples also support my broader argument: The interlocking discourses of national, civilizational, and environmental security employed by the Bush administration reinforce new/old policies of deterrence and containment and the racialized, xenophobic, and gendered boundaries of American identity upon which they are built. This discursively "justifies" the policing, punishment, and containment of those constructed as enemies of United States hegemony and empire: Peoples of color from the Global South who travel across the United States-Mexico border. I find it troubling that similar discursive dynamics characterize the so-called vigilante groups operating on the United States-Mexico border as part of its militarization.

5. Discourses of (In)Security, Militarization, and Paramilitaries

As with the dirty wars of the 1980s, the militarization of the United States-Mexico border under LIC doctrine is characterized by relationships among Border Patrol, military, local law enforcement officials, and "citizen groups." In this context, these groups include the Minutemen groups, American Patrol, Ranch Rescue, and other such groups, which the mainstream media commonly refer to as "vigilante" groups (Urban, 2008). By contrast, I refer to them as paramilitary groups. Border Action Network (2004b) explains:

> LIC has consistently employed the tactic of creating armed paramilitary groups that work in collaboration with government security forces to fur-

ther the propagation of fear. These groups operate with impunity as they engage in human rights abuses on behalf of security forces, which are afforded a measure of deniability for the worst transgressions of their policy.

At minimum, infrequent government denouncement of the behavior of these groups and infrequent investigation and prosecution of allegations of violence and intimidation, in tandem with statements from public officials celebrating these "citizen groups," support their definition as paramilitary groups. That groups like Ranch Rescue and American Border Patrol include retired military, INS, and police officials among its membership also helps explain the level of "law enforcement inaction, which becomes tacit approval of vigilantism and anti-immigrant activities" (Hammer-Tomizuka and Allen, 2002, p. 1). Their paramilitary role is also visible in their impersonation of law enforcement officials using camouflage outfits and homemade badges (ibid.).

Like the Bush administration, paramilitary groups seized upon 11 September 2001 to advance their agendas. Additionally, the actions and rhetoric of paramilitary groups support and reinforce the gendered and racialized representations of enemy Others that lay at the heart of the mutually supportive cluster between national, civilizational, and environment security discourses today. In addition, paramilitary groups operating on the border employ the old and new modes of containment and deterrence employed by the Bush administration.

Members of these paramilitary groups argue that their work is essential for defending private property and preserving national security. They even go so far as to characterize themselves as partners in the enforcement of border security. Glenn Spencer, leader of American Patrol, defines his group as "a little shadow Border Patrol" (Luke Turf, "The Border: Activist Tracks Migrants with High-Tech Network," *Tucson Citizen*, 21 July 2003). Chris Simcox, leader of the Minuteman Civil Defense Corps, similarly calls on the public to join as "force-multipliers" of Border Patrol to help them turn back "the tidal wave of people entering our country illegally," whom he characterizes as dangerous threats to national security (2005). Simcox also links his work to supporting the "war on terror" (and links civilizational and national security discourse in his construction of the Other as threat). He explains that anti-immigration groups operating on the border are only "doing what our president has asked us, which is to be vigilant and to report suspicious illegal activities to the proper authorities" (quoted in Daniel González, "Arizona Border Vigilantes Receive Jail Time, Area Groups Respond," *Arizona Republic*, 9 October 2003).

California Governor Arnold Schwarzenegger publicly praised the Minuteman organization saying, "they've done a terrific job. And they have cut down the crossing of illegal immigrants by a huge percentage" (quoted in Acuña, 2005). The specifics of their job tell a much different story. During 2002, Border Action Network worked with the communities of Douglas, Pirtleville, and Naco, Arizona to produce the report *Hate or Heroism* (Hammer-Tomizuka and Allen,

2002). The report reveals a pervasive pattern of violence, intimidation, and harassment by paramilitary groups, who "round-up" and detain people at gunpoint, which has led to injury and death. This pattern of violence and intimidation is neither an unforeseen nor an unrelated outcome of the border's militarization. Creating a climate of fear in this way is characteristic of the LIC doctrine under which the border is militarized, rendering Chris Simcox's (2005) characterization of the Minuteman Project as "one of the most important, socially responsible, and peaceful movements for justice since the civil rights movement of the 1960s," delusional at best.

Border Action Network, together with the Southern Poverty Law Center, civil and immigrant-rights attorney Jesus Romo Vejar, and the families they collectively represented, won a significant victory in 2006, against paramilitary violence in a civil suit against Roger Barnett. Barnett, the leader of Ranch Rescue, was found guilty of "intentionally inflicting emotional distress, negligence, unlawful imprisonment, and assault," and ordered to pay nearly $100,000 in damages (Allen, 2006). Adding to his already long history of violence (See Hammer-Tomizuka and Allen, 2002; Urban, 2008), Barnett yelled racist obscenities as he threatened Arturo, Ronald, Vanese, Angelique Morales, and Emma English (two adults and three children, nine and eleven years old at the time) with an assault rifle on 30 October 2004 (Border Action Network, 2007b). The trauma of the attack resulted in diagnoses of Post Traumatic Stress Disorder for the families (Border Action Network, 2007a). Yet, as Jennifer Allen, director of Border Action Network explains:

> We've already seen the courage the Morales and English girls as well as the jury had for standing up for what is right and fair. Now we are looking for the courage of our public officials to uphold human dignity and end vigilante impunity. (Allen, 2006)

By contrast, members of paramilitary groups often represent themselves as patriots fighting a war against invading, foreign, enemy forces. Roger Barnett claims, "I'm a patriot. God, country, the American flag, and sovereignty of our border" (Doty, 2001, p. 529). Simcox (2005) similarly represents Minuteman members as misunderstood but "truly patriotic nationalists." The rhetoric of invasion is extremely common. I found an interesting example in the "About Us" section of Chris Simcox's Minuteman Website (2008), which includes a text box and link with the statement "The Illegal Alien Invasion Continues" right next to his claim that his is one of the most socially responsible, peaceful movements since the civil rights movement (ibid.). Representations of invasion and patriotism by paramilitaries are used to "justify" violence.

Further, the rhetoric of invasion is deeply connected to the racism, sexism, and xenophobia perpetuated by paramilitary groups. I am not surprised that claims of patriotism juxtaposed with representations of enemy Others as security threats compel the actions of paramilitary groups. White supremacist groups have long operated in the United States targeting immigrants of color to "protect" the United States from "invasion," protect the "purity" of "American" identity, and protect United States national security. (See Hammer-Tomizuka and Allen [2002] for a historical overview of anti-Mexican hate groups operating in the region. ACLU [2000] also provides an important overview of anti-immigrant hostility and violence in the United States, especially during times of economic downturn.) In addition to engaging in direct violence, paramilitary groups on the United States-Mexico border continue a long history of creating a climate of fear on the border by engaging in ideological violence and spreading sexist, xenophobic, and racist messages representing Latinos/as as security threats. This climate of fear is emblematic of LIC doctrine.

President Bush and former Secretary of State Madeline Albright have publicly condemned what they call vigilante actions. Roxanne Lynn Doty argues that the actions of these groups legitimize those of the United States government, and importantly, make them appear rational:

> [t]he more familiar acts of statecraft by government officials would lack the legitimacy and constitutive force they generally have.... Government officials sitting in sanitized offices wearing faces of reason and making "rational" policies in a complicated world may seem far removed from gun-toting ranchers . . . but they are all engaged in the same project of statecraft. (Doty, 2001, p. 528)

I argue that not only are paramilitary groups involved in the same project of statecraft, but also, these groups operate as paramilitary groups within the broader militarization of the United States-Mexico Border under LIC doctrine. Their self-identification as force-multipliers and their actions, including dressing up as border officials and engaging in citizen arrests, intimidation tactics, and human rights abuses, all support my position. The dismissiveness with which some government officials treat the actions of these groups further supports my position. Arizona Representative Jim Kolbe for instance, calls Spencer's (of American Patrol) activities "fine because agencies need help identifying illegal entrants" (Turf, "The Border . . .," 2003).

Speaking again of the Barnett case, the Morales and English families were forced to file a civil suit instead of a criminal suit because public officials in Cochise County, Arizona, failed to file criminal charges. Southern Poverty Law Center explains that although there was enough evidence to charge Barnett with eight counts of felony aggravated assault and ten counts of misdemeanor disorderly conduct and intimidation, the Cochise County prosecutor refused to file criminal charges, allegedly telling Ronald Morales, "no jury in Cochise County will ever convict Roger Barnett" (Buchanan, 2006).

My labeling groups, such as the Minutemen and Ranch Rescue, as paramilitary groups is further supported by the explicit praise and support they have received from public officials. Not only did Governor Schwarzenegger publicly praise Minuteman's work, he invited them to work in Southern California (AFSC, Witness and ACLU, 2005). Senator Kay Bailey Hutchison also expressed her support of Minuteman, explaining, "[t]hese people have shown a commitment and a caring that should be acknowledged here in the United States Senate" (Moses, 2005).

Returning to the topic of environmental security, xenophobia and racism intersect with sexism within the environmental language adopted by many paramilitary groups. This is especially true of their Neo-Malthusian claims of "overpopulation." Not unlike Michael Chertoff, paramilitaries construct undocumented immigrations as "eco-terrorists" who destroy ranchers' lands with litter, harm the fragile desert with their traveling, and increase population, which they believe is to blame for environmental destruction in the United States. The argument about leaving behind litter is a common one. Less common is recognizing that what ranchers label as "trash" is often the personal belongings of crossers because Border Patrol officials routinely force them to leave their belongings behind when they arrest them (Border Action Network, 2004a).

Ranch Rescue Arizona uses environmental language in their (footpaths) argument that migrants trespass "on to private property in Cochise County in the *tens of thousands* each month, leaving behind a trail of environmental damage and property destruction" (2002, emphasis in original). Simcox similarly argues:

> Local support was unanimous as dozens of private property owners opened their gates to allow Minuteman Civil Defense Corps volunteers to keep watch over their homes and ranches, ravaged by the environmental and property damage of tens of thousands of illegal intruders. (2007)

Incidentally, none of the 150 community members interviewed for Border Action Network's 2002 *Hate or Heroism* report expressed support for the actions of Minuteman or other such groups (Hammer-Tomizuka and Allen, 2002). American Patrol (2003) also utilizes the resource depletor representation in its argument that "more than 30 million immigrants have settled in the United States since 1970. Now our cities, schools, health care systems, labor markets, and environment all need a break." Like mainstream ES discourse on immigration, paramilitary groups fail to engage in meaningful discussion about the structural realities behind migration. Apparently, along with the Clinton and Bush administrations, they find scapegoat immigrants of color easier, whether based on footpaths arguments or resource depletor representations.

In short, punitive immigration and population control policies and practices target undocumented immigrants of color. In so doing, state and paramilitary groups utilize highly gendered, racialized, and xenophobic representations of undocumented immigrants as enemy Others to argue that immigrants of color endanger the national, civilizational, and environmental security of the United States. As such, they represent immigrants of color crossing the United States-Mexico border as "deserving" a particular kind of motivated containment born of interlocking systems of power, privilege, and oppression. As previously noted, these systems intersect with apparently contradictory policies of deterrence through militarization on the one hand (to close the border to immigrants of color), and neo-liberal globalization on the other (to open the border to goods and services).

State and non-state proponents of population and immigration control hold a number of positions in common. The Clinton and Bush administrations for instance, demonstrate a remarkable faith in policies like NAFTA, and neo-liberal globalization more generally, for promoting democracy and freedom. As one Bush administration NSS proclaims:

> The concept of "free trade" arose as a moral principle even before it became a pillar of economics. If you can make something that others value, you should be able to sell it to them. If others make something that you value, you should be able to buy it. *This is real freedom*, the freedom for a person—or a nation—to make a living. (2002a, p. 18, emphasis added)

I believe that to say both administrations conflate global capitalism and neo-liberal globalization with democracy and freedom is more accurate.

State and non-state proponents of population and immigration control share a number of stunning silences: silence around the dramatic social, political, cultural, health, economic, and environmental consequences of neo-liberal globalization, including policies like NAFTA. Timothy Dunn reminds readers:

> Neither Congress nor the executive branch have debated, much less taken serious policy action, that addresses the underlying economic, political, social, and cultural factors that strongly contribute to the cross-border flows of immigrants and drugs. (2001, p. 20)

Contrary to its stated aims, NAFTA brought dramatic job loss, increases in poverty and environmental damage, and profound dislocation for people in the United States and in Mexico. As one example, Article 27 of the 1917 Mexican Constitution was amended in 1992 in anticipation of NAFTA, to allow the privatization of land that had been held communnally under the constitution (Willson, 1997). Hundreds of thousands of Mexican people lost their land and livelihoods. Remaining jobs suffered a significant drop in wages and the poverty rate rose dramatically to nearly half the population in 2001 (Akers, 2001). Job and land loss, along with the depression of wages "freed up" a tremendous amount of labor and compelled many to move northward in search of work.

NAFTA *stimulated* migration within Mexico and undocumented immigration into the United States from Mexico. Passage of the Southwest Border Strategy and NAFTA in 1994 helped provide the labor pool needed for the bourgening maquiladora industry. The maquiladora industry refers to the system located on the United States-Mexico border whereby companies, owned primarily by United States interests, "outsource the most labor-intensive part of the production process" (Aviva Chomsky, 2007, pp. 6–7). Maquiladora employees, who typically work in substandard conditions for little pay, process or assemble goods which are then exported, often to the United States. The maquiladora system is a central component of the free trade model advanced under NAFTA.

The negative consequences of neo-liberal trade policies, in tandem with the militarization of the border, support United States hegemony and empire. Dislocation in Mexico resulting from NAFTA coupled with the border's militarization under the Southwest Border Strategy, helped:

> restrict the mobility of workers to areas where labor-intensive industries, or the maquiladoras, are being placed, so that they can have an available labor supply and take advantage of low wages. (Phares, 2000)

Displacement in Mexico, together with militarization and criminalization, serves the needs of capitalism within the borders of the United States by creating conditions in which many workers, by virtue of their status as "illegal," are precariously positioned to protest for fair labor and broader human rights standards.

The destruction caused by NAFTA continues to push migration from Mexico northward. One significant mode of resistance to the destruction wrought by NAFTA is to migrate across the United States-Mexico border. Given the conditions created by neo-liberal policies like NAFTA, and given the restrictions on legal entry for immigrants of color from countries like Mexico, entering the United States without proper documentation is, I contend, an understandable form of civil disobediance (Chomsky, 2007, p. 57).

This shift in perception—that migration serves as not only a means of survival, but also a form of resistance for some—starts a crucial process of simultaneously breaking down anti-immigrant stereotypes and scapegoating on the one hand, and pointing to some of the root causes of global migration on the other. It also helps begin a process by which we can illuminate the true roots of environmental destruction and inequality. These include interlocking systems of white supremacist capitalist hetero-patriarchy, policies of neo-liberal globalization, legacies of colonialism, and militarization on the United States-Mexico border (and militarization around the world) in the service of United States hegemony and empire (Urban, 2008). Neither population growth nor undocumented immigration is the root cause of insecurity—environmental, national, civilizational, or otherwise.

The Bush administration strengthens systems of inequality by intensifying the militarization of the border, supporting policies such as NAFTA, and by having promoted a guest worker program that mirrors the extremely exploitative Bracero program of the 1930s–1960s. Like Bracero, the proposed guest worker program privileges the profit needs of United States corporations and agribusiness. It also reinforces the popular (albeit racist and xenophobic) assumption that immigrants can and should sell their labor in the United States, but need not, and indeed should not, enjoy civil, political, labor, or human rights in return. Put bluntly, neo-liberal globalization and militarization are not solutions, but are instead the causes of insecurity, violence, and inequality.

In summary, definitions of illegality under both administrations along with xenophobia, racism, and sexism serve capitalism and enhance exploitation and inequality by constructing "Third World Immigrant Others" as environmental resource depletors, thieves, and threats. Together, this allows undocumented immigration to be scapegoated by the state and paramilitary forces for the social, economic, political, and environmental insecurities and inequalities caused by neo-liberal globalization, militarization, legacies of colonialism, and interlocking systems of power, privilege, and oppression. State and paramilitary forces share a similar silence on the structural causes of insecurity, including the negative consequences of neo-liberal globalization. Silence and scapegoating not only divert attention away from the real causes of insecurity, but also allow them to flourish.

Scapegoating immigrants in times of economic distress and insecurity has been a common wedge strategy used throughout United States history (Hayes, 2001, p. 39). However, immigration (undocumented or otherwise) is not a strain on resources, nor do immigrants steal jobs from American citizens en masse. Instead, immigrants:

> enhance economic growth and create employment. They invest money, shop, pay taxes and use services, all of which contributes directly to the local economy. And they add skills, knowledge and labour to the workforce. ("Migration: The Facts," 1998, p. 19)

Despite the misinformation disseminated by state and non-state anti-immigration forces:

> Undocumented immigrants are not eligible for public benefits, including unemployment insurance and social security, but they pay for these programs through taxes and payroll deductions if they are employed. (Hayes, 2001, p. 36)

Deepa Fernandes (2007) highlights a Thunderbird Business School study that points to the financial contributions of Mexican immigrants in Arizona. The study calculated sales tax revenues and federal income tax contributions of

Mexican immigrants in Arizona in 2002 to be about $599 million; calculated the total costs of services for Mexican immigrants in Arizona to be $250 million; and calculated $31 million in uncompensated healthcare costs for undocumented Mexican people in Arizona. This left the state of Arizona with a *surplus* of $318 million. In addition, Fernandes points to federal government statistics indicating that undocumented workers (many of whom purchase false Social Security or identification cards instead of being paid "under the table"), contribute $7 billion to Social Security each year, money that, as undocumented workers, they will never see after they retire (Fernandes, 2007, p. 60). For more analysis of some common myths surrounding immigration, including the myths that "immigrants don't pay taxes," "immigrants take American jobs," and nineteen others, please see Aviva Chomsky (2007).

Despite evidence such as the aforementioned, economic-wedge strategies are commonly used and are not at all new. What may be relatively new is the identification of Latina immigrants as environmental threats as well as national and civilizational security threats.

6. Conclusion

I concur with Joni Seager, who, through an Intersectional Feminist lens, argues:

> In our current global context of endless (and endlessly expanding) warfare, at home and abroad, gender, race, immigration, and the environment are all militarized zones. At the same time, militaries and militarism, like race, immigration, and the environment, are all gendered zones. And, especially in the United States and other "western" countries, gender . . . militarization, and immigration are all racialized zones. (2003, p. 5)

Current modes of deterrence and containment advance militarization under LIC doctrine. This is in addition to the scapegoating of undocumented immigrants as national, civilizational, and environmental security threats. Added to this are the strategic silences around the material consequences of the intersection of militarization with neo-liberal globalization and systems of inequality, and the sacrifice of natural resources in the maintenance of American hegemony and empire. Taken together, it is not terribly difficult to see why the level of violence, repression, and insecurity on the United States-Mexico border has reached such high proportions. The physical and ideological violence—the Low Intensity Warfare—on the border harms more than just its immediate victims. It has a chilling effect for immigrants of color across the United States.

I am not suggesting that communities are not resisting; wherever and whenever there is violence and inequality, one will invariably find resistance. The work of Border Action Network provides a crucial case in point. The research, human rights and environmental documentation, analysis, and activism undertaken by members of Border Action Network help interrupt the normalization of violence under LIC doctrine and systems of inequality more broadly. Likewise, the framework of Intersectional Feminism I have used throughout this chapter helps interrupt the ideological bases of violence and insecurity through lenses that take seriously the existence and material consequences of interlocking systems of power, privilege, and oppression, along with strategies (such as the greening of hate) used to divert attention away from the root causes of environmental and national insecurity. Resistance and transformative change lies in visions of justice and security that do not rely on the greening of hate or any form of scapegoating or enemy construction, and do not rely on violence or oppression of any kind.

The Bush administration presents an interesting blend of old and new forms of containment and deterrence in addressing the United States-Mexico border in this post 11-September era. On one hand, the Clinton and Bush administrations share similar enemy construction strategies in relation to environmental, national, and civilizational security. Both administrations also rely heavily on the militarization of the United States-Mexico border under LIC doctrine (which includes the activities of paramilitary groups), although militarization is being enhanced under the Bush administration. Regardless, both administrations have created a warlike atmosphere for those living near the United States-Mexico border.

On the other hand, the Bush administration has presented some significant shifts, as illustrated most dramatically by its calls for permanent war and the policy of preemption. Permanent war and preemption require hegemony, and all three are intimately connected with empire building. The Bush administration conflates protection of the environment with protection of natural resources, which it only regards as valuable insofar as they serve the needs of, or can be sacrificed at the alter of, United States hegemony and empire. Interestingly, members of the administration even rationalize enhanced levels of militarization on grounds of environmental protection.

I reject the policies of militarization and neo-liberal globalization advanced by the Clinton and Bush administrations. I reject the representation of enemy Others that underlie militarization and the immigration policies associated with both administrations. The enemy-creation process characteristic of both administrations is related to interlocking discourses of national, civilizational, and environmental security, which form a mutually supportive cluster that (re)constructs and (re)enforces the boundaries of America and Americanness. It relies upon ideologies of racism, sexism and xenophobia to provide the "justifications" necessary for the criminalization of migration and the militarization of the United States-Mexico border under LIC doctrine.

Although logically absurd, the state strictly enforces interlocking discourses of national, civilizational, and environmental security through violent means. This discursive cluster also engenders powerful wedge strategies that divide potential allies from one another and divert attention away from the real causes of national, environmental, and economic insecurity: Intersecting systems of power, privilege, oppression, legacies of colonialism, neo-liberal globalization, militarization, and empire.

Critical and ongoing interrogation of the politics of representation and knowledge (re)production are crucial elements of engendering transformative, progressive change. I therefore argue that there is a very real need for Intersectional Feminist analysis and activism around the politics of representation, and the larger processes by which knowledge and policy are produced in the service of United States hegemony and empire. An Intersectional Feminist framework can foreground questions of how, why, and for whose benefit knowledge is produced. It can also illuminate the material consequences of knowledge production for social groups constructed and represented as enemy Others.

This framework, alongside the analysis and activism of members of Border Action Network, can highlight possibilities for transformative, progressive change, and modes of analysis, activism. It can contribute to policymaking that neither relies on gendered, racialized, or xenophobic constructions and representations of Others, nor on violence or inequality. As such, genuine possibilities exist for building coalitions aimed at creating a more just world for all, instead of strengthening the power bases of a privileged few.

Nine

SOLDIERING "GREEN CARD" IMMIGRANTS: CONTAINING UNITED STATES CITIZENSHIP

Jocelyn A. Pacleb

1. Introduction

Between February and May of 2006, a new wave of activism emerged, making visible the connection between the "war on terror" and the "war on immigrants" within the United States. Different immigrant rights groups filled the streets of major United States cities to take a public stand against HR 4437, a bill that would criminalize undocumented immigrants and those who assist individuals without proper documentation to stay in the United States. Passed on 16 December 2005, by the United States House of Representatives, HR 4437 was a major catalyst to one of the larger demonstrations in the young twenty-first century. Starting in February and peaking during March and May of 2006, the student walkouts in the Los Angeles area and the pro-immigration rallies in several American states were quite visible. Demonstrators equipped with cameras or video devices quickly posted what they captured from the rallies on the Internet, blogs, and YouTube.

One photo from the Los Angeles demonstration held in March 2006, provided a visual connection between the war on terror and the domestic war on immigrants. The image, captured by a photographer for *The Los Angeles Times*, showed a demonstrator holding a large sign of a United States flag. This was no ordinary flag. Superimposed over the fifty stars was a photo of a United States soldier dressed in fatigues. Hand-written in the white stripes of the flag was the message, "Sons of immigrants that are in the military, pray for justice!!!" (see Figure 1). This message informs us that the attacks on immigrants, legal and undocumented, are part of the same global war on terror declared by President George W. Bush immediately after the 11 September 2001 attacks in New York City and Washington, D.C.

The connection between the war on terror and the war on immigrants is more poignant when we consider the significant number of foreign-born women and men (many of whom are not United States citizens) currently serving in the United States military. According to one report, 5 percent of the United States armed forces on active duty service is comprised of 69,300 foreign-born soldiers. Within this group, 43 percent are non-United States citizens, over 100 of whom have died in Iraq and Afghanistan ("Immigrant Soldiers serve the U.S," *The Dallas Morning News* ([28 November 2006]).

Figure 1. Los Angeles, California, March 2006

Since the United States-led war in Iraq began in March 2003, legal non-citizens have enlisted, served, and died in the war effort. Often referred to as "green card soldiers," the military service of these women and men is hailed as the "ultimate act of patriotism" (Fact Sheet 2002; Keating, 2003). For many non-United States citizens, the military is a means of survival, especially for people with limited resources or no direct route to the middle class (the promised "American Dream").

Reporting on the demographics of the United States military and those who join the armed forces, Adam Adamshick states:

> The notion that those who answer our nation's call to serve are patriots, altruists and community stalwarts thinly veils a deeper understanding and acknowledgement of the opportunity sought by this nation's less empowered youths. (2005, p. 9)

In this chapter, I explore the need to understand that the patriotic rhetoric of Americanism has different meanings along race, gender, sexuality, and class lines. In an era of heightened xenophobia and vigilance over groups deemed unpatriotic, un-American, or plainly not worthy to be considered American, immigrants (and working poor, gay and lesbian, and communities of color) are forced to prove themselves as worthy citizens. The United States military provides a direct route to that goal. Non-United States citizens joining the armed forces inadvertently have become the new "model minority" of the twenty-first century.

Emerging from the political and social turmoil of the 1960s, the "model minority myth" constructed Asian American people as an example of a racialized immigrant group that has achieved the American Dream through hard work and as productive contributors to the state. In reality, the economic and social conditions of many Asian American people were very different from the purported myth that they were a successful minority group. For example, those from southeast Asia, who escaped war atrocities as a result of United States military interventions in Vietnam, Cambodia, and Laos, found themselves impoverished with few or no transferable skills in the United States (Fong, 2002; Thrupkaew, 2002).

Overlooking the diversity, class differences, and the historical arrivals of Asian immigrants in the United States, the so-called success of Asian American people reinforces unrealistic ideologies of United States meritocracy and equality. Coming from those in power and not from Asian American people themselves, their narrative as the model minority identifies and constructs a group along race and class lines as being comprised of good, productive workers who have realized the American Dream with no assistance from government programs such as welfare and affirmative action (Fong, 2002, p. 61). This construction makes the group worthy to be included within the state as an exemplar for other minority groups, but with the understanding that they will never be equal to white American citizens (Chan, 1991; Fong, 2002).

This ideological delineation is significant especially concerning what is happening in the current situation with green card soldiers serving in the war on terror. Low military enlistment rates and the need for soldiers have pushed the Pentagon and military recruiters to turn to immigrants to fill their enlistment ranks. Along similar lines, the war on terror and the war on immigrants are forcing noncitizens to turn to the military for reasons beyond patriotism. Within the United States-led wars in Iraq and Afghanistan, the discourse of patriotism and the on-going immigration debates in various media outlets portrays green card soldiers as a new "model minority" group. Unlike the previous model minority myth, the news accounts of non-United States soldiers as a distinct and worthy immigrant group has made visible the state's domestic aggression in terms of economic, social, and political containment of all immigrant communities in the United States and its territories.

In this chapter, I examine the unintended ways that the pro-immigration marches and newspaper reports on green card soldiers have unveiled a war on immigrants that reveals a unique kind of containment effort: the containment of the immigrant's body in the United States military.

2. "The Few. The Proud"

The United States military of the early twenty-first century is far more racially, ethnically, linguistically, and culturally diverse than it was several decades ago. From 1980 until 2002, minority soldiers increased from 23.2 to 35.8 percent (Adamshick, 2005, p. 3). In a 2003 report from the Congressional Research Service, among the 1.4 million active duty personnel in the four United States military branches, 2.6 percent are foreign nationals (Lee and Wasem, 2003, p. 6). The number of foreign nationals is also high in the Selected Reserves with 20.8 percent (ibid.).

Although these percentages indicate the number of green card soldiers in the military, they are not equally represented in the different military branches. The Navy has an overwhelmingly large number of noncitizens, with 27.8 percent, followed by the Army, with 20.2 percent (ibid.). A significant number of green card soldiers in the Navy are from the Philippines, a former colony of the United States. Other immigrant soldiers come from Mexico, Jamaica, El Salvador, Haiti, Dominican Republic, Colombia, South Korea, Trinidad and Tobago, and Peru (ibid., p. 7; Hattianagadi, et al., 2005).

On 3 July 2002, President Bush signed Executive Order 136269 that provided expedited naturalization to "aliens" and noncitizen national residents serving the armed services during this current war on terrorism (Bush, 2002). The 2004 National Defense Authoritarian Act (NDAA) made the following changes to expedite the naturalization process for immigrants in the armed forces:

1) The waiting period for citizenship application was reduced from three years to one year;
2) Noncitizen soldiers serving in the United States military are granted emergency leave and priority government transportation to complete citizenship processing;
3) All application fees are waived;
4) Military citizenship applications may be finalized at United States consulates, embassies, and overseas United States military installations. (Hattianagadi, et al., 2005, p. 38)

The 2004 NDAA also includes the granting of posthumous citizenship for noncitizen soldiers who die during active duty (ibid.). Immediate family members of a deceased soldier receive special preference for immigration purposes.

Keeping in mind the lack of economic opportunities in local communities, we should not be surprised that a large proportion of young women and men enlist with the armed forces. Rather than patriotism, green card soldiers likely see the military as a potential worksite to earn wages and earn skills. And perhaps equally importantly, the possibility of becoming naturalized citizens provides a sense of security and permanency that noncitizens do not have.

3. "An Army of One": Americanizing the Immigrant Soldier

Simona Garibay, mother of fallen Marine Corporal José Angel Garibay who died in Nasiriyah, Iraq, in 2003, movingly captures what is at stake for immigrants and the "sons [and daughters] who are in the military": "On one side, they're sending them to war. On the other, they want higher fences on the border so

Mexicans don't come" (Riley, 2005). Garibay's statement illustrates what Aihwa Ong (1996) puts forth as the contradictory experiences of immigrants as they are made into subjects of a nation-state. Garibay and her son immigrated to the United States from Mexico. Her son, a legal resident, died for his adopted country, a country that has waged war on immigrants since 11 September 2001.

The war on terror, globalization, and transnational migrations have made theorizing citizenship in terms of assimilation difficult because these processes not only involve non-citizen subjects, but also involve the state, which makes the final decision on who belongs to the nation. In addition, the state has become more vigilant and controlling. It has put more effort into the containment of citizens and the sorting of citizens into "good" ones and "bad" ones. These distinctions are always present when different elements of the media recycle debates ignited by the latest proposed legislation on immigrants.

The state uses race, gender, class, and sexuality as markers to differentiate those who are to be included within or excluded from the nation's political body. That is to say, the state uses markers to contain different groups within its fold. Within this hierarchal power structure of containment, Ong points out that those wanting to be included within the state go through a "dual process of self-making and being-made within webs of power linked to the nation-state and civil society" (1996, p. 738). In this self-making, Ong elaborates:

> hegemonic ideas about belonging and not belonging in racial and cultural terms often converge in state and nonstate institutional practices through which subjects are shaped in ways that are at once specific and diffused. (Ibid.)

Ong's work is useful in underscoring the "webs of power" that immigrant soldiers must negotiate and the ways in which immigrants are differentiated from others during times of war.

Because of such differentiation, immigrant soldiers must negotiate a contradictory terrain. The military, as an instrument and a guardian of the state, has turned to immigrants as a viable labor pool to fill its armed forces due to low enlistment rates, especially in this current war. The job description for soldiers is explicitly delineated. Kenneth S. Coates and William R. Morrison explain the role of soldiers in the following way: "[their] primary task is to defend the political and ideological boundaries of the nation, assist its allies, and extend its control over enemy territory during times of war" (1993, p. 274). As guardians and laborers of the state, immigrant soldiers are sent, along with non-immigrant ones, to places where they must defend with their lives the varied, though primarily economic, interests of the United States. To carry out the defense of the nation, all soldiers regardless of legal status, are socialized through boot camp training to become American soldiers, an "army of one."

Perhaps another way to explain the contradictory terrain that green card soldiers have to navigate is to examine what people are posting in various sites on the Internet. The Internet has dramatically changed how information is disseminated and controlled. It provides a space for people to express their opinions, ideas, and in many cases, opposition to dominant ideologies. One video provides a twist on an Army advertisement targeting Latinos, especially those in the eighteen–twenty-four years age group.

The video clip starts with a scene of a man in fatigues with a camouflaged face in a helicopter. A male voice begins the narration, "As a Latino in the U.S. Army, I use cutting edge technology and my Mexican sensing skills to protect the U.S. from illegal aliens." A second male voice shouts out, "No jobs for you!" The earlier male voice continues:

> Because I am a Latino I can think like a Latino and find where they are hiding. I never thought I'd use a sixty million dollar Apache to catch Mexicans but here we are. The Army needs a few good Mexicans to catch a lot of bad ones. What kind of Mexican are you?

The video clip ends with a low steady voice, "*Yo soy el Army* (I am the Army)," and ends with, "Help catch Mexicans" (jsjkim, 2006). This YouTube post is a satire but it illustrates the contradictory terrain and the "webs of power" that aims to contain and differentiate "good" and "bad" immigrants. The employer of immigrant soldiers is the same entity that has proposed and enforced some of the most restrictive immigration legislation in the last few decades. Within this context, immigrant soldiers who also enforce immigration legislation as part of their assignments, are constructed as worthy American people. This forced negotiation on green card soldiers implies allegiance to the state that rejects these soldiers' ethnic group.

The discourse used in this satirical clip is similar to President Bush's use of dichotomous, "You're either with or us or against us." The video includes a binary that identifies a "good Mexican" and "bad Mexican." The good Mexican is the one wearing Army fatigues, pursuing the bad Mexican—the one crossing the border. In "'The War on Terror' and Same-Sex Marriage: Narratives of Containment and the Shaping of U.S. Public Opinion," Mary K. Bloodsworth-Lugo and Carmen Lugo-Lugo (2005) argue that containment processes construct those who are American and un-American, instituting and maintaining "the American" and "the un-American" boundaries. Because of this complicated process, the American has become an increasingly narrow and guarded class of citizens, while the un-American has become a site of attack (ibid., p. 471).

4. "It's Not Just a Job . . ."

One of the challenges in discussing the United States military as an institution is that in our society, emotive images evoking patriotism and heroism are much more prevalent than images of soldiers as workers for the state. The media embellishes reports of fallen soldiers with the narrative of heroism, which ultimately obscures the reasons why these soldiers might chose to join the military. At the same time, the military markets itself as a means for gaining skills and as a potential jumping-off point for careers after military service. This was especially appealing to Marine Corporal José A. Garibay. Family and friends remembered him as a friendly young man who wanted to become a police officer. Prior to enlisting with the Marines, Garibay spoke with a teacher about his future career goals. Garibay was told by his teacher, a colonel in the Army Reserve, that "he might do better in the Army, where he could advance faster and earn his spurs as a military officer" (Mark Arax, Daniel Hernandex, Robert J. Lopez, and Jennifer Mena, "Green Card Marines; Just Looking to Fit In," *Los Angeles Times* [26 May 2003]). Sadly, Garibay never fulfilled his dream.

Similar to José Garibay and many other immigrant soldiers, those from communities of color and the working poor join the armed forces to gain skills or earn money for college with the G.I. Bill. John J. Hisnanick's (2003) work that studies African American enlistees provides significant insights regarding their enlistment during the early 2000s:

> For many of these individuals [African American men] military service means a chance to be employed, learn a skill and the opportunity to receive an education upon discharge. Moreover, for some, military service can be a second chance, a place of equal acceptance and involvement despite prior social disadvantages, a chance to get ahead and an avenue for social and career mobility. (ibid., p. 41)

The economic situation of these groups connects immigrant soldiers with communities of color and the working poor.

Adamshick (2005) provides further insight into the demographics of those who enlist with the United States military. He found that the level of education, race, and whether someone was born in the United States were factors that correlated with the decision to enlist in the armed forces. Educational level attained and academic success also influenced whether an individual joined the military. Those who attained less education and those who did poorly in school were more willing to join the armed forces than those who did well in school. Finally, the military provides an avenue for non-United States born enlistees to secure better income than the meager civilian wages they might earn. Adamshick elaborates:

> Non-natives [non-United States born] or children of non-natives might be less-privileged than their native counterparts. Many non-native citizens struggle to find employment or initially situate in low income jobs. (Ibid., p. 14)

Under these narrow opportunities for economic and social mobility, the poor and racialized youths are most vulnerable to becoming pliable laborers for the military.

In a report published by the Pew Hispanic Center (2003), Latino students tend to have lower levels of high school completion when compared with other racial and ethnic groups. For instance, in 2002, the high school completion rate for Latino people older than twenty-five years of age was 57 percent. Compared to the percentage of White (88 percent) and African American (78 percent) people who have completed high school, the difference is quite disturbing (Castillo and Bishop, 2005). This population is more likely to be underemployed and have a lower rate of college attendance by comparison with their counterparts. In addition to these alarming statistics, the Latino population is rapidly growing. Jorge Mariscal writes:

> Huge increases in the number of new immigrants from Latin America during the decade of the 1990s (over 4.5 million legal arrivals) mean recruiters will be busy in Latino communities for decades to come. (2003, p. 349)

The combination of low-level education attainment rates and the increased growth of Latinos have made this group a military recruiter's "paradise." The United States military has eyed the Latino population since it began to grow into the largest racial minority: "Latinos make up less than 10 percent of the active-duty forces, but they comprise 16 percent of the 18- to 24-year-old U.S. population" (Linda Bilmes, "Uncle Sam Really Wants Usted," *Los Angeles Times* [21 August 2005]). Based on these statistics, the Pentagon has made efforts to double the enlistment number of Latinos by focusing recruitment on areas with a high Latino population such as Los Angeles, Phoenix, and Sacramento (ibid.).

One strategy to increase Latino enlistments is through Spanish-language military advertisement campaigns that appeal to the Latino family. A representative from Cartel Creativo, a San Antonio-based advertising company known for making Army's recruitment advertisement "*Yo Soy El Army*," explains how their current advertisements incorporate Latino cultural and family values, "We search for cultural insights and determine how to leverage Hispanic values and beliefs" (ibid.). Spanish-language advertisements such as "*Yo Soy el Army*" is given air time on popular Spanish-language and radio stations and networks such as Univision and Telemundo (Lizette Alvarez, Lizette, "With Charm and Enticements, Army is Drawing Hispanic Recruits, and Criticism," *New York Times* [9 February 2006]). The irony of this military advertisement campaign is best illustrated in the following:

> The military's successful Latino marketing campaign is the flip side of our government's failure to provide socioeconomic opportunities for all. It is a tragic irony that many young people are heading for Iraq, trying to reach the American dream unattainable at home. (Reyes, 2006)

Given these facts, that only a few scholarly works have examined the relationship between the United States military and these racialized and less privileged groups is alarming. Jorge Mariscal's (2004) work on the "economic draft" or "economic conscription" aimed at the Latino community makes visible the recent military recruiting campaigns targeting this community. Underscoring the bleak economic reality of many Latinos in urban areas and the high death rates among this group, Mariscal (2003, p. 93) states, "In effect, these young men and [women] died trying to become students." Under the guise of patriotism, loyalty, and "Americaness," immigrant youth are most vulnerable to manning the current domestic war on terror. At the same time, these communities are forced to align themselves with "Americanness" to prove their worthiness as citizens.

5. You and the DREAM Act: Full Speed Ahead

In 2003, the Senate voted on a proposal regarding the military recruitment of daughters and sons of undocumented parents. Referred to as the Development, Relief, and Education for Alien Minors (DREAM) Act, this proposed policy would provide a pathway for undocumented children in the United States to have conditional permanent residency that can turn into permanent resident status (Darem Briscoe, "Los Angeles; Rally Backs Effort to Help Immigrant Students," *Los Angeles Times* [13 April 2003]; Batalova and Fix, 2006). Individuals can achieve the conditional permanent residency status either by completing two years of college or serving honorably in the military for a minimum of two years. At the time of this writing, the DREAM Act is stalled in Congress but politicians and organizations are making concerted efforts to revive the DREAM Act.

Though the aim of the DREAM Act is to help the children of undocumented parents to achieve legal permanent resident status, the legislation is taking place within the context of the war on terror and an escalation of military deployment. The Migration Policy Institute estimated that if the DREAM Act passed in 2006, it would have resulted in 279,000 eligible persons for college enrollment or the military (Batalova and Fix, 2006, p. 1). The estimates of how many immigrant youths would choose college over the military is difficult to predict, but given the reality of budget cuts to higher education and the increasing cost of tuition, the option to serve in the military to earn the right to stay in the United States may become a forced choice.

In many states (with the exceptions of Texas, California, Utah, Washington, New York, Oklahoma, Illinois, Kansas, New Mexico, and Nebraska), undocumented students have to pay out-of-state tuition for college. Even those allowed to pay in-state tuition find doing so difficult, as funding for these students is limited and many have work schedules that include full time jobs in addition to attending classes.

Student organizations such as Improving Dreams, Equality, Access, and Success (IDEAS) at the University of California, Los Angeles are working hard to educate the public in an effort to garner support for the DREAM Act so that undocumented students can have a path to legal resident status (McGray, 2006).

However, there are those who see the measure as a military recruitment tool for undocumented immigrants. Carlo Guerra writes:

> This measure certainly has humanitarian aspects. Considering the financial situation of most of these young people, the likelihood is that most will opt for the military, not college. That could also pave the way for the creation of a culturally distinct American warrior class. That's too risky. ("Will Iraq and Afghanistan Wars Produce a Thorny New Dilemma?" *San Antonio Express-News* [30 December 2006])

The military route to legal resident status is no doubt an unresolved issue, but in conversations with individuals working to pass the DREAM Act, the supporters believe that through education, undocumented youths would be deterred from joining the military.

6. "It's a Great Way to Serve"

The attention to green card soldiers has further connected the war on terror with the war on all immigrants. On one hand, there are those such as Max Boot, a conservative analyst with the Council on Foreign Relations, who views the enlistment of undocumented immigrants as a commitment that "foreigners" make to the country as a sort of rite of passage to become a member of this society. He states:

> Would foreigners sign up for Uncle Sam? I don't see why not, because so many people are desperate to move here. Serving a few years in the military would seem a small price to pay, and it would establish beyond a doubt that they are the kind of motivated, hardworking immigrants we want. ("Defend America, Become American," *Los Angeles Times* [16 June])

Foreigners who serve and sacrifice their lives in the military are construed as ideal immigrants, a twenty-first century version of the "model minority." Others share Boot's views on how immigrants, legal and undocumented, can serve the in the military to prove themselves as worthy subjects for United States citizenship. Richard T. McCarthy writes in an editorial piece:

> My question is why should we seek new immigrants when the country is bursting with millions of illegal immigrants who are already here. Why not offer those who are within the right age group of a way to become legal [by enlisting in the armed forces]. Citizenship could be an offer they couldn't refuse.

Out of the many millions that are here, I'm sure that there are many men and women who would accept such a deal. And they wouldn't be accused of bypassing the normal route to legal entry. This could address both problems with a viable solution ... Give some of them the opportunity, and I'm sure they would apply for entrance into the military. ("Let Illegal Immigrants Earn Citizenship in Military," *The PatriotLedger* [8 December 2006])

The statements made by Boot and McCarthy illustrate important points relevant to this chapter. The presence of undocumented immigrants in the United States is seen as a problem and as a solution. Those who choose not to serve in the United States armed forces are a problem and have yet to prove themselves as motivated and hardworking immigrants that the United States wants. Boot and McCarthy also propose that immigrants, especially undocumented, are the solution to the low military enlistment rates. As immigrant soldiers in the war on terror, they demonstrate that they are a desired immigrant group. To view immigrants as a potential source for military recruitment also illustrates that the American government sees this group as a potential labor pool. Primarily due to economic necessity, these women and men enlist in the military to do the work that many American citizens are not willing to do. Serving in the United States military would greatly influence youth, especially in a time of economic downturns and unrelenting war such as the current one.

In early April 2008, Albert Huerta-Cruz, a green card soldier in the United States Army, died in action serving a country that was engaged in two wars, the war on terror abroad and the war on immigrants in the United States. In a newspaper commentary, JoAnn Lee Frank raises a crucial question regarding the enlistment of immigrants in the military:

So in other words, it's all right for immigrants like [Albert] Huerta-Cruz, a legal resident but not a citizen, to give the ultimate sacrifice for a country that isn't theirs, but it's not all right for them to take a job in order to make a decent living. Why is that I don't hear anyone complaining that Huerta-Cruz took their job by becoming a soldier? ("Immigrants Face Double Standard," *St. Petersburg Times* [1 May 2008])

This cogent question demonstrates the containment of immigrants and the contradictory terrain that they face in the present militarized and xenophobic era. Frank's statement reveals the rampant hypocrisy in the current discourse on immigrant recruitment in the United States military. The immigrant considered acceptable and eligible for citizenship is one contained in the United States military.

The current debates on United States citizenship, immigration, and military service have to consider the war on terror being waged against immigrant communities. A link exists between race, social class, and strong incentives to join the military. However, serving in the military is no guarantee of citizenship for green card soldiers. The containment of immigrant soldiers and the bestowal of citizenship are intricately linked to the webs of power of the nation-state and civil society (Ong, 1996, p. 738). Race is a factor in the final granting of United States citizenship, especially upon racialized green card soldiers.

In a 2008 report in the *New York Times*, about 7,200 honorably discharged service members had their citizenship application pending (Santos, Fernanda. (2008) "After the War, a New Battle to Become Citizens," *The New York Times* [24 February]). Though green card soldiers are supposed to be given priority for naturalization, many find themselves waiting to hear about their cases. Noncitizen soldiers such as Mustafa Aziz (H. G. Reza, "For Citizenship Delayed, 10 Taking U.S. To Court," *Los Angeles Times* [1 August 2006]) and Abdool Habibullah (Santos, 2008) have yet to know the status of their citizenship status even though they filed their applications a few years before their honorabe discharge from the military.

Citizenship and Immigration Services (USCIS) has cited stronger national security measures and the backlog of paperwork to explain the delayed conferral of United States citizenship to green card soldiers. Race may also have a major role in the naturalization process. Leslie B. Lord, an Army liaison to the Citizenship and Immigrations Services, stated, "But even the soldier with the cleanest of records, if he has a name that's very similar to one that's in the F.B.I. bad-boy and bad-girl list, things get delayed" (ibid., p. 1).

The pattern of delayed citizenship to noncitizen soldiers is a part of the webs of power. In the context of the dual wars on terror and immigrants, green card soldiers enlist with the military and they are self-made into "good" immigrants. In this self-making process, the state makes the ultimate decision about whom it deems worthy and to whom it awards citizenship. At the same time, the state can also undo the self-making of green card soldiers as in the case of Aziz and Habibullah. Though these two cases are in the contemporary period, the delayed conference of citizenship to soldiers is not new.

In 1941, President Franklin D. Roosevelt signed an order that called for the military service of Filipinos to fight alongside American soldiers to end the Japanese occupation of the Philippine Islands. He promised Filipino soldiers United States citizenship and military benefits in return. However, in 1946, a year after World War II ended, the Rescission Acts rescinded the promises made in the military order of 1941. After forty-nine years, the 1990 Immigration Act passed and made Filipino World War II veterans eligible for United States citizenship (Cabotaje, 1999).

While there has been a long history involving the recruitment of people of color into the United States military, enlistment has proven to be a way for immigrants and racialized groups to prove their worthiness for citizenship in the United States. But the cases of Aziz, Habibullah, and Filipino World War II Veterans serves as a constant reminder that service in the military is no guarantee that citizenship will be awarded.

7. Conclusion

In an era of increased anti-immigrant sentiments and restrictive immigration laws, immigrants, legal and undocumented, encounter an American society that confines them as either worthy or unworthy subjects in the United States. The government recognizes green card soldiers such as José Garibay and Albert Huerta-Cruz for their military service to their adopted country and sees them as members of an ideal minority immigrant group. Some have called the military service of noncitizen immigrant soldiers the "ultimate act of patriotism." However, this population, which the military heavily targets for recruitment, is subject to a socioeconomic reality far different from what such praise might suggest.

Green card soldiers must contend with a landscape that forces them to prove their loyalty and Americaness in the face of rejection of their own ethnic communities by the very same state that employs them. This terrain exemplifies the complex webs of power that both make and unmake subjects in a nation. Yet, the pretense of the rhetoric of patriotism is apparently not lost in the popular minds of those who post satirical materials in the Internet, and this is especially not lost in those who participated in the pro-immigration marches that took place in the United States.

The pro-immigration marches of 2006 remind us that even under repressive conditions by which the state seeks to contain groups it deems unworthy (un-American), some people are taking a visible stand to end the war on terror and the war on immigrants. During 2006, news of students walking out of schools in Los Angeles and in other cities to protest H.R. 4437 was but one example of people taking a stand against racism and xenophobia. Many protestors evinced knowledge of what was at stake if H.R. 4437 passed in the Senate: the possible criminalization or the deportation of their family members and friends. The students understood that the war on immigrants and the war on terror are connected.

These students also appeared to understand that the high cost of tuition makes access to higher education more difficult, but on many high school campuses, students have seen more military recruiters than college counselors (Furumoto, 2005). Through these massive demonstrations, we see the contradictory terrain that marginalized groups, especially green card soldiers, often have to navigate to prove their worthiness of belonging. Here, we also see organizations and individuals from all walks of life actively unravel the webs of power.

Ten

THE BRACERO, THE WETBACK, AND THE TERRORIST: MEXICAN IMMIGRATION, LEGISLATION, AND NATIONAL SECURITY

Luz María Gordillo

1. Introduction

During the Great Migration of the twentieth century, 1900–1930, approximately 46,000 Mexican people immigrated into the United States. Still, Mexican immigrants did not take center stage until the inception of the Bracero Program in 1942, one of the first official bilateral labor agreements between the United States and Mexico. Before that, efforts of agribusiness and wealthy growers to advocate for the importation of more Mexican workers were counteracted by growing concern from nativist groups and civil society about the increase in numbers of Mexican immigrants in the United States. This sentiment resulted in the illegal deportation, during the Great Depression of the 1930s, of up to two million Mexican people, of whom as many as 60 percent were born in the United States or had become legal citizens. Called the Mexican Reparation, its purported intent was to free up jobs for "real" Americans. President Herbert Hoover authorized this action, which many state and local governments continued even after President Franklin Roosevelt ended federal support for the program (Valenciana, 2006).

With the advent of World War II, the need for agricultural workers became a national concern and imminent necessity. The Bracero Program sought to enroll young strong men from Mexico to work in agricultural fields and railroad maintenance crews in the United States to alleviate labor shortages during the war. Civil rights movement leaders, who brought to light the systematic exploitation and mistreatment of Mexican laborers for two decades, condemned the Bracero Program and helped end it in 1964.

Since then, the discourse on Mexican immigration in the United States has become the property of politicians, social commentators, academicians, the media, religious leaders, and political groups. This discourse either has "erased" or "praised" Mexican immigrants depending on the economic, political, social, and cultural atmosphere in the United States. While the United States has placed a historical demand on Mexican labor, social constructions of the Mexican laborer have oscillated between the "good" and "docile" worker and the "dangerous" predator threatening to contaminate cultural integrity.

2. Historical Aspects of the Mexican Image

The ideologies and legislation behind the creation of the Bracero Program during the 1940s cemented the schizophrenic game the United States has played with the importation and deportation of Mexican labor. We had begun to see the beginnings of this game a decade before with the forced repatriation campaigns during the Depression. Undoubtedly, the economic and social atmosphere in the United States has dictated the image and legality of the Mexican immigrant. That image is of outmost importance for the argument of this chapter, as it appears to shift and mold to the needs of powerful interest groups, infecting the views of the public in the process.

A constellation of agriculturalists, industrialists, and conservative politicians along with small businesses and segments of civil society who capitalize on cheap labor glorify the image of Mexican people as the good and docile Mexican worker. Contrary to this perspective is the demonized and perilous Mexican posed as a predator who endangers the future of the United States by threatening its political, economic, social, and cultural "integrity." Though both perspectives have been part of the national discourse, it has been the second one that has permeated public discourse for the past twenty years since the militarization of the Mexico-United States border and the inception of Operation Gatekeeper in 1994. Together with the militarization of the border, social constructions of Mexican immigrants as dangerous threats to the security of the nation consolidate the Mexican immigrant as the quintessential danger to the United States national security.

Since 2006, Euro-American and international media have covered and headlined Mexican immigration in the United States. Because of historical selective memory, mainstream media has focused on and portrayed events instigated by proposed immigration reform under H.R. 4437, Border Protection, Antiterrorism, and Illegal Immigration Control Act of 2005, as if it were a new phenomenon. These measures would change the current immigration system—the family reunification system—to a point system based on immigrants' skills, favoring those who are better educated. This proposal appeared to be a culmination of concerns about national security present in the United States since the 11 September 2001 attacks on the United States. Within this framework, the immigration "problem" has become synonymous with Mexican people, while Mexican people have become synonymous with terrorism and drug and sex trafficking. Collective paranoia about immigration is such that, in 2006, President George W. Bush proposed the deployment of the National Guard to "protect" and "control" (read contain) the border between the United States and Mexico.

This chapter will map the history of United States legislation toward Mexican immigration, starting with the Bracero Program in 1942 and continuing into the twenty-first century. It will underline severe "schizophrenic" behavior the United States has demonstrated by simultaneously recruiting aggressively and actively curtailing Mexican labor. Understanding the history of these legislative changes will shed new light on the severe "migraphobia" that has sparked nativist groups to resuscitate private organized vigilante violence in the name of civil duty and pride exemplified by the Minute Man Project.

Examining historic efforts to contain Mexican people can also shed some light on efforts to contain Mexican immigrants and the Mexican border during the last years of the twentieth and earlier years of the twenty-first century. More importantly, this chapter will emphasize the legislative parallels between past legislation and the proposed new legislation. While previous legislation severely restricted the entrance of Mexican nationals into the United States, it was also unable to curtail the increase of undocumented immigrants entering the United States. In most cases, as with the Bracero Program, the legislation actually mobilized domestic migration to the North of Mexico and at the same time increased undocumented immigration into the United States:

> In its 1951 report, President Harry S. Truman's Commission on Migratory Labor noted that the Bracero Program also seemed to have contributed to an unprecedented population buildup in Northern Mexico as people used northern Mexican cities as staging grounds from which to enter the United States. Between 1940 and 1950, for example, the population of the Mexican border town of Mexicali grew by 240 percent; of Tijuana, by 259 percent; of Ciudad Juárez, by 149 percent; and of Matamoros, by 179 percent. (Gutiérrez, 1995, p. 72)

Justin Akers Chacón articulates it:

> "Illegalized" Mexican labor migration became the preference of United States capital, which ultimately dismantled the last vestiges of "legal" labor migration. Undocumented workers were now responsible for providing their own transportation, housing, and food while still working for subsistence wages, relieving the United States government of the last of its responsibilities. (Akers and Davis, 2006, p. 147)

Within the Bracero Program, many farmers aggressively recruited undocumented migrants either to bypass the program's labor contracts that demanded decent housing and fair wages and working conditions, or to avoid doing the paper work to process Braceros legally. This allowed Mexican laborers to cross the border many times, either legally as Braceros or illegally according to familial or economic needs.

These processes underline a silent, but quite volatile, cat and mouse game between United States agencies like the Border Patrol and several groups who have historically had vested interests in Mexican labor. The multiple agendas coming from different stakeholders, however, had as a common denominator the disposability of the Mexican worker. Furthermore, these programs also encouraged the dependency of both the United States on Mexican labor and Mexican labor on United States labor demand contingent upon the United States economic landscape. A very good example of this dysfunctional and unequal economic and social relationship is the forced repatriation campaigns carried out during the Great Depression:

> [A]s nationwide unemployment reached six million by the end of 1930 and eleven million by the end of 1932, Mexican workers were singled out as scapegoats in virtually every locale in which they lived in substantial numbers. In this atmosphere the nativist litany that had been employed against Mexicans in the 1920s—charges that they were disease ridden, that they committed crimes, that they displaced American workers, and that they were, in short, singularly un-American—was raised with new vehemence. (Gutiérrez, p. 72)

A similar pattern, with a similar nativist litany has developed in the United States since 11 September 2001. These current efforts at containing the Mexican population, though similar to those engaged by multiple stakeholders over fifty to seventy years ago, are compounded by the specter of terrorism. Still, it is important to emphasize the historical connections, for they shed some light on how these processes operate.

Neo-liberal economic structures such as the North American Free Trade Agreement (NAFTA) and Structural Adjustment Policies (SAPs) imposed by the International Monetary Fund (IMF) and World Bank (WB) not only have dispossessed and displaced many peasants in Mexico, they have done much more than create an economic dependency of the United States to Mexican labor and vice versa. Cultural and social influences have also served as direct conduits by which transnational communities take shape in the United States and Mexico. Within this transnational context, Mexican people slowly construct an immigrant experience particular to historical moments and geographical locations.

The Bracero Program exemplified the beginning of a formalized system of labor exploitation supported by both the United States and Mexican Governments. As a gendered program, the Bracero Program only recruited Mexican men that would ultimately substitute Asian workers. After many years of United States capital's aggressive recruitment of Asian labor—Chinese, Japanese and Filipino respectively—racist ideologies, along with domestic paranoia and competition for available resources, sought to be rid of Asians. By then the construction of the "dangerous Asian" was consolidated and normalized within the cultural and social fabric.

Asian immigration legislation illustrates the racist attitudes toward Asian immigrants starting from the end of the nineteenth century and continuing for the first three decades of the twentieth century exemplified by the Chinese Exclusion Act of 1882. In the first decade of the twentieth century, after this collective paranoia against Chinese immigrants had been temporarily appeased, the nativist and xenophobic boomerang struck again. This time, it turned its social and socio-economic paranoia toward Japanese imported labor. Its legislative justification came in form of the Gentleman's Agreement of 1907 in which Japan—pressured by the United States—agreed to curtail Japanese immigration. This inflamed anti-Asian sentiment, which persisted several decades into the twentieth century. Exemplifying these racist sentiments during World War II was the way the United States forcibly relocated Japanese immigrants, many of whom were naturalized American citizens, into internment camps. This anti-Asian sentiment was not limited to Chinese and Japanese immigrants. Philippine laborers were also the targets for these legislative changes. A few decades into the twentieth century, the portability, geographic proximity, and easy access to Mexican labor became an asset and a great justification for its constant, aggressive recruitment throughout the twentieth century and into the new millennium.

3. The Bracero

The Bracero Program began as a guest worker program; however, the structure provided the means to support a more permanent workforce due to the aggressive recruitment of Mexican immigrants. While the war in Europe demanded Euro-American, African American, and Mexican American labor to help the United States become a world power, the need for social survival in the United States demanded Mexican labor to support the United States' rise as a world power after World War II. Unlike the soldiers acclaimed as heroes and martyrs of Democracy in their effort to combat enemies on the other side of the ocean, Mexican people, originally recruited through the Bracero Program to help with the war effort, were routinely subjected to discrimination and had their labor rights constantly violated.

The stipulations that guaranteed basic labor rights in their contracts were systematically violated depriving Mexican American people of civil rights to which they were legally entitled under the program's guidelines. Even though the Bracero Program was referred to as a "guest worker" program and the United States designated as the "host" country, the process created an open and vulnerable space where Mexican people were exposed to mistreatment, forced to work under deplorable conditions, and paid meager wages—an "exploitable guest." The Bracero Program laid the foundation for a self-sustained exploitative and corrupted mechanism against Mexican labor supported by both the United States and Mexico.

Historically, the institutionalization of migration and the commoditization of Mexican labor had a tremendous impact affecting economic, political, social and cultural spheres in Mexico and the United States. It is important to analyze some of the processes by which both governments sanctioned not only the overt exploitation of Mexican laborers, but also the corruptive measures they encouraged through the different institutions used to administer and control the operation of the Bracero Program, especially between 1942 through 1954. A letter from the Mexican Viseconsul written in 1952 from a Reception Center stated:

> Continued violations to the workers' contracts and irregularities in the agents from United States Employment Services (USES) are the main complaints that our Mexican laborers are filing. An example is how our workers are being forced under threats by a "tyrannical" government representative to sign contracts with specific companies. This is a violation of their contracts that stipulates that our workers are free to choose their employers. (ARE, 1952, TM-3–8)

The first fourteen years of the program's operation was the primary time for both nations to negotiate and shape the outlines of the international agreement. Both countries received a lot of resistance from Mexican Nationalists who believed that only the loss of thousands of laborers, urban and agricultural, could sabotage the progress of Mexico. They were also well aware of the recent massive deportations from the United States of Mexican immigrants during the depression years. Wholesale civil rights violations against Mexican immigrants and Mexican American citizens by United States authorities were rampant.

Mexican politicians, artists, and businesspersons interceded, albeit in vein, to stop the exportation of Mexican laborers. Paradoxically, most of these same individuals in the United States agreed with their counterparts in Mexico, but their reasons for opposition were radically different. United States nativists were afraid that Mexican immigrants would contaminate cultural life and the social fabric of the United States. Racist images constructed and disseminated by interested stakeholders, illustrated the discourses on both sides of the Mexican immigration debate:

> The Mexican is a quiet, inoffensive necessity in that he performs the big majority of our rough work, agriculture, building and street labor. They have no effect on the American standard of living because they are not much more than a group of fairly intelligent collie dogs. (Akers and Davis, 2006, pp.192–193)

On the other side of the argument, while introducing legislation to deport Mexican immigrants, Congressman John Box commented:

> [E]very reason which calls for the exclusion of the most wretched, ignorant, dirty, diseased, and degraded people of Europe or Asia demands that the illiterate, unclean, peonized masses moving this way from Mexico be stopped at the border. (Ibid.)

Demonization of the Mexican worker and patriotic nativist sentiments sparked and inflamed by the Cold War continued at a dissonant crescendo for the next decades of the twentieth century. The Cold War and xenophobic attitudes would mark a new era of legislative production—the McCarran Internal Security Act of 1950. It blocked members of "subversive" groups, those determined to be dangerous to the political or democratic national health, from citizenship—keeping out "undesirable immigrants." Citizen-members could be denaturalized.

Congress terminated the Bracero Program in 1964 as the result of the efforts of a civil rights coalition that protested against Mexican workers' inhumane working conditions and the constant violation of their contracts as stipulated in the guidelines of the Bracero Program.

Anti-Mexican legislation, along with general paranoia on illegal immigration, became evident with the implementation of immigration reform that explicitly curtailed Latin American immigration regardless of the country of origin. In an effort to curtail Mexican laborers in 1965, Congress passed a bill planned for implementation in 1968 that limited the number of visas available across the entire Western Hemisphere to 120,000. The consequences were serious because family reunification became next to impossible for Mexican people, who had been aggressively recruited during the Bracero Program and who had managed to legalize their residence in the United States. Waiting periods were unrealistically long. Jorge Durand has argued, "undocumented migration would probably not have grown after the demise of the Bracero Program had it not been followed immediately by the imposition of new limits on the legal immigration of Mexicans" (Massey, Durand, and Malone, 2003, p. 23). It became obvious that family reunification, then, was a primary target of the imposition affecting many Mexican laborers residing in the United States.

4. The Wetback

The 1965 visa-limit legislation meant that all countries, regardless of their economic ties to the United States, were to abide by these immigration reforms. This meant ignoring global bridges established by capital in developing countries that facilitated not only the flow of goods but also the flow of people. This capitalist enterprise leads to the dual dependence of capital on cheap Mexican labor and Mexican labor on immigration to the United States.

While the United States imposed visa limits to curtail Latin American migration, it mobilized Mexican migration to the north by setting up factories all along the Mexico-United States border. In 1965, the United States negotiated with Mexico the implementation of the Border Industrialization Program (BIP). This program gave tax incentives for United States investors to set up huge industrial plants called maquilas all across the Mexico-United States border. These spaces, located on the South side of the border, are known as "free trade zones." Since the implementation of the BIP, these locations have become sites where United States capital and Mexican labor engage in a complicated, inequitable labor exploitation that favors the capital and makes labor vulnerable to exploitative techniques used to manage these plants.

Although the BIP locale is within Mexican territory, economic transformations in Mexico—brought about by neo-liberal ideologies that favor export oriented economies—and new financial strategies in the United States have made these free zones a lucrative investment for capital. This lucrative capital gain became evident within the first decade of the program, when "nearly a third of the value for all U.S. components sent abroad went to Mexico, and by 1977 more than $1 billion worth of maquiladora-assembled products [were] being returned to the United States every year" (Akers and Davis, 2006, p. 117). Slowly, with the aid of the BIP and other political and economic structures, Mexico became one of the more important trading partners of the United States. The economic impact of this program, along with the slow deindustrialization of the Mexican economy pressured by an export-oriented economy, slowly drove many urban Mexican people to migrate north and find jobs in Maquiladora Land.

The program would prove to be obsolete for the many men who ventured North and those who were already near the border location. These were mainly undocumented workers—"leftovers" of the Bracero Program and largely encouraged by farmers who wanted to overstep the Bracero Program's contract stipulations, which included transportation costs and a minimum wage for braceros. They had well-established networks that guaranteed a constant supply of undocumented workers. As Bill Ong Hing states:

> [D]espite all the economic advantages of the Bracero program, it did impose burdens on employers that could be avoided by using undocumented workers. While recruitment and transportation of legally contracted Braceros cost United States' taxpayers about $450 apiece for the 4.5 million legal laborers, the program spurred the long-term migration of millions of undocumented workers (at no direct cost to taxpayers' money) who continued to support U.S. farming. (2004, p. 128)

Even though the BIP initially intended to provide returning braceros and undocumented workers with available industrial jobs, the maquila hiring system proved to be the complete opposite by mostly recruiting young females. At the same time, it provided new corridors of capital-labor relationships that have facilitated the movement of labor from Mexico to the United States, "In export manufacturing, the main cause of the disruption of traditional work structures is the massive recruitment of young women into jobs in the new industrial zones" (Sassen, 1996, p. 219).

Although scholars disagree on the effects of the feminization of the labor force—whether it granted women more access to political and economic capital or continued to exploit women by keeping them in low-skilled positions:

> most of the manufacturing in these zones is of the sort that also employs women in the developed countries—apparel, electronics assembly, toys, textiles, and garments account for the largest share of all jobs in export zones and factories producing for export. (Ibid.)

Unquestionably, the BIP changed the gendered immigration dynamics previously established by the Bracero Program.

Much of the focus in the early maquiladora literature concerned the fact that 80 percent or more of the labor force was composed of young women. The government had hoped that those hired would be unemployed male migrant agricultural workers prevented from working legally in the United States as braceros during the 1960s. However, women were attracted to the unskilled assembly work that was almost the exclusive domain of the early maquiladoras (Kopinak, 1995, p. 31). The BIP contributed to incrementing the number of Mexican immigrant women pulled by aggressive recruitment campaigns launched by multinational corporations that purposely looked for a "vulnerable" labor force. Young women from all states in Mexico would take the trip North to work at the assembly plants. Two dissonant cultural images emerged: one on the Mexican side with its shanty towns and poverty stricken population; the other on the Euro-American side with a landscape of shopping malls and capitalist consumerism.

This dividing image of the border continues to illustrate the recurrent schizophrenic attitude of the United States' implementation of restrictive immigration policy aimed at the exclusion of "unacceptable immigrants" through severe limitations on visas allocated to Latin American countries. On the one hand, maquila workers are expected to contribute to the economic well-being of the United States, but on the other, their own dire living conditions, low wages and continuous [sexual] abuse are systematically ignored.

Familial dislocations are at the core of many immigrants' everyday experiences and the implementation of restrictive legislation was responsible for further incrementing the curtailment of Mexican immigrants. By restricting the number of visas available to Mexican nationals while at the same time launching the Border Industrialization Program with Mexico, the United States continues to dispense of Mexican labor on an economic whim. The Border Industrialization Program not only drew more Mexican workers north but it encouraged and enhanced United States investment in Mexican territory through tax exemption enticements by the Mexican government that granted United States capital exorbitant increments in profit calculated through the hiring of a cheap exploitable labor force. The primary advantage for a United States company to operate a maquila is the lower cost of labor in Mexico. Studies have found that the process of "maquiladorizing" results in severely reduced wages. Other advantages include more favorable labor law in Mexico and fewer union-driven work rules. In other instances, maquilas fill jobs that United States workers are no longer willing to work (ibid., p. 35).

Once more, the United States was severely curtailing immigration and family reunification from Latin American countries, and in particular Mexico, which had been the largest supplier of Latino labor in the United States. While implementing immigration reforms that were not positively affecting Mexican immigrants, the United States at the same time was formalizing a trade agreement that proved to be incredibly lucrative for the United States. The United States enforced the 20,000 country visa limits despite the growing numbers of immigrant women lured by the BIP to the border towns of Mexico— and more often than not into the United Sates—and the braceros' families seeking residency. Two decades before NAFTA, restrictions on family reunification would become a growing concern in Mexico-United States politics of immigration.

The struggle for family unification by Mexican nationals during the 1970s emphasized how much American society needed Mexican laborers, but not for permanent residence. In 1976, Congress passed legislation applying the preference system for family reunification. This was a harsh blow to Mexican immigrants, because children of undocumented parents, who were American citizens, had to be twenty-one years old to sponsor their parents' permanent residency. This made undocumented Mexican nationals with children who were citizens, more vulnerable. It forced many families to marginalize themselves even more. At the same time, it imposed the 20,000-visa limit in the Western Hemisphere regardless of the size of the countries of origin and ignored long trade patterns between the United States and countries in Latin America, including Mexico. The 1970s opened the door to newly recycled restrictive legislation against Mexican immigration. During the 1970s, severe migraphobic sentiments began to rise in tandem with the increasing numbers of undocumented immigrants in the United States.

The United States has historically maintained exploitative hiring practices that have been dependent upon immigrant labor. Such practices have served to either recruit or curtail immigrants from laboring within the United States. These unstable labor practices have also fostered the notion of the "bad immigrant." Mexican immigrants have become the repositories of racial eco-political instabilities, while most of these socially constructed images stand in front of the heroic façade of a nation state struggling and building against all odds. The pride of having a past rooted in a long gone and imagined myth of a nation built by "immigrant forefathers" has as its binary opposition the historical criminalization of different immigrant groups in the United States.

Those who are criminalized do not look or act like "acceptable immigrants." These immigrants are socially catalogued as Others in a very complicated system of human taxonomies focusing on racial distinctions to define those who are unacceptable immigrants regardless of their immigration status. United States' history demonstrates repressive and racist policies and attitudes directed toward these "Other immigrants"—Chinese, Japanese, Philippinos, and Latinos—those immigrants whom the state believes are more difficult to "assimilate." The definition for assimilation of immigrants in the United States has—as has any other socially constructed definition—undergone multiple historical changes. Underlining most of these changes is a social expectation that we can interpret as a process of "whitening." A person of Mexican descent residing or desiring to live permanently in the United States has little it can do to become an "eligible" participant in American society. For Mexican immigrants, the 1970s marked the prelude to what was to become one of the more disruptive immigration reforms: The Immigration and Reform Control Act (IRCA) of 1986.

Mainstream media followed a predictable pattern by producing cartoons and commentaries supporting restrictionist and racist attitudes. Media images corroborated policy-making decisions by demonizing and criminalizing Mexican immigrants while imbuing society with a collective paranoia surrounding the danger of an imaginary "invasion" of Mexican workers and possible criminals. The number of Mexican immigrants in the United States had risen significantly during the 1970s. In response, on 17 May 1975, in a headline entitled, "500 Illegal Aliens Seized At Los Angeles Factory," *The New York Times* expressed existing sentiments by reporting, "as many as 500 illegal aliens, most of them Mexicans, were taken into custody today at handbag factory by agents of the Immigration and Naturalization Service."

Following a decade of hostile responses to Mexican workers, documented or undocumented, the IRCA promised to ensure a cheap labor force by granting leniency to agricultural workers. IRCA offered a guest worker program through which workers could obtain H2A or H2B visas. With these visas, Euro-American corporations could contract with workers for specified periods. The H2A visa is designed for agricultural labor, while the H2B visa can be granted to any company that "proves" local domestic laborers are in shortage. The difficulty with both visa programs is that they make no demands of employers in terms of ensuring fairness to workers. Immigrants are most vulnerable to exploitation under the H2B visa, since there are no provisions in workers' contracts for protections against corruptive measures often used by employers. Such measures include refusal to cover the costs of laborers' transportation to place of work, failure to provide decent living conditions, violations around the amount of work promised and the amount delivered, and leverage used by employers to solicit loyalty and fear through constant threats of deportation.

Recruitment within these enterprises is, in and of itself, a process of convincing poor farmers to borrow money—usually from persons ("coyotes") arranging trips to the United States—at high interest rates. Many Mexican immigrants—forced by coyotes—use as collateral the deeds of their humble dwellings in their communities of origin. At the same time that IRCA announced its regulations, which included "amnesty" for undocumented workers, the H2A and H2B visas were part of a package that guaranteed a constant flow of cheap and exploitable labor not protected by any labor laws that guaranteed basic rights of workers (fair wages, decent living conditions, and access to medical attention).

IRCA also granted amnesty to illegal "aliens" who could prove that they had resided in the United States since 1984. At the same time, Congress, influenced by wealthy farmers' needs for inexpensive labor, enacted Special Agricultural Workers (SAW) as an integral component of IRCA. Mexican agricultural workers who could prove that they had been working in any agricultural field for a minimum of one year prior to the amnesty, would be granted permanent residency. Despite complaints by politicians, lobbyists, and civil groups, the bill passed with a minority of votes in Congress supporting the amnesty. The Bill granted permanent residency to undocumented immigrants despite the extremely high numbers of Mexican people whom Congress predicted would seek legalization (which varied from two to sixteen million). Ultimately, the United States granted amnesty to two million Mexican immigrants. Of those, one million were under the SAW program (Hing, 2004, pp. 162–164). Thus, the majority in Congress did not support amnesty for Mexican workers. It came as an appeasement component to a larger goal and mission—penalizing employers that knowingly hired undocumented workers. Extending the funding and personnel for the Border Patrol and the SAW program came as a consolation for wealthy growers.

Despite its obvious goals, IRCA did not curtail undocumented immigration to the United States nor did it legalize most of the undocumented labor force. The process to become "legal" during IRCA entailed several steps, which became a cultural barrier for many Mexican people to apply. These included fraudulent transactions from predators that charged high fees from Mexican immigrants promising a path to citizenship but delivering nothing. The amnesty, which terrified most members of Congress and civil society, worked more efficiently as a trigger to evoke xenophobic sentiments than to render a solution to the "Mexican Immigration Problem"—or, more colorfully, "the wetback problem."

5. The Terrorist

In the aftermath of IRCA, the 1990s solidified the militarization of the United States-Mexico border. This militarization unfolded as the United States, Mexico, and Canada were preparing to sign NAFTA—an agreement intended to revolutionize the way geopolitical entities would conduct global business into the twenty-first century. While images of the Mexican immigrant in the 1990s replicated stereotypes of Mexican people "stealing" available "good old American jobs," draining the welfare system, and endangering the cultural and social fabric of the United States, a new identity emerged that would come to haunt Mexican nationals into the next millennium: the drug dealer.

The drug dealer identity was typically a perverted individual who corrupts and endangers the minds and lives of Euro-American youth. The marked correlations among social ailments, such as the sale and consumption of drugs and blaming minorities for such social illnesses in the United States, is not new. During the drug scare of the 1930s, the dominant society systematically blamed African American people for being the cause of their crime-infested neighborhoods due to their smoking marijuana.

Mexican people and the consumption of illegal drugs in the United States have been historically synonymous with collective negative sentiments against immigrants. Marijuana was and continues to be the quintessential drug associated with Mexican immigrants and with criminal behavior. This behavior is associated with the belief that Mexican immigrants are impossible to assimilate into America as "acceptable immigrant[s]." Clayton Mosher and Scott Akins state:

> Illegal drug use has also been demonized through claims that minorities, immigrants, and foreign nationals are the primary users and traffickers of illegal drugs. Through this strategy, both the external cause and internal problems associated with drug use can be attributed to something that is foreign and clearly "un-American." (2007, p. 35)

Mexican immigrants have always been subject to such assumptions about un-Americanism or the alleged connection to drug abuse and trafficking.

Just as the United States has used techniques of racial scapegoating with linkages to drugs in the past, anti-Mexican immigrant sentiment during the 1990s associated Mexican people with methamphetamine consumption, addiction, production, and sales. During the late 1990s and early 2000s, several articles on the methamphetamine asserted, "Mexican organized crime groups were becoming involved in the methamphetamine trade" (Mosher and Atkins, p. 34). The United States-Mexico border has been porous, and the smuggling of drugs between Mexico and the United States has been a growing concern. However, drugs trafficked through Mexico are not always run by Mexican drug cartels. Generalizing Mexican people as the main suppliers of these drugs—disregarding other countries' contributions to this lucrative business and the consumption of these harmful and illegal substances by United States citizens—is misleading. It aggravates the image of Mexican people as inherent criminals.

Notwithstanding the general social atmosphere created against the Mexican immigrant during the 1990s, President George Herbert W. Bush and Mexican president Salinas de Gortari signed NAFTA, which became effective on 1 January 1994. In the same year, Border Control Chief Sylvester Reyes—now head of the intelligence committee in the United States House of Representatives—was implementing Operation Blockade in El Paso, Texas. At the same time, Governor Pete Wilson in California released a video, *Border under Siege*, which fostered alarm surrounding undocumented immigrants' numbers and their endangerment to the United States economy and cultural integrity.

While United States policy encouraged the free trade of technology, information, consumer goods, etc., it was maintaining a strict and vigilant system of restriction and containment toward labor. This continued the rendering of Mexican workers as invisible in the United States and emphasized their existence as disposable labor. Once again, legislation toward Mexican workers at all levels—local, regional, and federal—contoured the historical patterns of unfair and illegal implementation of legislation against Mexican immigrants.

San Diego's Operation Gatekeeper in 1994 exemplifies legislative changes, influenced by politicians and policy makers imbued with racist attitudes toward Mexican immigrants. The series of legislative changes directed in major cities and towns along the United States-Mexico border illustrate the collaborative efforts by the United States government to conduct political "raids" to appease social paranoia while representing itself as the major global trade partner of Mexico and Canada (with NAFTA). The historically discordant attitude of the United States toward Mexican immigrants had never been as serious as after the implementation of Operation Gatekeeper and its offspring: Operation Safeguard (1995), in Nogales, Arizona (extended East and West during 1999); Operation Hold the Line (1997, extended ten miles West into New Mexico); Operation Rio Grande (1997, expanded thirty-six miles along the southeast Texas Border).

Experts estimate that approximately 300 Mexican nationals have died every year while trying to cross the border since the implementation of Operation Gatekeeper in San Diego and the other immigration deterrent Operations along the United States-Mexico border. The California Legal Assistance Foundation reported that between 1998 and 2000, 1,186 migrants died crossing the border. The most common causes of death were hypothermia or heat stroke, drowning, accident, and homicide. One way to view these data is to say that the United States launched a fully militarized "low-intensity" war against Mexican nationals that cost hundreds of lives while, at the same time, economically benefitting from NAFTA and a constant flow of cheap labor from Mexico. Capital demand and cheap labor supply required a Mexican labor force regardless of its immigration status. Although immigration scholars recognize this historical pattern, the cost of Mexican lives in the last decade of the twentieth century marks a new attitude adopted by the United States toward Mexican nationals. This new attitude cynically marks the perpetuation of exploitative programs sanctioned by the government and operated by local authorities and rich capitalists.

By the end of the 1990s, the Mexican immigrant had secured its place in the collective imagination of American civil society. Many American people envisioned Mexican people as invaders, criminals, and a danger to the environment. As early as the 1970s, environmental groups such as Federation for American Immigration Reform (FAIR) and the Sierra Club had joined in the antagonism against Mexican immigrants. These organizations' core ideology espoused the imminent dangers of environmental decay due to overpopulation and misuse of available resources by "unwanted" immigrants.

In the new millennium, the 11 September 2001 attacks crystallized the Mexican immigrant as a possible threat to United States national security. Congress passed the United States Uniting and Strengthening America by Providing Appropriate Tools Required to Intercept and Obstruct Terrorism Act of 2001 (PATRIOT Act). The PATRIOT Act has deputized local, regional, and state institutions of authority as full-time enforcers of federal immigration laws by enacting [anti-]immigration laws as they see fit. Racial profiling has often resulted in an extremely restrictive space open to ethnic scrutiny—regardless of immigration status. This circumstance has come to weigh heavily on people of Latin American descent, especially Mexican people.

The militarized United States-Mexico border has come to symbolize containment and deterrence. The Mexican immigrant has come to represent many things that American fears, including the contamination and pollution of the so-called ideal American. As in the past, political and economic stressors serve as the main social triggers for continuing the mistreatment of Mexican nationals. Reflective of historical amnesia, the Mexican immigrant becomes a contested site for collective social anxieties created by a combination of media carnivalesque imagery. Unstable immigration policy and a general social unrest, instigated and compounded by the war in Iraq, further complicates the picture.

As a consequence of the demonization, dehumanization, and criminalization of Mexican immigrants within several venues (including the media, the political arena, among lobbyists, and within private organizations), civil paramilitary groups are taking action and introducing civilian techniques of terror directed, with impunity, toward Mexican peoples. As Hing remarks, "Once dehumanized and rendered voiceless, the immigrant's actions, status and dreams may be criminalized. The process is completed: problematize, demonize, dehumanize and then criminalize" (2006, p. 206).

Privatized vigilante groups such as The Minuteman Project exemplify the effects that all of these processes have at the most fundamental, organic levels of society. This is reminiscent of, and in tandem with, Ku Klux Klan ideology, the Minutemen focus on phenotypes to argue for a "better America," the continuation of "United States traditional values," and the "dissemination of a National language." Of great danger today is the naturalization of these nativist and xenophobic sentiments lost in patriotic rhetoric that reflect the continuation and replication of racist ideologies and attitudes toward Mexican immigrants in the United States.

Legislation production continues to influence, and be influenced by, general collective images of "undesirable" citizens. The United States Supreme

Court continues to grant a growing number of (illegal) liberties to the Border Patrol. These liberties include making evidence found in an illegal search admissible in a deportation case which perpetuates anti-Mexican attitudes. In the last seven years, states are beginning to reconsider local and regional laws regarding Mexican immigrants. While legislative and media production continue to shape and reshape each other, civil society's consensus becomes the accusatory force behind racist and inhumane policies directed at Mexican immigrants. Most recently, in 2008 in St Helens, Washington, in the county of Columbia, a prosperous construction entrepreneur, Wayne Mayo, proposed a bill that would fine landlords renting to undocumented immigrants, and set up an "emergency civilian hot line" for "responsible" citizens to call and denounce anyone they might suspect of being an illegal immigrant. Mayo's bill calls for the county to hang signs that would read "Illegal Worker Free County."

Antagonistic sentiments on both sides of the border have created legal, social, and cultural hostilities that continue to recycle pernicious stereotypes of Mexican immigrants. This antagonism has also triggered rampant criminal acts against Mexican people through a combination of unreasonable immigration policies, collective pejorative stereotypes, xenophobic and migraphobic sentiments, and the normalization of all of these into one hegemonic discourse. While Congress, wealthy growers, businesspersons, politicians, and civil stakeholders in general continue to advocate for the importation of Mexican labor, the United States has waged a war on the United States-Mexico border against a country and its people who have not been at war with the United States. This war against unarmed immigrants continues to take its toll in the alarming number of Mexican immigrants dying on the border, as well as the horrible displacement of families that this newly revived and generated xenophobia has created. Mexican immigrants feel forced to choose between survival and familial preservation.

In this taxonomy of citizenship and historically systematized exclusion of particular "undesirable" immigrants to the United States, the Mexican immigrant ranks among the most unwanted. This is partly because of the geographical proximity between Mexico and the United States, and partly because of United States imperialist and expansionist agendas. The Mexican has historically inhabited the Euro-American imagination as an unwanted transgressor. Since the Mexican-American War (1846 to 1848), when the United States invaded and colonized half of the Mexican territory, Mexican people have figured in the collective imagination of Euro-American people as inherent invaders. The United States-Mexico border has come to symbolize this historical phenomenon within the United States' systems of oppression and labor exploitation where racial hierarchies serve as justifications for capital's growth and survival.

The United States has engineered a social system that grounds its domestic capitalist agenda in demonizing unwanted migrants and justifying their social, economic, and political segregation and marginalization in the name of patriotic and nationalist integrity and safety. In this era of social paranoid containment, and against a backdrop of fear of terrorism (where foreign policy, the War on Terror, and domestic policy collide), the social and political construction of the Mexican immigrant has become a double depository of United States nationalist insecurity and dissonant attitudes. My research shows that this morbid attitude toward Mexican immigrants that in the past encouraged a semi-innocent game of cat and mouse has now turned into a very dangerous game where Mexican immigrants' lives are the price to pay.

6. Concluding Remarks:
11 September 2001, Mexican People, and Terrorism

Since 11 September 2001, Mexican people have become the quintessential "non-Arab terrorists" threatening—according to hegemonic discourses—the cultural, racial, economic, and political integrity of the United States. Furthermore, some states are reconfiguring their laws granting local authorities the power to enforce–with little or no training—[anti]immigration laws. On 27 July 2007, *The New York Times* reported on a key decision by federal judge James M. Munley that "struck down ordinances adopted by the City of Hazleton in Pennsylvania to bar illegal immigrants from working or renting homes there, the most resounding legal blow so far to local efforts across the country to crack down on illegal immigration." Judge Munley's decision came after local officials began to enforce illegal anti-immigration policies. The town of Hazleton represents one of many localities that have tried to enforce anti-immigrant laws with impunity. After the Judge's decision, the town's mayor, Louis J. Barletta, vowed to continue efforts to enforce anti-immigrant laws in his town. This national headline illustrates how the nation is responding to the social and cultural xenophobic sentiments directed at Mexican immigrants. It also points to the racial and social conflicts arising from legislative production and civil society's involvement and participation in this newest response to Mexican immigration.

The historically restrictionist attitudes toward Mexican immigration have resuscitated old and created new demons in the form of strict and severe legislative changes. These legislative changes have aggravated and instigated contested racial, economic, political, and social relations in the United States. The historicity of these legislative actions, in tandem with Mexican immigrants' experiences, documents the injustices committed by the United States against Mexico, its labor, and its nationals. My findings have shown how the intersections of legislative production and ideas of cultural and economic integrity and national security are dialectical. In turn, they contribute to shaping a collective construction of who is an acceptable citizen and who is not.

The politics of movement in the twenty-first century demand that we reconsider the ways we categorize "citizen," "border," and "international labor." We need to reexamine and reconfigure legislative changes toward immigration policy in the United States to accommodate the new, globalized mobility triggered and deployed by labor structures within the global economy and chosen by international laborers adjusting to global markets. Mexican immigrants—regardless of immigration status—have been, and continue to be, active participants in the social, economic, and political structure of the United States. Historical legislative production, in conjunction with ideologies created and disseminated through different social structures, have proven time and again that national containment rooted in racist ideologies and capitalist strategies for profit has less to do with national security and more to do with the maintenance and endorsement of a dysfunctional and exploitative kind of globalized socio-political and economic containment.

This new kind of containment advocates legislative abuses such as Operation Gatekeeper and unfair international agreements such as NAFTA, and it no longer integrates a semi-safe labor contracting game with Mexican workers but purposely forces Mexican workers to national border death traps. This new kind of containment relies on cheap labor to maximize profit, while it promotes the deadliest international labor turnover in the history of immigration legislation to curtail Mexican immigration. The historical production of immigration legislation in the United States underlines a historicity rooted in ideas of containment and collective xenophobia. Unfortunately, legislative decision-making in the new millennium promises no immediate changes. We need to critically understand that dehumanizing and criminalizing immigrants from different ethnic groups is more of a practical tool for capitalist profit-making and a detrimental attempt for white supremacists to maintain dominance than it is a deterrent for immigrants. It is time that we decide who we want to be as a nation: a nation rooted in racialized and xenophobic national forms of containment, or a nation that recognizes and integrates the social, economic, and political participation of all its agents–such as Mexican immigrants—as acceptable global citizens with deserving labor rights, civil rights, and human rights.

WORKS CITED

Chapter One: Bloodsworth-Lugo, Lugo-Lugo

ABC News, "Gay Marriage/Nationally," ABC News Election Coverage, 2 November 2004.
Advocate.com. "Voters in 11 States Overwhelmingly Vote Against Same-Sex Marriage," (3 November), http://www.advocate.com/news_detail_ektid06891.asp (accessed 27 February 2008).
Associated Press. (2003) "Poll: 70% Believe Saddam, 9-11 Link," *USA Today* (6 September), http://www.usatoday.com/news/washington/2003-09-06-poll-iraq_x.htm (accessed 28 February 2008).
Bash, Dana. (2004) "Bush Renews Call for Same-Sex Marriage Ban," CNN.com (17 May), http://www.cnn.com/2004/ALLPOLITICS/05/17/bush.gay/index.html (accessed 27 February 2008).
Brinkley, Alan. (2001) "The Illusion of Unity in Cold War Culture." In Kuznick and Gilbert, *Rethinking Cold War Culture*.
Bush, George W. (2001) "Address to a Joint Session of Congress and the American People," Office of the Press Secretary, Washington, D.C., (20 September), http://www.whitehouse.gov/news/releases/2001/09/20010920-8.html (accessed 27 February 2008).
———. (2002) "Iraq: Denial and Deception," Office of the Press Secretary, Washington, D.C. (7 October), http://www.whitehouse.gov/news/releases/2002/10/20021007-8.html (accessed 27 February 2008).
———. (2003) "The State of the Union," White House, Washington, D.C. (28 January), http://www.whitehouse.gov/news/releases/2003/01/20030128-19.html
———. (2004a) "President Calls for Constitutional Amendment Protecting Marriage," Office of the Press Secretary, Washington, D.C. (24 February), http://www.whitehouse.gov/news/releases/2004/02/20040224-2.html (accessed 27 February 2008).
———. (2004b) "The State of the Union," The White House, Washington, D.C. (20 January), http://www.whitehouse.gov/stateoftheunion/2004/ (accessed 27 February 2008).
"Bush: States Shouldn't Change Marriage: President Stops Short of Endorsing Amendment," (2004) CNN.com (21 January), http://www.cnn.com/2004/ALLPOLITICS/01/20/same.sex.marriage/index.html (accessed 27 February 2008).
Butler, Judith. (1993) *Bodies That Matter: On the Discursive Limits of "Sex."* New York: Routledge, pp. 227–228.
CBS News. (2003a) "Canada's 1st Same-Sex Wedding: Two Men Tie the Knot Hours after Court Overturns Ban," CBS News, Toronto (11 June), http://www.cbsnews.com/stories/2003/06/11/world/main558150.shtml?source=search_story (accessed 27 February 2008).
CBS News. (2003b) "High Court Rejects Sodomy Law: Also Rules on Sex Abuse Cases, Death Penalty," Washington (26 June), http://www.cbsnews.com/stories/2003/06/26/supremecourt/main560508.shtml?source=search_story (accessed 27 February 2008).

CBS News. (2003c) "Poll: Bush Iraq Rating at New Low," Washington (17 September), http://www.cbsnews.com/stories/2003/09/17/opinion/polls/main573774.shtml?source=search_story (accessed 27 February 2008).

CBS News. (2003d) "Poll: Legalize Same-Sex Marriage?: 55 Percent Polled by CBS/NY Times Said No; 40 Percent Said Yes," New York (30 July), http://www.cbsnews.com/stories/2003/07/30/opinion/polls/main565918.shtml?source=search_story (accessed 27 February 2008).

CBS News. (2004) "Bush Sticks to Guns on Iraq," (12 July), http://www.cbsnews.com/stories/2004/07/13/iraq/main629358.shtml?source=search_story (accessed 27 February 2008).

Chomsky, Noam. (2003) *Power and Terror: Post 9/11 Talks and Interviews*. New York: Seven Stories Press.

———. (1996) *World Orders: Old and New*. New York: Columbia University Press.

Cloud, John. (2004) "The Battle Over Gay Marriage," *Time* (February 16), p. 56.

Curry, Tom. "Gay Marriage in Play as 2004 Issue," MSNBC.com, http://www.msnbc.msn.com/id/3070820/%5Benter%20URL%5D (accessed 27 February 2008).

De Hart, Jane. (2001) "Gender, Sexuality, and National Identity in Cold War America." In Kuznick and Gilbert, *Rethinking Cold War Culture*.

D'Emilio, John. (1992) *Making Trouble: Essays on Gay History, Politics, and the University*. New York: Routledge.

Gallup. (2003) "American Public Opinion about Gay and Lesbian Marriages," http://www.gallup.com (accessed 27 May 2004).

———. (2003) "Six Out of 10 Americans Say Homosexual Relations Should Be Recognized as Legal," (15 May), http://www.gallup.com/poll/8413/Six-Americans-Say-Homosexual-Relations-Should-Recognized-Legal.aspx (accessed 27 February 2008).

———. (2004) "Gay and Lesbian Marriages," gpns *Focus On*, http://www.gallup.com/poll/10432/Gay-Lesbian-Marriages.aspx (accessed 27 February 2008).

Hulse, Carl. (2004) "Defeat of Federal Marriage Amendment," *The New York Times* (14 July), http://mysite.verizon.net/lardil/id16.html (accessed 27 February 2008).

Ireland, Doug. (2003) "Republicans Relaunch the Antigay Culture Wars," *The Nation* (20 October), http://www.thenation.com/doc/20031020/Ireland (accessed 27 February 2008).

Khalilzad, Zalmay. (1995) *From Containment to Global Leadership?: America and the World after the Cold War*. Santa Monica, Calif.: Rand.

Kniderbocker, Brad. (2004) "Ballot Wars Over Same-Sex Marriage," *Christian Science Monitor* (8 October), http://www.csmonitor.com/2004/1008/p03s01-uspo.html (accessed 27 February 2008).

Kranish, Michael. (2007) "Gay Marriage Bans Passed," *The Boston Globe* (3 November), http://www.boston.com/news/nation/washington/articles/2004/11/03/gay_marriage_bans_weighed/ (accessed 27 February 2008).

Kuznick, Peter and James Gilbert. (2001) "Introduction: U.S. Culture and the Cold War." In *Rethinking Cold War Culture*.

———, eds. (2001) *Rethinking Cold War Culture*. Washington: Smithsonian Institution Press.

Lochhead, Carolyn. (2004) "S. F.'s Gay Marriages Trouble President," *The San Francisco Chronicle* (19 February), http://www.sfgate.com/cgi-bin/article.cgi?f=/c/a/2004/02/19/SAMESEX.TMP (28 February 2008).

Max, Sarah. (2001) "Consumers Seek Comfort: America Copes by Flying the Flag, Spending on Things Fostering Safety, Comfort," *CNNMoney* (9 November), http://money.cnn.com/2001/11/09/saving/q_consumer/index.htm (28 February 2008).

Meyerowitz, Joanne, ed. (1994) *Not June Cleaver: Women and Gender in Postwar America, 1945–1960*. Philadelphia, Pa.: Temple University Press.

Morris, David, and Gary Langer. (2004) "Same-Sex Marriage: Most Oppose It, but Balk at Amending Constitution," (21 January), http://abcnews.go.com/sections/us/Relationships/same_sex_marriage_poll_040121.html (accessed 28 February 2008).

Mrozek, Donald. (1980) "The Cult and Ritual of Toughness in Cold War America." In Ray B. Browned. *Rituals and Ceremonies in Popular Culture*. Bowling Green, Ohio: Bowling Green University Popular Press.

Newport, Frank. (2003) "Same-Sex Marriage in the News," Gallup News Service, http://www.lmfct.org/ (accessed 15 May 2003).

Stevenson, Richard. (2004) "Winning While Losing." *The New York Times* (24 July), http://query.nytimes.com/gst/fullpage.html?res=950DEED9173AF936A25754C0A9629C8B63&scp=4&sq=Winning+while+Losing&st=nyt (accessed 27 February 2008).

Wallerstein, Immanuel. (1998) *Historical Capitalism with Capitalist Civilization*. London: Verso.

Warner, Michael. (2000) *The Trouble with Normal: Sex, Politics, and the Ethics of Queer Life*. Cambridge: Harvard University Press.

World Net Daily. (2004) "Homosexual Marriage Sparks Nationwide Backlash: Massachusetts Decision 'Awakening' Majority of Americans," (5 February), http://worldnetdaily.com/index.php?fa=PAGE.view&pageId=23109 (accessed 27 February 2008).

Chapter Two: Gay

Ackerman, Peter, and Jack Duvall. (2000) *A Force More Powerful: A Century of Nonviolent Conflict*. New York: St. Martin's Press.

American Friends Service Committee. (n.d.) "Surviving Militarism, Racism, & Repression: An Emergency Preparedness Kit for LGBT & Queer Youth," http://www.afsc.org/lgbt/YM/default.htm (accessed 25 April 2008).

———. (n.d.) "Is Opposing the War an LGBT Issue?" http://www.safeschoolscoalition.org/LGBTAntiWar.pdf (accessed 25 April 2008).

The Audre Lorde Project. (2003) "Open Letter to LGBTST Communities Opposing War" American Friends Service Committee (27 February), http://www.alp.org/whatwedo/statements/antiwar (accessed 7 September 2008).

BBC News. (2002) "War on Terror Cloaks Rights Abuses" (17 January), http://news.bbc.co.uk/1/hi/world/americas/1766038.stm (accessed 25 April 2008).

Bloodsworth-Lugo, Mary K., and Carmen R. Lugo-Lugo. (2005) "'The War on Terror' and Same-Sex Marriage: Narratives of Containment and the Shaping of U.S. Public Opinion," *Peace and Change*, 30:4, pp. 469–488.

Bush Administration, George W. (2002) National *Security Strategy of the United States of America* The White House (September), http://www.whitehouse.gov/nsc/nss.html (accessed 25 April 2008).

Etzold, Thomas H. and John L. Gaddis, eds. (1978) *Containment: Documents on American Policy and Strategy, 1945–1950*. New York: Columbia University Press.
Gay, William C. (1994) "The Prospect for a Nonviolent Model of National Security." In *On the Eve of the 21st Century: Perspectives of Russian and American Philosophers*. Edited by William C. Gay and T. A. Alekseeva. Lanham, M.D.: Rowman & Littlefield, pp. 119–134.
———. (2004) "Economic Democracy: The Final Frontier." In *Democracy and the Quest for Justice: Russian and American Perspectives*. Edited by William C. Gay and T. A. Alekseeva. Amsterdam: Rodopi, pp. 121–136.
———, and Michael Pearson. (1987) *The Nuclear Arms Race*. Chicago: American Library Association.
Holmes, Robert. (1989) "Terrorism and Violence: A Moral Perspective." In *War and Peace: Philosophical Inquirie*. Edited by Joseph C. Kunkel and Kenneth H. Klein. Wolfeboro, N.H.: Longwood Academic, pp. 115–127.
Kant, Immanuel. (1983) *Perpetual Peace and Other Essays*. Translated by Ted Humphrey. Indianapolis, Ind.: Hackett, 1983), p. 135.
Lakoff, George. (1991) "Metaphor and War: The Metaphor System Used to Justify War in the Gulf," *Peace Research*, 23, pp. 25–32.
LGBT Program. (2002) American Friends Service Committee, "A Statement Opposing the War form the LGBT Program," (8 November), http://www.afsc.org/lgbt/antiwar.htm (accessed 23 April 2008).
Lifton, Robert J. (1968) *Death in Life: Survivors of Hiroshima*. New York: Random, 1968).
Routley, Richard. (1984) "Metaphysical Fall-Out from the Nuclear Predicament," *Philosophy and Social Criticism*, 10:3–4 (Winter), pp. 19–34.
Scagliotti, John, Dan Hunt, Janet Baus, and Reid Williams. (2003) "Dangerous Living: Coming Out in the Developing World," After Stonewall Productions, http://www.afterstonewall.com/press.html#dl (accessed 23 April 2008).
Signorille, Michelangelo. (2001) "Hate Crimes: Like the Taliban, America's Middle East Allies, Tyrannize Gays, and Women," http://www.glas.org/ahbab/Articles/signor.htm (accessed 25 April 2008).
U.S. Department of State. (2007) "United Arab Emirates: Country Reports on Human Rights Practices–2006" (6 March), http://www.state.gov/g/drl/rls/hrrpt/2006/78865.htm (accessed 25 April 2008).

Chapter Three: Guerrero

Bah, Abu B. (2006) "Racial Profiling and the War On Terror: Changing Trends and Perspectives," *Ethnic Studies Review* (Summer 2006).
Boykin, Keith. (1996) *One More River to Cross: Black and Gay in America*. New York: Anchor/Doubleday.
Farrow, Kenyon. (2007) "Is Gay Marriage Anti-Black?" *ChickenBones: A Journal* (29 September), http://www.nathanielturner.com/isgaymarriageantiblack.htm (accessed 28 February 2008).
Hemphill, Essex. (1992) *Ceremonies*. San Francisco: Cleis Press.
Lustick, Ian S. (2006) *Trapped in the War on Terror*. Philadelphia: University of Pennsylvania Press.

McBride, Dwight. (2005) *Why I Hate Abercrombie and Fitch*. New York: New York University Press.

Chapter Four: Streamas

Adler, Margot. (2006) "Artist Botero Turns to Abu Ghraib in New Paintings," *NPR Weekend Edition* Saturday (11 November), http://www.npr.org/templates/story/story.php?storyId=6470129 (accessed 28 February 2008).
Adobe Creative Team. (2004) *Adobe Photoshop CS Classroom in a Book*. San Jose, Calif.: Adobe Systems.
Batchelor, David. (2000) *Chromophobia*. London: Reaktion.
Danner, Mark. (2004) *Torture and Truth: America, Abu Ghraib, and the War on Terror*. New York: New York Review of Books.
Davis, Mike. (2006) *Planet of Slums*. London: Verso.
Ebony, David, ed. (2006) *Botero: Abu Ghraib*. Munich: Prestel Verlag.
Gage, John. (1993) *Color and Culture: Practice and Meaning from Antiquity to Abstraction*. Berkeley: University of California.
Galeano, Eduardo. (2004) *Upside Down: A Primer for the Looking-Glass World*. New York: Picador.
Hersh, Seymour M. (2004) "The Gray Zone," *The New Yorker* (24 September).
Michaels, Walter Benn. (2006) *The Trouble With Diversity: How We Learned To Love Identity and Ignore Inequality*. New York: Metropolitan.
Scheper-Hughes, Nancy. (2002) "Coming to Our Senses: Anthropology and Genocide." In *Annihilating Difference: The Anthropology of Genocide*. Edited by Alexander Laban Hinton. Berkeley: University of California Press.
Simpson, David. (2004) "Theory in the Time of Death; Review of *After Theory*, by Terry Eagleton," *Critical Quarterly*, 48:1 (Spring), pp. 126–135.
Sontag, Susan. (2003) *Regarding the Pain of Others*. New York: Picador.
Sze, Julie. (2007) *Noxious New York: The Racial Politics of Urban Health and Environmental Justice*. Cambridge, Mass.: MIT Press.
Williams, Kristian. (2006) *American Methods: Torture and the Logic of Domination*. Boston: South End Press.

Chapter Five: King

Churchill, Ward. (2001) "Some People Push Back: On the Justice of Roosting Chickens," A supplement of *Dark Night Field Notes, Pockets of Resistance* 11 (12 September), http://www.ratical.org/ratville/CAH/WC091201.html (accessed 08 March 2008).
Doumani, Beshara. (2006) "Between Coercion and Privatization: Academic Freedom in the Twenty-First Century." In *Academic Freedom after September11*. Edited by Doumani. Cambridge: Zone Books, pp. 11–57.
D'Souza, Dinesh. (2006). *The Enemy at Home: The Cultural Left and Its Responsibility for 9/11*. New York: Random House.
Giroux, Henry A. (2004) "War on Terror: The Militarising of Public Space and Culture in the United States," *Third Text*, 18:4, pp. 211–221.
———. (2006) *Stormy Weather: Katrina and the Politics of Disposability*. Boulder, Colo.: Paradigm Publishers.

———, and Susan Searls Giroux. (2004) *Take Back Higher Education: Race, Youth, and the Crisis of Democracy in the Post-Civil Rights Era*. New York: Palgrave Macmillan.

Horowitz, David. (2004) *Unholy Alliance: Radical Islam and the American Left*. Washington, D.C.: Regnery Publishing.

Jackson, Richard. (2005) *Writing the War on Terrorism: Language, Politics, and Counter-Terrorism*. Manchester, UK: Manchester University Press.

Kaplan, Robert D. (2004) "Indian Country: America's Military Faces the Most Thankless Task in the History of Warfare." *Wall Street Journal* (25 September), http://opinionjournal.com/extra/?id=110005673 (accessed 10 March 2008).

Llorente, Marina A. (2002) "Civilization versus Barbarism." In *Collateral Language: A User's Guide to America's New War*. Edited by John Martin Collins and Ross Glover. New York: New York University Press, pp. 39–51.

Newman, Bob. (2005) "Ward Churchill: Treason in the Teepee," *MND*, http://www.mensnewsdaily.com/archive/m-n/newman/2005/newman020605.htm (accessed 29 February 2008).

O'Reilly, Bill. (2005) "What's Left for American Universities?" http://www.billoreilly.com (accessed 28 February 2005).

Owen, B. (2005) "Letter on Ward Churchill," http://www.thedenverchannel.com/4151452/detail.html (accessed 10 February 2005).

Paine, Jim. (2005) "The Imam of Indigenism," (13 February), http://www.pirateballerina.com/blog/entry.php?id=307 (accessed 28 February 2008).

Puar, Jasbir K., and Amit S. Rai. (2002) "Monster, Terrorist, Fag: The War on Terrorism and the Production of Docile Patriots," *Social Text*, 72, pp. 117–148.

Text of House Resolution on Churchill. (2005) Colorado House Joint Resolution 1011 (3 February), https://portfolio.du.edu/portfolio/getportfoliofile?uid=86996 (accessed 29 February 2008).

University of Colorado Department of Ethnic Studies. (2005) "An Open Letter from the Department of Ethnic Studies, University of Colorado at Boulder to the Board of Regents, Betsy Hoffman, and Phil DiStefano" (25 April), http://www.coloradopeace.org/2005/WardChurchill/UcbEthnicStudies-2005apr 25.html (accessed 10 March 2008).

Zieve, Sher. (2005) "Ward Churchill—Another Leftist Allowed to Promote Sedition and Treason" (10 February), http://web.archive.org/web/20060823155621re_/www.theconservativevoice.com/articles/article.html?storyid=2816 (accessed 20 March 2008).

Chapter Six: Lee

Bellavia, Timothy D. (2000) *We Are All the Same Inside*. New York: T.I.M.M.-E. Co.

Bernasconi, Robert. (2001) "The Invisibility of Racial Minorities in the Public Realm of Appearances." In *Race*. Malden, Mass.: Blackwell, pp. 284–299.

Carlson, Nancy L. (2002) *There's a Big, Beautiful World out There!* New York: Viking.

Fest, Joachim C. (1974) *Hitler*. New York: Harcourt Brace Jovanovich.

Foucault, Michel. (2003) *Society Must Be Defended: Lectures at the Collège De France, 1975–76*. Translated by Mauro Bertani, Alessandro Fontana, François Ewald, and David Macey. 1st ed. New York: Picador.

Hanson, Victor Davis. (2004) "A Return to Childhood, the New Immaturity." *National Review Online* (6 August), http://www.nationalreview.com/hanson/hanson 200408060837.asp. (accessed 12 August 2008).
H. Byron Masterson Elementary School (Kennett, Mo.). (2002) *September 12th: We Knew Everything Would Be All Right*. New York: Scholastic.
Jacobs, Gerard, and David Meyer. (2006) "Psychological First Aid: Clarifying the Concept." In *Psychological Interventions in Times of Crisis*. Edited by Laura Barbanel and Robert J. Sternberg. New York: Springer, pp. 57–71.
Jonell, Lynne. (2002) *Bravemole*. New York: G. P. Putnam's Sons.
Kant, Immanuel. (1996) "An Answer to the Question: What Is Enlightenment? (1784)." In *Practical Philosophy*. Edited by Mary J. Gregor. New York: Cambridge University Press, pp. 11–22.
MacLean, Christine Kole, and Mike Reed. (2002) *Even Firefighters Hug Their Moms*. New York: Dutton Children's Books.
Marsh, Carole. (2001) *The Here & Now Reproducible Book of the Day that Was Different: September 11, 2001: When Terrorists Attacked America*. Peachtree City, Ga.: Gallopade International.
Metropolitan Transportation Authority, 2007, http://www.mta.info/mta/security/index.html (accessed 1 September 2008).
Miller, J. Hillis. (2000) "Friedrich Schlegel and the Anti-Ekphrastic Tradition." In *Revenge of the Aesthetic: The Place of Literature in Theory Today*. Edited by Michael Clark. Berkeley: University of California Press., pp. 58–75.
Mitchell, W. J. T. (2002) "911: Criticism and Crisis," *Critical Inquiry*, 28, no. 2: pp. 567–572.
Osborne, Mary Pope, Steve Johnson, and Lou Fancher. (2002) *New York's Bravest*. 1st ed. New York: A. A. Knopf.
Poffenberger, Nancy M., and Val Gottesman. (2002) *September 11, 2001: A Simple Account for Children*. Cincinnati, Ohio.
Schmitt, Carl. (1976) *The Concept of the Political*. New Brunswick, N.J.: Rutgers University Press.
Schnurr, Rosina, and John Strachan. (2002) *Terrorism: The Only Way Is Through: A Child's Story*. Ottawa, Canada: Anisor Publishers.
Sedgwick, Eve Kosofsky. (1993) *Tendencies*, Series Q. Durham, N.C.: Duke University Press.
Shepard, Aaron. (2001) "What's Good for the Children's Book Business," Society of Children's Book Writers & Illustrators, http://www.scbwi.org/pubs/scbwi_pubs/shepherd/whats_good.htm (accessed 12 August 2008).
Sontag, Susan. (2001) "Talk of the Town." *The New Yorker* (September 24).
Sutherland, Shelley B. (2002) "Review of *There's a Big, Beautiful World out There!*" *School Library Journal*, http://www.schoollibraryjournal.com/ (accessed 20 June 2007).
Swanson, Susan Marie. (2002) "Trouble, Fly." In *This Place I Know: Poems of Comfort*, 1st ed. Edited by Georgia Heard. Cambridge, Mass.: Candlewick Press.
Wheeler, Jill C. (2002) *September 11, 2001: The Day That Changed America, War on Terrorism*. Edina, Minn.: Abdo.

Chapter Seven: Nicholls

Agamben, Giorgio. (2000) *Means without End: Notes on Politics.* Translated by Vincenzo Binetti and Cesare Casarino. Minneapolis: University of Minnesota Press.
———. (2004) "No to Bio-Political Tattooing," *Le Monde* (10 January), http://www.ratical.org/ratville/CAH/totalControl.html (accessed 29 February 2008).
———. (2005) *State of Exception.* Translated by Kevin Attell. Chicago, Ill.: University of Chicago Press.
Aguayo, Terry. (2006) "Padilla Pleads Not Guilty; Bail Is Denied," *The New York Times* (13 January), http://www.nytimes.com/2006/01/13/politics/13padilla.html (accessed 29 February 2008).
Amnesty International. (2005) "USA: Further Information on Incommunicado Detention/Detention without Charge/Legal Concern/Fear of Torture/Ill-Treatment: Jose Padilla (also known as Abdullah al-Mujahir)," *Amnesty International Library* (24 November) PUBLIC AI Index: AMR 51/190/2005, http://archive.amnesty.org/library/index/engamr511902005 (accessed 29 February 2008).
BBC (2006a) "Annan Backs UN Guantanamo Demand," BBC.co.uk (17 February), http://news.bbc.co.uk/go/pr/fr/-/1/hi/world/americas/4722534.stm (accessed 29 February 2008).
———. (2006b) "Guantánamo 'Damages Terror Fight,'" BBC.co.uk (23 February), http://news.bbc.co.uk/go/pr/fr/-/1/hi/uk_politics/4741780.stm (accessed 29 February 2008).
———. (2006c) "US denies terror suspect torture." BBC.co.uk (5 May), http://news.bbc.co.uk/go/pr/fr/-/2/hi/americas/4974852.stm (accessed 29 February 2008).
———. (2007) "Profile: Jose Padilla," BBC.co.uk (16 August), http://news.bbc.co.uk/1/hi/world/americas/2037444.stm (accessed 29 February 2008).
Beauvoir, Simone de. (1948) *The Ethics of Ambiguity.* Translated by Bernard Frechtman. New York: Citadel Press.
Blum, William. (2000) *Rogue State: A Guide to the World's Only Superpower.* Monroe, Maine: Common Courage Press.
Blumner, Robyn. (2007) "Habeas Corpus," *St. Petersburg Times* (4 March), http://www.sptimes.com/2007/03/04/News/Habeas_corpus.shtml (accessed 29 February 2008).
Butler, Judith. (2004) *Precarious Life: The Powers of Mourning and Violence.* London: Verso.
Elsea, Jennifer. (2001) "Terrorism and the Law of War: Trying Terrorists as War Criminals before Military Commissions," CRS Report for Congress (11 December) Congressional Research Service: The Library of Congress. Order Code RL31191.
Foucault, Michel. (2003) *"Society Must Be Defended": Lectures at the Collège de France, 1975–76.* Edited by Mauro Bertani and Alessandro Fontana. Translated by David Macey. New York: Picador.
Goodman, Amy. (2007) "How U.S. Interrogators Destroyed the Mind of Jose Padilla," *Alternet* (17 August), http://www.alternet.org/story/59958/?page=1 (accessed 29 February 2008).
Greenberg, Karen J., ed. (2006) *The Torture Debate in America.* New York: Cambridge University Press.
Henry, Ed and Barbara Starr. (2006) "Bush: 'I'm the Decider' on Rumsfeld," CNN.com (18 April), http://www.cnn.com/2006/POLITICS/04/18/rumsfeld/ (accessed 29 February 2008).

Works Cited

Hentoff, Nat. (2006) "The CIA's 'Black Sites,'" *The Village Voice* (24 February), http://www.villagevoice.com/news/0609,hentoff,72320,6.html (accessed 29 February 2008).

Human Rights First. (2003) "Cubans on Floating Truck Returned to Cuba by U.S.: U.S. Should Change Its Interdiction Practices," Human Rights First: Refugee Protection (28 July), http://www.humanrightsfirst.org/asylum/torchlight/newsletter/newslet_18.htm (accessed 29 February 2008).

Human Rights Watch. (2000) "U.S. Government Efforts to Undermine the International Criminal Court (ICC) Treaty," Human Rights Watch *Campaigns* (25 May), http://www.hrw.org/campaigns/icc/docs/news-hrw-statement.htm (accessed 29 February 2008).

———. (2002) "U.S. Circumvents Courts With Enemy Combatant Tag," *Human Rights News* (12 June), http://hrw.org/english/docs/2002/06/12/usdom4040.htm (accessed 29 February 2008).

———. (2003) "U.S. Again Uses Enemy Combatant Label to Deny Basic Rights," *Human Rights News* (23 June), http://hrw.org/english/docs/2003/06/23/usdom 6177.htm (accessed 29 February 2008).

Jacobs, Ron. (2004) "American Exceptionalism: A Disease of Conceit," *Counterpunch* (21 July), http://www.counterpunch.org/jacobs07212004.html (accessed 29 February 2008).

Karon, Tony. (2002) "The 'Dirty Bomb' Suspect: Lots of Questions, Few Answers," *Time* in partnership with CNN (11 June), http://www.time.com/time/nation/article/0,8599,261119,00.html (accessed 29 February 2008).

Kipling, Rudyard. (1899) "The White Man's Burden: The United States and The Philippine Islands," *McClure's Magazine* (February 1899).

Latour, Bruno. (2002) *War of the Worlds: What about Peace?* Edited by John Tresch, Translated by Charlotte Bigg. Chicago: Prickly Paradigm Press.

Military Advantage, "The Spanish-American War: The Splendid Little War." Military.com (2006), http://www.military.com/Resources/HistorySubmittedFileView?file=history_spanishamericanwar.htm (accessed 29 February 2008).

Office of the United Nations High Commissioner for Human Rights. (1949) "Geneva Convention Relative to the Treatment of Prisoners of War," (12 August), http://www.unhchr.ch/html/menu3/b/91.htm (accessed 29 February 2008).

Parker, John. (2003) "A Nation Apart," *The Economist* (6 November), http://economist.com/surveys/displayStory.cfm?story_id=2172066 (accessed 29 February 2008).

PBS.org. (2002) "Handling Haitian Refugees." *Online News Hour* (30 October), http://www.pbs.org/newshour/bb/international/july-dec02/haiti_10-30.html (accessed 29 February 2008).

Reynolds, Paul. (2005) "Defining torture in a New World War," BBC News (8 December), http://news.bbc.co.uk/go/pr/fr/-/1/hi/world/americas/4499528.stm (accessed 29 February 2008).

Scherer, Michael. (2006) "Will Bush and Gonzales Get Away with It?" (2 August), http://hrw.org/english/docs/2003/06/23/usdom6177.htm (accessed 29 February 2008); stable URL at Salon.com, http://www.salon.com/news/feature/2006/08/02/cronin/print.html (accessed 25 August 2006).

Tocqueville, Alexis de. (1945/1831) "Future Condition of Three Races–Part 7." Translated by Henry Reeve. In *Democracy in America*, vol. 1. Edited by Phillips Bradley, Henry Reeve, and Francis Bowen. New York: A. A. Knopf, pt. 7, chap. 18.

United States Supreme Court. (1942) *Ex Parte Quirin*, 317 U.S. 1, 63 S.Ct. 1, 87 L.Ed. 3.
USA Today. (2006) "'Decider' Bush Responsible for Rumsfeld—and the War." (19 April), http://www.usatoday.com/news/opinion/editorials/2006-04-19-rumsfeld_x.htm (accessed 29 February 2008).
Vagts, Detlev F. (2007) "Military Commissions: A Concise History," *The American Journal of International Law*, 101:1 (January), pp. 35–48.
Wasem, Ruth Ellen. (2005) "U.S. Immigration Policy on Haitian Migrants," CRS Report for Congress. Congressional Research Service: The Library of Congress, Order Code RS21349 (21 January).
Weaver, Robert C., Jr. (2006) "No Man's Land: Report from Guantánamo," *Commonweal* (6 October), pp. 9–11.
Wilson, Jamie. 2005 "Torture Claims 'Forced US to Cut Terror Charges,'" *The Guardian* (25 November), http://www.guardian.co.uk/print/0,3858,5341292-110878,00.html (accessed 29 February 2008).

Chapter Eight: Urban

Acuña, Rodolfo.(2005) "A Tolerance of Violence On the Border," *ZNet/Activism* (20 June), http://www.zmag.org/content/showarticle.cfm?ItemID=8123 (accessed 26 February 2008).
Akers, Justin. (2001) "Operation Gatekeeper: Militarizing the Border" *International Socialist Review*, 18 (June–July), http://www.isreview.org/issues/18/gatekeeper.shtml (accessed 7 May 2008).
Allen, Jennifer. (2003) *Justice on the Line: The Unequal Impacts of Border Enforcement in Arizona Border Communities*. Edited by Zoe Hammer-Tomizuka. Border Action Network, pp. 1–18, http://www.borderaction.org/PDFs/ justice_on_the_line.pdf (accessed 26 February 2008).
———. (2006) "Jury to AZ Border Vigilante: Guilty!" Press Release. Border Action Network, http://www.borderaction.org/press2.php?articleID=29 (accessed 26 February 2008).
American Civil Liberties Union. (2000) "The Rights of Immigrants—ACLU Position Paper" ACLU, http://www.aclu.org/immigrants/gen/11713pub20000908.html (accessed 26 February 2008).
———. (2004) *America's Disappeared: Seeking International Justice for Immigrants Detained after September 11*, http://www.aclu.org/FilesPDFs/un%20report.pdf (accessed 7 May 2008).
———. (2006a) "ACLU of Texas Shares United Nation's Concern about Increased Level of Militarization on Border," Press Release (28 July), http://www.aclu.org/intlhumanrights/gen/26274prs20060728.html (accessed 26 February 2008).
———. (2006b) *Dimming the Beacon of Freedom: U.S. Violations of the International Covenant on Civil and Political Rights*. U.N. Committee on Human Rights Concerning the International Covenant on Civil and Political Rights, http://www.aclu.org/pdfs/iccprreport20060620.pdf (accessed 26 February 2008).
American Friends Service Committee, and Witness and American Civil Liberties Union. (2005) *Rights on the Line Vigilantes at the Border*. Witness.
American Friends Service Committee and National Youth Advocacy Coalition. (2003) "Is Opposing the War an LGBT Issue?" In Gluckman, Kamel, and Hartman. *Militarized Zones*, pp. 33–38.

American Patrol. (2003) "Tancredo Introduces Immigration Moratorium Bill," http://www.americanpatrol.com/CONGRESS/TANCREDO/HR946 MoratoriumBill030301.html (accessed 26 February 2008).

Barnett, Jon. (2001) *The Meaning of Environmental Security*. London and New York: Zed Books.

Barsamian, David. (2001) "Immigration and Racism: An Interview with Miriam Ching Louie and Cathi Tactaquin," *Z Magazine/ZNet Online* (November), http://www.zmag.org/Zmag/articles/nov01barsamian.htm (accessed 26 February 2008).

Basham, W. Ralph. (2006) "Ask the White House," The White House (4 August), http://www.whitehouse.gov/ask/print/20060804.html (accessed 26 February 2008).

Bhattacharjee, Anannya. (1997) "The Public/Private Mirage." In *Feminist Genealogies, Colonial Legacies, Democratic Futures*. Edited by Jacqui Alexander and Chandra Mohanty. New York: Routledge, pp. 308–329.

Border Action Network. (2002) "What is Militarization?" Border Action Network (formerly SWARM Southwest Alliance to Resist Militarization), http://web.archive.org/web/20021122042320/http://www.resistmilitarization.org/whatis.htm (accessed 7 May 2008).

———. (2003) "JTF-6 and Militarization," Border Action Network (27 June), http://www.borderaction.org/campaigns3.php?articleID=33 (accessed 26 February 2008).

———. (2004a) *Environmental Protection on the Line. Untold Environmental Impacts of Arizona/Mexico Border Enforcement* pp. 1–26, http://www.borderaction.org/PDFs/environment_report.pdf (accessed 26 February 2008).

———. (2004b) "Low Intensity Conflict Along the Border," Border Action Network, http://www.borderaction.org/oldSite/lowintensity.html (accessed 25 February 2008).

———. (2007a) "Arizona Vigilante Violence on Trial—Final Day to Highlight Pattern of Violence," Border Action Network (23 February), http://www.borderaction.org/web/index.php?option=com_content&task=view&id=116&Itemid=27 (accessed 7 May 2008).

———. (2007b) "Civil Lawsuit Filed Against Vigilante Roger Barnett" Border Action Network, http://www.borderaction.org/campaigns3.php?articleID=56 (accessed 22 May 2008).

Buchanan, Susy. (2006) "Border Vigilante Ordered to Pay Damages on SPLC-Sponsored Suit" Southern Poverty Law Center, http://www.splcenter.org/intel/news/item.jsp?aid=93 (accessed 7 May 2008).

Bush, George W. (2002a) *The National Security Strategy of the United States of America*. The White House, Washington D.C., http://www.whitehouse.gov/nsc/nss.pdf (accessed 26 February 2008).

———. (2002b) *Securing the Homeland Strengthening the Nation*. The White House, Washington, D.C., http://www.whitehouse.gov/homeland/homeland_security_book.pdf (26 February 2008).

———. (2006a) "President Bush Addresses Nation on Immigration Reform," The White House, Washington, D.C. (15 May), http://www.whitehouse.gov/news/releases/2006/05/20060515-8.html (accessed 26 February 2008).

———. (2006b) "President's Address to the Nation," The White House, Washington D.C. (11 September), http://www.whitehouse.gov/news/releases/2006/09/20060911-3.html (accessed 26 February 2008).

———. (2006c) *The National Security Strategy of the United States of America*. The White House, Washington D.C. (March), http://www.whitehouse.gov/nsc/nss/2006/nss2006.pdf (accessed 26 February 2008).

Butts, Kent Hughes. (1999) "A Healthy World is a Safe World," *Forum for Applied Research and Public Policy*, 14, p. 117.

Chomsky, Aviva. (2007) *They Take our Jobs!: And 20 Other Myths about Immigration*. Boston, Mass.: Beacon

Clinton, William Jefferson. (1994) *Accepting the Immigration Challenge: The President's Report on Immigration*. Washington D.C.: U.S. Office of the President (For sale by the U.S. G.P.O., Supt. of Docs.; ISBN: 016045350X 9780160453502).

Department of Defense, United States. (2005) *The National Defense Strategy of the United States of America*. (March), http://www.comw.org/qdr/fulltext/0503nds.pdf (accessed 26 February 2008).

Department of Justice, INS. (1996) "Building a Comprehensive Southwest Border Enforcement Strategy." Washington D.C.: INS, Public Affairs, Federal Publication, Government Documents Collection, Depository Item (October), pp. 1–8.

Doty, Roxanne Lynn. (2001) "Desert Tracts: Statecraft in Remote Places," *Alternatives*, 26:4, pp. 523–543.

Dunn, Timothy. (2001) "Border Militarization via Drug and Immigration Enforcement," *Social Justice*, 28:2 (Summer), pp. 7–30.

Ehrlich, Paul. (1968) *The Population Bomb*. New York: Ballantine Books.

———, Anne Ehrlich, and Gretchen Daily. (1993) "Food Security, Population and the Environment," *Population and Development Review*, 19:1, pp. 1–32.

Eisenstein, Zillah. (2004) *Against Empire: Feminisms, Racism, and the West*. New York: Zed Books.

Fernandes, Deepa. (2007) *Targeted*. New York: Seven Stories Press.

Gaddis, John. (2002) "Grand Strategy of Transformation," *Foreign Policy*, 133 (Nov/Dec), pp. 50–57.

Gluckman, Ryn, Rachael Kamel, and Betsy Hartmann, eds. *Militarized Zones: Gender, Race, Immigration, Environment*, special issue, *Political Environments*, no. 10. Edited by Ryn Gluckman, Rachael Kamel, and Betsy Hartmann, http://popdev.hampshire.edu/projects/militarized_zones.pdf (accessed 26 February 2008).

Hammer-Tomizuka, Zoe. (2008) "Inventing Just Futures: Organizing for Human Rights in the Sonoran Desert," Presentation at Humboldt State University (7 February).

———, and Allen, Jennifer. (2002) *Hate or Heroism: Vigilantes on the Arizona-Mexico Border*. Edited by Sahee Kil, Patrisia Macias Rojas, and Bryn Jones. Border Action Network, http://www.borderaction.org/PDFs/vigilante_report.pdf (accessed 26 February 2008).

Hardin, Garrett. (1968) "The Tragedy of the Commons," Garrett Hardin Society, http://www.garretthardinsociety.org/articles/art_tragedy_of_the_commons.html (accessed 26 February 2008).

———. (1974) "Lifeboat Ethics," Garrett Hardin Society, http://www.garretthardinsociety.org/articles/art_lifeboat_ethics_case_against_helping_poor.html (accessed 26 February 2008).

———. (1999) *The Ostrich Factor*. New York: Oxford University Press.

———. (2003) "Garrett James Hardin Curriculum Vitae," Garrett Hardin Society, http://www.garretthardinsociety.org/gh/gh_cv.html (accessed 26 February 2008).

Hartmann, Betsy. (2006) "Why Population Control Undermines Human Rights," *Committee on Women, Population and the Environment*, http://cwpe.org/files/whypopcontrol.pdf (accessed 26 February 2008).
———. (2004) "Conserving Racism: The Greening of Hate at Home and Abroad," *Different Takes* 27 (Winter), http://popdev.hampshire.edu/projects/dt/pdfs/DifferenTakes_27.pdf (accessed 26 February 2008).
———. (1999) "Population, Environment, and Security: A New Trinity." In Silliman and Bhattacharjee. *Policing the National Body*, pp. 1–23.
———. (1995) *Reproductive Rights and Wrongs*. Cambridge, Mass.: South End Press.
Hayes, Helene. (2001) *U.S. Immigration Policy and the Undocumented*. Westport, Conn.: Praeger.
Homer-Dixon, Thomas. (1999) *Environment, Scarcity, and Violence*. Princeton, N.J.: Princeton University Press.
———. (1998) "Environmental Scarcities and Violent Conflict: Evidence from Cases." In *Green Planet Blues*. Edited by Ken Conca and Geoffrey Dabelko. Boulder, Colo.: Westview Press, pp. 287–297.
hooks, bell. (2000) *Feminism is for Everybody*. Cambridge, Mass.: South End Press.
Hyunhye Cho, Eunice (2003) "The New War on Immigrants." In Gluckman, Kamel, and Hartman. *Militarized Zone*, pp. 19–23.
Jhally, Sut. (1997) *bell hooks: Cultural Criticism and Transformation*. Video recording. Northampton, Mass.: Media Education Foundation.
———. (2002) *Edward Said: On "Orientalism,"* Video recording. Northampton, Mass.: Media Education Foundation.
Kirk, Gwyn, and Margo Okazawa-Rey, eds. (2007) *Women's Lives: Multicultural Perspectives*. New York: McGraw-Hill.
La Resistencia. (2001) "Deadly US Border Operations Strike Again 14 Die in Arizona Desert! Enough is Enough!" http://www.refuseandresist.org/imm/061601lares arizona.html (accessed 7 May 2008).
Lindsley, Syd. (2002) "The Gendered Assaults on Immigrants." In Silliman and Bhattacharjee. *Policing the National Body*, pp. 175–196.
———. (2000) "Gendered Assaults: The Attack on Immigrant Women," *Z Magazine*, ZNet Daily Commentaries, Sustainers (3 December), http://www.zmag.org/Sustainers/Content/2000-12/03lindsley.htm (accessed 26 February 2008).
Lynn, Richard. (2003) "Garrett Hardin, PhD—A Retrospective of his Work: Tribute to Garrett Hardin," Garret Hardin Society, http://www.garretthardinsociety.org/tributes/tr_lynn_2001.html (accessed 26 February 2008).
Martinez, Demetria. (1996) "Paranoia is Busy Protecting Our Borders" *National Catholic Reporter*, 34:15 (13 February).
Martinez, Elizabeth, and Arnoldo García. (2000) "What is 'Neo-Liberalism'? A Brief Definition," *Global Exchange* (26 February), http://www.globalexchange.org/campaigns/econ101/neoliberalDefined.html (accessed 26 February 2008).
"Migration: The Facts," (1998) *The New Internationalist*, 305, p. 19.
Milliken, Jennifer. (1999) "Intervention and Identity." In *Cultures of Insecurity*. Edited by Jutta Weldes, Mark Laffey, Hugh Gusterson, Raymond Duvall. Minneapolis: University of Minnesota Press, pp. 91–118.
Moses, Greg. (2005) "Vigilante Wedge," *ZMagazine*, ZNet (4 May), http://www.zmag.org/content/showarticle.cfm?ItemID=7783 (accessed 7 May 2007).

National Security Council. (1997) *A National Security Strategy for a New Century*. Washington D.C.: Government Printing Office (May), http://clinton2.nara.gov/WH/EOP/NSC/Strategy/ (accessed 26 February 2008).

Office of Homeland Security. (2002) *National Strategy for Homeland Security*. The White House, Washington D.C., http://www.whitehouse.gov/homeland/book/nat_strat_hls.pdf (accessed 26 February 2008).

Palafox, José. (1996) "Militarizing the Mexico-U.S. Border," *Covert Action Quarterly* (March).

Persaud, Randolph. (2002) "Situating Race in International Relations." In *Power, Postcolonialism, and International Relations: Reading Race, Gender, and Class*. Edited by Geeta Chowdhry and Sheila Nair. New York: Routledge, pp. 56–81.

Phares, Rebecca. (2000) "The US-Mexico Border: A Strategy of Low-Intensity Conflict, Interview with Maria Jimenez, Dir. Immigration Law Enforcement Monitoring Project of the American Friends Service Committee," *Social Justice*, 27:4 (Winter).

Prashad, Vijay. (2000) "The Hunt for Mexicans," *Z Magazine*, ZNet Daily Commentaries (16 July), http://www.zmag.org/sustainers/content/2000-07/16prashad.htm (accessed 26 February 2008).

President's Council on Sustainable Development. (1996) *Sustainable America: A New Consensus for Prosperity, Opportunity, and a Healthy Environment for the Future*, http://clinton2.nara.gov/PCSD/Publications/TF_Reports/amer-top.html (accessed 26 February 2008).

Ranch Rescue Arizona (2002) Website Home Page, Arizona Chapter, http://www.ranchrescue.com/arizona.htm (accessed 7 June 2002; Website since taken offline and not archived).

Roberts, Dorothy. (1998) *Killing the Black Body*. New York: Vintage.

Rutherford, Stephanie. (2005) "Constructing Global and National Nature: Population, Immigration and the Greenwashing of Racism and Misogyny," *Women and Environments International Magazine*, 68:9, pp. 20–21.

Seager, Joni (2003) "Introduction." In Gluckman, Kamel, and Hartmann. *Militarized Zones*, pp. 5–9.

Sferios, Emanuel. (1998) "Greentide: Population, Immigration, and the Environment: Eco-fascism and the Environmental Movement," *Z Magazine* ZNet (June), http://www.zmag.org/ZMag/articles/sferiosjune98.htm (accessed 26 February 2008).

Silliman, Jael, and Anannya Bhattacharjee, eds. (2002) *Policing the National Body*. Cambridge, Mass.: South End Press.

Silliman, Jael, and Ynestra King, eds. (1999) *Dangerous Intersections*. Cambridge, Mass.: South End Press.

Simcox, Chris (2005) "About Us," The Minuteman Civil Defense Corps, http://www.minutemanhq.com/hq/aboutus.php (accessed 26 February 2008).

Simcox, Chris. (2007) "Minuteman July 4th Operation a Success," The Minuteman Civil Defense Corps, http://www.minutemanhq.com/hq/article.php?sid=11 (accessed 26 February 2008).

Smith, Andrea. (2002) "Better Dead than Pregnant: The Colonization of Native Women's Reproductive Health." In Silliman and Bhattacharjee. *Policing the National Body*, pp. 123–146.

Works Cited 181

Southern Poverty Law Center. (2007) "New SPLC Report: Nation's Most Prominent Anti-Immigration Group has a History of Hate, Extremism," Southern Poverty Law Center *New @ the Center* (11 December), http://www.splcenter.org/news/item.jsp?aid=295 (accessed 26 February 2008).

———. (2006) "The Groups: In the World of 'Academic Racism,' Four Groups Play Leading Roles," Southern Poverty Law Center Intelligence Report (Summer), http://www.splcenter.org/intel/intelreport/article.jsp?sid=370 (accessed 7 May 2008).

Sullivan, Eileen, Associated Press. (2007) "Chertoff: Border Fence is Good for the Environment," *The Huffington Post* (1 October), http://www.huffingtonpost.com/2007/10/01/chertoff-border-fence-is_n_66705.html (accessed 26 February 2008).

Thomas, Gerald. (1997) "U.S. Environmental Security Policy: Broad Concern or Narrow Interests," *Journal of Environment and Development*, 6:4.

Urban, Jessica LeAnn. (2001) *Constructing Blame: Overpopulation, Environmental Security and International Relations*. Working Paper #273, Michigan: Women and International Development.

———. (2004) The Politics of "Blame:" Nation, Immigration, and Environmental Security in International Relations. PhD diss., Northern Arizona Univ.

———. (2007) "Interrogating Privilege/Challenging the 'Greening of Hate,'" *International Feminist Journal of Politics*, 9:2 (June), pp. 251–263.

———. (2008) *Nation, Immigration, and Environmental Security*. New York: Palgrave MacMillan.

U.S. Commission on National Security/21st Century. (2001) *Road Map for National Security: Imperative for Change* (February 15), http://govinfo.library.unt.edu/hnssg/PhaseIIIFR.pdf (accessed 26 February 2008).

U.S. Immigration and Naturalization Service. (1999) *Backgrounder: INS' Southwest Border Strategy*. Washington, D.C.: U.S. Department of Justice, Immigration and Naturalization Services.

West, Cornel. (2004) "Race Matters." In *Race, Class and Gender: An Anthology*. Edited by Margaret L. Anderson and Patricia Hill Collins. Belmont, Calif.: Wadsworth, pp. 121–126.

Willson, Brian. (1997) "The Slippery Slope: U.S. Military Moves into Mexico, Section III: Poverty and Misery in Mexico," *Global Exchange*, http://www.globalexchange.org/countries/americas/mexico/slope/index.html#top (accessed 7 May 2008).

Zinn, Howard. (2007) "Foreword." In Deepa Fernandes. *Targeted*. New York: Seven Stories Press, pp. 13–18.

Chapter Nine: Pacleb

Adamshick, Adam. (2005) "CIRCLE Working Paper 32: Social Representation in the U.S. Military Services," *CIRCLE* (9 May), http://www.civicyouth.org/PopUps/WorkingPapers/WP32Adamshik.pdf (accessed 4 June 2008).

Batalova, Jeanne, and Michael Fix. (2007) "DREAM Act: Basic Information," *National Immigration Law Center*, http://www.nilc.org/immlawpolicy/DREAM/dream_basic_info_0406.pdf (accessed4 June 2008).

Bloodsworth-Lugo, Mary K. and Carmen R. Lugo-Lugo. (2005) ""The War on Terror" and Same-Sex Marriage: Narratives of Containment and the Shaping of U.S. Public Opinion," *Peace and Change*, 30:4, PP. 469–488.
Bush, George W. (2002) Executive Order 13269 of July 3, 2002, *Federal Register* 67:130, p. 45287, http://www.immigration.com/newsletter1/expeditenatuarmy.pdf (accessed 4 June 2008).
Cabotaje, Michael A. (1999) "Equity Denied: Historical and Legal Analyses in Support of the Extension of U.S. Veterans' Benefits to Filipino World War II Veterans," *Asian Law Journal*, 6, pp. 67–97.
Castillo, Juan, and Bill Bishop. (2005) "Texas Hispanic Soldiers Dying at Higher Rate," *Austin American-Statesman* (27 February), http:www.statesman.com/metrostate/content/metro/stories/02/27wardead.html (accessed 4 June 2008).
Chan, Sucheng. (1991) *Asian Americans: An Interpretive History*. Boston: Twayne.
Coates, Kenneth S., and William R. Morrison. (1993 "Soldier-Workers: The U.S. Army Corps of Engineers and the Northwest Defense Projects, 1942–1946," *Pacific Historical Review*, 62:3, pp. 273–304.
Bush, George W. (2002) "Fact Sheet: Honoring Members of American's Armed Services." Office of the Press Secretary (4 July), http://www.whitehouse.gov/news/releases/2002/07/20020704.html (accessed 4 June 2008).
Fong, Timothy P. (2002) *The Contemporary Asian American Experience: Beyond the Model Minority*. 2nd ed. New Jersey: Prentice Hall.
Furumoto, Rosa. (2005) "No Poor Child Left Unrecruited: How NCLB Codifies and Perpetuate Urban School Militarism," *Equity & Excellence in Education*, 38, pp. 200–210.
Hattianagadi, Anita U., Aline O. Quester, Gary Lee, Diana S. Lien, Ian MacLeod, David L. Reese, and Robert Shuford. (2005) "Non-Citizens in Today's Military," CRM D0011092.A2/Final (April), http://www.cna.org/documents/D0011092.A2.pdf (accessed 4 June 2008).
Hisnanick, John J. (2003) "A Great Place to Start: The Role of Military Service on Human Capital Formation," *Labour*, 17:1, pp. 25–45.
"Hispanics in the Military," Fact Sheet (2003) Pew Hispanic Center (27 March), http://pewhispanic.org/files/reports/17.pdf (accessed 4 June 2008).
jsjkim (*sic*), 2006. "Anti-Recruitment Ad #3: Latino Soldiers." Video clip, http://www.youtube.com/watch?v=lPaWv9pewoE (accessed 4 June 2008).
Keating, Raymond J. (2003) "Immigrants Fight for U.S., Deserve Welcome," *Newsday* (8 April), http://www.latinamericanstudies.org/immigration/fight.htm (accessed 4 June 2008).
Kobach, Kris W. (2006) "The Senate Immigration Bill Rewards Lawbreaking: Why the DREAM Act is a Nightmare," *Backgrounder* published by The Heritage Foundation (14 August), http://www.heritage.org/Research/Immigration/upload/bg_1960.pdf (accessed 4 June 2008).
Lee, Margaret Mikyung, and Ruth Ellen Wasem. (2003) "Expedited Citizenship through Military Service: Policy and Issues." CRS Report for Congress (30 September), http://www.fas.org/sgp/crs/natsec/RL31884.pdf (accessed 4 June 2008).
Mariscal, Jorge. (2003) "Latinos on the Frontlines: Again," *Latino Studies*, 1, pp. 347–351.
———. (2004) "No Where Else to Go: Latino Youth and the Poverty Draft," *Marxist Thought Online* (November), http://www.politicalaffairs.net/article/articleview/295/1/36/ (accessed 4 June 2008).

Ong, Aihwa. (1996) "Cultural Citizenship as Subject-Making: Immigrants Negotiate Racial and Cultural Boundaries in the United States," *Current Anthropology*, 37:5, pp. 737–762.
Reyes, Raul. (2006) "Hispanic Recruiting: Double-Edged Sword," *USA Today* (3 March), http://www.hispanictips.com/2006/03/03/hispanic-recruiting-double-edged-sword/ (accessed 4 June 2008).
Riley, Michael. (2005) "Citizen Soldiers Immigrants' Sacrifices Honored Posthumously, Some Families are Pained by Calls for Border Crackdowns as Loved Ones are Dying for their Adopted Country," *Denver Post* (30 May), http://www.wkconline.org/resources/word/Riley-Citizen_Soldiers.doc (accessed 4 June 2008).
Thrupkaew, Noy. (2002) "The Myth of the Model Minority," *The American Prospect*, 13, http://www.totse.com/en/ego/literary_genius/modelmin.html (accessed 4 June 2008).

Chapter Ten: Gordillo

ARE Archivo de Relaciones Exteriores, Mexico City Fondo de Braceros: Contratación de Trabajadores Agrícolas en EU. *Departamento de Contrataciones.*
Akers, Justin, and Davis, Mike. (2006) *No One Is Illegal: Fighting Racism and State Violence on the U.S.-Mexico Border.* Chicago, Ill.: Heymarket Books.
Gutiérrez, David. (1995) *Walls and Mirrors: Mexican Americans, Mexican Immigrants, and the Politics of Ethnicity.* Berkeley, Los Angeles and London: University of California Press.
Hing, Bill Ong. (2004) *Defining America through Immigration Policy.* Philadelphia, Pa.: Temple University Press.
———. (2006) *Deporting Our Souls: Values, Morality and Immigration Policy.* Cambridge: Cambridge University Press.
Kopinak, Kathryn (1995) "Gender as a Vehicle for the Subordination of Women Maquiladora Workers in Mexico," *Latin American Perspectives*, 22:1 (Winter, 1995).
Massey, Douglas S., Jorge Durand, and Nolan J Malone. (2003) *Beyond Smoke and Mirrors: Mexican Immigration in an Era of Economic Integration.* New York: Russell Sage Foundation.
Mosher, Clayton, and Akins, Scott. (2007) *Drugs and Drug Policy: The Control of Consciousness Alteration.* Thousand Oaks, Calif.: Sage.
Sassen, Saskia. (1996) "US Immigration Policy Toward Mexico in a Global Economy." In *Between Two Worlds: Mexican Immigrants in the United States.* Edited by David Gutiérrez. Washington, Del.: A Scholarly Resources Inc. Imprint, 1996.
Valenciana, Christine. (2006) "Unconstitutional Deportation of Mexican Americans during the 1930s: A Family History and Oral History," *Multicultural Education*, 13:3 (Spring), pp. 4–9, http://wwweric.ed.gov/ERICDocs/data/ericdocs2sql/content_storage_01/0000019b/80/2b/48/ad.pdf (accessed 30 July 2008).

ABOUT THE AUTHORS

MARY K. BLOODSWORTH-LUGO, associate professor of comparative ethnic studies at Washington State University, has taught and published in the areas of race and ethnicity, gender and sexuality, embodiment/theories of the body, identity, popular culture, film, and contemporary continental political philosophy. Bloodsworth-Lugo is author of *In-Between Bodies: Sexual Difference, Race, and Sexuality* (2007), and her recent work on United States administrative rhetoric and "the War on Terror," with Carmen R. Lugo-Lugo, has appeared in *Peace & Change: A Journal of Peace Research, International Journal of Contemporary Sociology, Reconstruction: Studies in Contemporary Sociology*, and *Cultural Studies*. Their co-authored book, *Browned Bodies: Immigrants, Same-Sex Couples, and Terrorists after 9/11*, is in progress.

WILLIAM C. GAY, professor of philosophy at University of North Carolina at Charlotte, is editor of the Concerned Philosophers for Peace Special Series on "Philosophy of Peace" (with Rodopi's VIBS). He is past President and past Executive Director of Concerned Philosophers for Peace, and has published many articles and book chapters on issues of peace, justice, and nonviolence. His monographs and edited collections include *Capitalism with a Human Face: The Quest for a Middle Road in Russian Politics* (with T. A. Alekseeva, 1996); *On the Eve of the 21st Century: Perspectives of Russian and American Philosophers* (with T. A. Alekseeva, 1994); *The Nuclear Arms Race* (with Michael Pearson, 1987); and *Global Studies Encyclopedia* (with I. I. Mazour and A. N. Chumakov, 2003).

LUZ MARÍA GORDILLO, assistant professor of women's studies at Washington State University Vancouver, focuses on the historical processes of Mexican immigration between the United States and Mexico, emphasizing gender relations in the context of the immigrant experience. Her book, *Engendering Transnational Ties: Mexicanas and the Other Side of Immigration, 1942–2000*, is under contract with the University of Texas Press for inclusion in their prestigious series, Chicana Matters. Gordillo highlights social, cultural, and economic production by Mexicanas experiencing the migratory flow between a small town San Ignacio Cerro Gordo in Jalisco, Mexico, and Detroit, Michigan. Her most recent work focuses on the history of Mexicanas, Immigration Law, and ideas of National Security since 1942.

LISA GUERRERO, assistant professor of comparative ethnic studies at Washington State University, teaches and publishes in the areas of African American literature, black masculinity, African American popular culture, satire, and African American humor, and race, and commodity culture. She has published articles in several anthologies and journals. Her edited collection, *Teaching Race in the 21st Century: College Professors Talk about the Fears, Risks, and Rewards*, is forthcoming, as is her co-authored book with David J. Leonard, *African Americans in Television* (Praeger Publishing).

C. RICHARD KING, associate professor of comparative ethnic studies at Washington State University, has written extensively on the changing contours of race in post-Civil Rights America, the colonial legacies and postcolonial predicaments of American culture, and struggles over Indianness in public culture. His work has appeared in a variety of journals such as *American Indian Culture and Research Journal, Journal of Sport and Social Issues, Public Historian,* and *Qualitative Inquiry.* He is also the author/editor of several books, including *Team Spirits: The Native American Mascot Controversy* (a CHOICE 2001 Outstanding Academic Title), *Postcolonial America,* and *Visual Economies of/in Motion: Sport and Film.*

KYOO LEE, assistant professor of philosophy at John Jay College of Criminal Justice, City University of New York, writes in the intersecting fields of aesthetics, critical theory, cultural studies, gender studies, literary theory, post-phenomenology, and translation. Her academic essays have appeared in *Angelaki, The Comparatist, Encyclopedia of Nineteenth-Century Thought, How to Talk to Photography, Mythos and Logos, Parallax, Philosophical Writings, Poetry Review, SOAS Literary Review,* and *Social Identities.* At John Jay, she teaches, in addition to philosophy, interdisciplinary courses for the Justice Studies and Gender Studies programs.

CARMEN R. LUGO-LUGO, assistant professor of comparative ethnic studies at Washington State University, engages in research on Empire, the "War on Terror," and popular culture. She has co-authored (with Mary K. Bloodsworth-Lugo) several articles on the rhetoric behind the War on Terror and its link to discourse surrounding particular groups. She has published an article on the Puerto Rico/United States relationship and several articles on the representation of Latinos and other minoritized groups within the United States. Lugo-Lugo is currently revising a manuscript titled, *An Island of Coloniality: Women, Vieques, and The Invisibility of the Third World Commonwealth of Puerto Rico,* and co-writing (with Mary K. Bloodsworth-Lugo) a book titled, *Browned Bodies: Immigrants, Same-Sex Couples, and Terrorists after 9/11.*

TRACEY NICHOLLS, assistant professor of philosophy at Lewis University, and co-director of their Women's Studies Program, engages in teaching and scholarship around issues of power, oppression, marginalization, and social justice. She received her PhD from McGill University and held a postdoctoral appointment at the Centre de Recherche en Éthique de l'Université de Montréal. She writes and presents in the areas of aesthetics, feminist political philosophy, critical race theory, and decolonization. Her manuscript in preparation explores connections between improvised music and human rights. She argues that aesthetic pluralism and political pluralism are indispensable and mutually reinforcing commitments of a truly multicultural society.

JOCELYN A. PACLEB, assistant professor in the Ethnic and Women's Studies department at California State Polytechnic University Pomona, has taught Introduction to Ethnic Studies; Introduction to the Study of Women and Men in Society; Gender, Ethnicity, and Film: Filipina/o Americans; Ethnic Identity: Filipinos; Women in Global Perspectives; Ethnicity, Race, and Sexuality; and Asian American Contemporary Issues. Her research interests include Asian American studies, ethnic studies, Filipina/o Americans, militarism and militarized diasporas, gender, labor, immigration, and globalization.

JOHN STREAMAS, associate professor of comparative ethnic studies at Washington State University, teaches courses in introductory Ethnic Studies and Asian Pacific American Studies in addition to Asian Pacific American literature, culture and power, theories of race and ethnicity, Asian Pacific American women, and technologies of time and space. He has published stories, poems, journalism, and reviews. His book, *Japanese Americans and Cultures of Effacement*, is forthcoming from the University of Illinois Press. Currently, he is researching the cultural and political implications of time, space, and color.

JESSICA LEANN URBAN, assistant professor at Humboldt State University, teaches in the Women's Studies Program and the Multicultural Queer Program, as well as the Environment and Community Masters Program. She received her Ph.D. in Political Science from Northern Arizona University. Her research and teaching interests vary widely, but are grounded in an interrogation of interlocking systems of power, privilege, and oppression, in addition to a commitment to exploring and growing coalitional strategies for environmental, reproductive, and social justice. Some of her other writings include *Nation, Immigration and Environmental Security* (2008), and "Interrogating Privilege/Challenging the 'Greening of Hate'" in *International Feminist Journal of Politics*.

INDEX

Abu Ghraib prison, 3, 6, 19, 52, 53, 55–61, 63, 89, 91
academic life, 74
Accepting the Immigration Challenge (Clinton), 116
activism, 113, 132, 134, 135
Adamshick, Adam, 136, 141
affirmative action, 53, 137
Afghanistan, 7, 14, 33, 50, 60, 65, 93, 97, 98, 136, 137, 144
African American people, 43–45, 47, 48, 161
  gay A. A. people, 46
  A. A. high school completion rate, 142
  A. A. labor, 153
  A. A. military enlistees, 141
After Theory (Eagleton), 61
Agamben, Giorgio, 91–93, 98, 101
  State of Exception, 92
Agent Orange sprayings, 95
agribusiness, 131, 149
Akins, Scott, 161
al Qaeda, 9, 14, 19, 25, 27, 55, 101
Alberti, Leon Battista, 62
  On Painting, 62
Albright, Madeline, 127
Alexander, Michelle, 44
alien(s), the, 108
  a. enemies, 65
  extraterrestrial a., 85
  illegal a. (undocumented migrants), 103, 104, 126, 138, 140, 143, 159, 160
Allen, Jennifer, 126
allies, 2, 30–33, 97, 98, 133, 135, 139
al-Marri, Ali Saleh Kahlah, 98, 101
al-Mujahir, Abdullah. *See* Padilla, José
al-Sayeed, Darwyn, 81
America, 2, 3, 5, 6, 9, 13, 15, 18, 20, 21, 23, 24, 36, 40–45, 48, 49, 65, 68, 73, 75–82, 85–87, 89, 94–96, 100, 104, 110, 144, 161, 163. *See also* United States

Anglo-A., 5, 77, 78
Latin A., 105, 157, 158, 163
L. A. migration, 142, 155
United States-driven proxy wars in L. A., 114
American Border Patrol, 125
American Civil Liberties Union (ACLU), 107, 119, 120, 127
American Council of Trustees and Alumni, 68
American Dream, 136, 137, 142
American Eugenics Society, 111
American Patrol, 106, 114, 124, 125, 127, 128
Americanness, 2, 6, 10, 12, 104, 119, 133, 143
"Americans Don't Have Faith in Same-Sex Marriages, Poll Finds" (Wolfe), 16
Americans United to Preserve Marriage, 22
amnesia, historical, 163
amnesty, 160
anarchists, 65
animal rights activists, 65
"An Answer to the Question: What is Enlightenment?" (Kant), 76
anti-Asian sentiment, 153
anxieties, 66, 163
The Arab Mind (Patai), 60
Asian American people, 136, 137
asylum, political, 96, 97
"Attack Anniversary Is Living History Lesson" (Field), 86
atrocities, war, 137
Aubry, Larry, 45
  "Racial Profiling in Spotlight after 9/11," 45
Aziz, Mustafa, 146

Bah, Abu B., 45
Barletta, Louis J., 165
Barnett, Jon, 121
Barnett, Roger, 126, 127

Batchelor, David, 54, 55, 57–59
  Chromophobia, 54
Bauer, Gary, 23
BBC News, 34
Benjamin, Walter, 92
Bhattacharjee, Anannya, 107
Bildung, 5, 75, 76
Bildungsroman, 75
binarization, racialized, 77
biopolitics, 93
black special access program, 55
black(ness) (men of color)
black-and-whiteness, 54, 55, 57
blood, 56–59
blood purity laws, 54
Bloodsworth-Lugo, Mary K., 1, 9, 31, 32, 140
Blum, William, 95
bomb(ing)(s), 43, 44, 81, 100, 101
Boot, Max, 144, 145
Border Action Network, 120, 123–126, 128, 132–134
  Environmental Protection on the Line, 123
  Justice on the Line, 120
  Hate or Heroism, 125, 128
Border Industrialization Program (BIP), 155–158
Border Patrol, 103, 115, 118–120, 124, 125, 128, 151, 160, 163
Border Protection, Antiterrorism, Illegal Immigration Control Act of 2005 (H.R. 4437), 150
Border under Siege (Wilson), 161
Botero, Fernando, 52, 57–59
boundaries, 70
  American(ness) b., 6, 10, 104, 119, 124, 133, 140
  body b., 26
  flesh and site of torture, b. between, 59
  geographical b., 107
  identity b., 113
  ideological b., 107, 108, 139
  inclusive/exclusive, b. between, 85
Box, John, 154
Boykin, Keith, 47, 48

"Whose Dream," 47
Bracero Program, 7, 131, 149–158
Bravemole (Jonell), 83, 84
Broder, John, 122, 123
  "With Congress's Blessing, a Border Fence May Finally Push Through to the Sea" (Broder), 122, 123
bromides, self-congratulatory, 76
Brown, Lester, 109
brutalities, 55
Bull, Chris, 18
  Justice Served, 18
burden(s), 34, 40, 73, 90, 95, 97, 102
  Bush's b., 5, 89, 91, 93, 95, 102
  b. imposed on employers by Bracero Program, 156
  white man's b., 5, 73, 89, 90, 95, 97
bureaucratic formality, 78
Bush, George W., 2, 6–11, 14–24, 26, 27, 32, 33, 40, 49, 50, 60, 61, 76, 89–92, 95, 97, 100–102, 106, 120, 121, 127, 135, 138, 140, 150, 161. See also burden, Bush's
  B. administration, 1, 6, 10, 13, 17, 23, 25, 32, 33, 35, 36, 44, 49, 55, 61, 89, 91, 93, 95, 97–99, 101–105, 115, 117–125, 128, 129, 131, 133
Bush, George Herbert W., 95, 161
Butler, Judith, 10, 26, 90–93, 101
  Precarious Life, 90

Cairo 52, 30, 32, 33
California Legal Assistance Foundation, 162
Cambone, Stephen, 55, 60
Campus Watch, 69
capitalis(m)(ts), 9, 29, 87, 105, 129–131, 155, 157, 162, 164, 166
Carl Schmitt-Walter Benjamin debate, 92
Central American people, 107
Central Intelligence Agency (CIA), 98, 110
Chacón, Justin Akers, 151
Cheney, Lynn, 68
Cheney, Richard Bruce "Dick," 68
Chertoff, Michael, 123, 124, 128

Index 191

children, 21–24
  comfort for post-9/11 American c., 5, 75–78, 83–87
  c. of non-native military enlistees, 141
  c. of undocumented parents, 113, 126, 143, 158
    American citizen c. of u., 158
Chinese Exclusion Act of 1882, 103, 108, 153
Chomsky, Aviva, 105, 106, 108, 132
Chomsky, Noam, 13, 27
  Power and Terror, 27
Chretien, Jean, 15
chromophobia, 54
Chromophobia (Batchelor), 54
Churchill, Ward, 4, 5, 65–68, 70–73
  "Some People Push Back," 4, 66
citizen(ry)(s)(ship), 44, 97
  color, c. denied to people of, 108, 109
  denaturalization of c. for subversive activity, 155
  global c., 166
  Japanese-American c., 153
  jobs, immigrants "stealing" c.'s jobs 131
  Mexican-American c., 149
  Mexican immigrants, path to c. for, 160
  c. militias, 44, 124, 125, 127
  non-native/naturalized c., 141
  second-class c., 32
  soldiers, non-c., 135–139, 145–147
  c. of the state, 75
  terrorization of c. by their government, 30
  undesirable c., images of, 163, 165
  United States c., 1, 6, 7, 10, 16, 27, 39, 40, 41, 68, 70, 82, 85, 89–92, 99, 101, 105, 107, 108, 112, 117, 119, 135, 137, 140, 158, 164, 165
    color, U.S. c. of, 43
    evil, U.S. c. saved from evil by government, 36
    illegal drug use by U.S. c., 161
  worthiness of c. (good/bad), 139, 143, 144
Citizenship and Immigration Services (USCIS). *See* Immigration and Naturalization Service (INS)

civil liberties, 34, 36, 40, 44, 45, 91, 92, 102, 107
civil rights, 42, 43, 47, 48, 53, 153–155, 166
  c. r. movement, 126, 149
Civil Rights Act, 42
civil unions, 16, 20, 23, 39, 50
civilian-court prosecution, 100
civilization, 1, 4, 5, 20–22, 24, 65, 72, 73, 90, 99, 103, 106, 107
  c. discourse, 6, 7, 70, 103, 105, 106, 113, 120, 125
  c. security, 103–107, 109, 117, 119, 121, 123, 124, 129, 130, 133
  c. threats, 106, 132
  Western C., 27, 69, 71
classism, 105
Clinton, William Jefferson "Bill," 112
  Accepting the Immigration Challenge, 116
  C. administration/presidency, 6, 90, 99, 105, 110, 114, 118, 119, 121, 122, 128, 129, 133
  C.'s southwest border strategy, 115, 116
Cold War, 1, 12–14, 25, 29, 31, 32, 97, 155
  c. clichés, 71
  containment, C. W. definition of, 121
  c. discourse, 72
  post-C. W. era, 89, 90, 95
colonialism, 105, 122, 123, 130, 131, 134
  neocolonial war on terror, 73
  post-c. theroists, 90
  United States era of c., 104
colonization, 105, 113
color blindness, 83
color, 4, 42, 55, 62, 63, 80, 86, 87
  c. blindness, 83
  c.-blind racisim, 53
  c.-coded boundaries, 85
  communities/people of c., 3, 31, 34, 40, 48–50, 108, 109, 111, 136, 141, 146
  gay people of c., 41
  men of c., 42, 43, 50
  immigrants of c., 6, 104, 107, ,112, 119, 124, 127–130, 132
  female i. of c., 113, 117

color, *con't.*
  politicized c., 4, 52–54
  race/color hierarchy, 97
  c. of shame, 56–59
  social c. lines, 85
  c. of terror alerts, 43
comfort books, 5, 75, 77, 78–80, 86
communism, 13, 14, 97, 113
  anti-c., 12
confidence, nationalist, 78
conservatism, nationalist, 78
Constitution of Mexico, 129
Constitution of the United States, 1, 19, 78
  civil liberties, c. guarantee of, 44, 92, 100, 101
  free speech, c. guarantee of, 71
  same-sex marriage, proposals to amend against, 1, 20–23, 27, 49
  threat, c. manipulation to contain, 49
containment, 1–14, 25, 26, 29, 31, 57, 68–70, 73, 77, 89, 90, 96, 101, 121, 132, 133, 140, 163, 164, 166
  c. of American identity, 124, 12
  c. of black bodies/color, 39, 41, 44, 46, 47, 59–63
  c. of borders, 107, 113, 119, 129
  economic c., 166
  c. of enemy others, 104, 113, 118
  c. of immigrants, 137, 139, 145, 146
  c. of labor, 162
  c. of LGBT community, 31, 32
  c. of poor, 51–54
  c. of "them," 108
  c. of threat, 49
Copper Green program, 55
"At the Corner of Progress and Peril" (Fletcher), 42
corporatization, 69
Council on Foreign Relations, 144
Council on Sustainable Development, President's, 116
CounterPunch, 94
coyotes, 159
critical thinking, 66, 68, 69
Cuban refugees, 6, 89, 96, 97

Dahlvang, Rosalie, 20
Daniels, Gregory, 47
Danner, Mark, 52, 55, 56
D'arcy, Janice, 23
  "Voters Citing 'Moral values' Win it for Bush," 23
Davis, Mike, 51, 63
de Gortari, Salinas, 161
De Hart, Jane, 12, 13
de Tocqueville, Alexis, 94
death-in-life, ,52
Delay, Tom, 22, 23
DeLeon, Virginia, 22
  "Judge Says Gays May Wed," 22
  "Pastors in Region Gather to Denounce Gay Marriage" (with Zheng), 22
D'Emilio, John, 13
democracy, 11, 29, 42, 44, 69, 78, 90, 94–97, 99, 110, 129, 153
Democracy Matters (West), 42
demons, 42, 165
deportation, 107, 147
  d. of Mexican labor, 8, 150
  d. of illegal entrants from United States based on illegal liberties granted to Border Patrol, 163
  illegal d. of Mexican people during Great Depression, 149, 154
  threats of d., 159
de-subjectivation, 91
detention, 1, 49, 50, 62, 97
  Afghanistan, American d. practices in, 98
  arbitrary d., 107
  d. at Guantánamo Bay, 60
  indefinite d., 93, 98
  war-related d., 97
deterrence, 104, 114, 115, 118–122, 124, 125, 129, 132, 133, 163
development, 66
  cognitive d., 83
  sustainable d., 116
Development, Relief, and Education for Alien Minors Act (DREAM), 143, 144

Index

difference(s), 4, 33, 43, 44, 53–56, 61, 62, 70, 79, 93, 102
   class d., 137
   constructed d., 57
   containing d., 80
   ethnic d., 94
   political d., 57
dignity, 37, 57, 99, 126
diplomacy, 30
Dirty Thirty, 69
disappearance, 40
discourse of security/threat/LGBT issues, 1, 2, 5–10, 13, 17–21, 23, 27, 29, 66, 70, 72, 77, 78, 85, 87, 89, 90, 95, 99, 103–107, 118–120, 124, 125
   d. combined with environmental security (ES) issues, 104–106, 109, 111, 113, 116–118, 121, 123, 128, 133
   hegemonic d., 164, 165
disposability, 40, 152
dissent, 4, 5, 13, 30, 31, 65, 68, 69
distancing, 85
distrust, 40
diversity, 53, 54, 61, 137
doomsday scenarios, Neo-Malthusian, 6, 104, 123
Doty, Roxanne Lynn, 127
Doumani, Beshara, 69
Downing, William L., 22
drugs, illegal, 24, 44, 58, 118, 121, 129, 161
D'Souza, Dinesh, 68
due process, 90, 100
Dunn, Timothy, 129
Duvalier dictatorship, 96, 97
Duvalier, François, 96
Duvalier, Jean-Claude, 96

Eagleton, Terry, 61
   After Theory, 61
Ebony, David, 58
economy, 15, 49, 118, 131
   global e., 162
   market e., 29
   Mexican e., 156
      export-oriented e., 156

   United States e., 162
"Editing a Mask" (Adobe Creative Team), 4, 53
education, 13, 15, 49, 50, 66, 68, 69, 71, 75, 105, 112, 113, 141–144, 147
Ehrlich, Anne, 110
Ehrlich, Paul, 109, 110
Eisenstein, Zilla, 105
11 September 2001 era, post, 1–3, 5, 6, 8, 10, 11, 14, 17, 18, 25, 27, 29–36, 41–45, 66–69, 71, 73, 75–83, 85–87, 89, 90, 92–94, 96, 100, 104, 105, 107, 109, 117–120, 123–125, 135, 139, 150, 152, 163, 165
"11 States Pass Amendments Banning Same-Sex Marriage" (Wire Reports), 23
enem(ies)(y), 5, 7, 12, 14, 15, 18, 25, 40, 49, 65, 72, 77, 80, 82, 85, 91, 104, 113, 117, 119, 121, 124–126, 129, 134, 153
   e. combatants, 1, 6, 89, 93, 97, 98, 100, 101
   e.-creation process, 105, 106, 133
   gays/lesbians/blacks, e. status of, 41, 50, 65
   racialized e., 118, 123
   e. territory, 139
England, Lynndie, 56, 61
English, Emma, 126, 127
Enlightenment, German, 75
environmental activists (see if we have environment alone; put the environmental under that if possible)
Environmental Change and Security Program, 110
environmental degradation/destruction, 104, 109–111, 113, 116, 118, 119, 121, 123, 124, 128, 130
Environmental Protection on the Line (Border Action Network), 123
Environmental Security (ES) discourse, 104, 106, 109–113, 116–118, 121, 123, 128

"Episcopalians Wrestle with Issues of Gay Marriage, Bishop" (*The Spokesman-Review*), 16
equality, 49, 66, 87, 105, 106, 130–134, 137
espionage, 13, 97
Euro-American
   E.-A. corporations, 159
   E.-A. imagination, 164
   E.-A. labor, 153
   E.-A. media, 150
   E.-A. side of United States-Mexico Border, 157
   E.-A. youth, 161
Even Firefighters Hug Their Moms (MacLean and Reed), 83
evil(s), 10, 14, 33, 36, 70, 71, 80–82
   e. spirits, 21
Ex parte Quirin, 97, 98, 101
exceptionalism, 99
   American e., 94, 101, 102
   racialized e., 96
exclusion, 5, 18, 40, 80, 84, 107, 154, 157, 164
   inclusion-e., 78, 85
expansionism, territorial, 29
   Soviet e., 31

F.B.I. bad-boy list, 146
familial dislocations, 157
familialism, 85
family structures, 49
family values, 10, 13, 21, 25, 40, 49, 142
Farrow, Kenyon, 48
farsightedness, 36
fear, 2, 3, 6, 12, 24, 27, 30–32, 34–37, 39–41, 43, 44, 50, 60, 77, 80, 81, 83, 84, 86, 87, 95, 96, 103, 104, 107, 114, 120, 125–127, 159, 163, 165
Federation for American Immigration Reform (FAIR), 162
fenc(e)(ing), United States-Mexico border, 118, 122–124
Field, Monique, 86
   "Attack Anniversary Is Living History Lesson," 86

Fields, Sadie, 23
fifth column, 69
Filipino World War II verterans, 146
"500 Illegal Aliens Seized At Los Angeles Factory" (*The New York Times*), 159
Fletcher, Michael A., 42
   "At the Corner of Progress and Peril," 42
foreign aid, 32–34
foreigners, 34, 144
Foucault, Michel, 91, 93, 94, 95
Frank, JoAnn Lee, 145
free markets, 11, 110
free trade, 129, 130, 162
free trade zones, 156
freedom, 5, 61, 73, 77, 78, 81, 82, 87, 95, 107, 129
   academic f., 66, 69–71

G. I. Bill, 141
Gage, John, 62, 63
Galeano, Eduardo, 51, 63
Garibay, José Angel, 138, 139, 141, 147
Garibay, Simona, 138
Gatekeeper
Gay Pride Week, 17
gay rights, 47
"Gays Want to Ruin Marriage" (Roloff), 21
gay(ness)(s), 2, 3, 10, 15–19, 25–27, 29, 32, 34, 136
   Arab g. men, 33, 34
   black g. men, 39–41, 45–48
   g. enemy, 50
   white g. men, 48, 49
Gay, William C., 2, 3, 29
gender hierarchies, 74
Geneva Convention, 6, 55, 91, 97, 98, 100, 101
genocide, 62, 63, 99
Gilbert, James, 12
Giuliani, Rudolph, 51
globalization, 105, 113, 123, 129–134, 139
Goethe, Johann Wolfgang, 75
Goldsmith, Lord Peter Henry, 102
Goldwater Nichols Act of 1986, 110
Goldwater Range, Barry M., 124

Gonzales, Alberto, 91
good (versus evil)
Gordillo, Luz María, 7, 8, 149
Gore, Al, 110
governmentality, 91, 92
gray zones, 3, 4, 51, 53, 54, 57, 61, 62, 63
"The Gray Zone" (Hersh), 3, 52
Great Depression, 149, 152
Great Migration, 149
green card immigrants, 7, 135
green card solder(ing)(s), 7, 136–140, 144–147
Guantánamo Bay military prison, 60, 89, 91, 93, 98
Guerra, Carlo, 144
  "Will Iraq and Afghanistan Wars Produce a Thorny New Dilemma?" 144
Guerrero, Lisa, 3, 39
guest worker programs, 131, 153, 159

Habibullah, Abdool, 146
Haitian refugees, 6, 89, 96, 97, 100
Hardin, Garrett, 111, 112, 116, 117
  "Lifeboat Ethics," 116
  "The Tragedy of the Commons," 116
hate, 47, 53, 76, 81, 87, 104, 107, 111, 112, 113, 124, 127, 133
hate group(s), 112, 127
Hate or Heroism (Border Action Network), 125, 128
Hathaway, Alden, 16
"Heavy Breathing" (Hemphill), 39
hegemony, 121
  American h., 85, 105, 113, 122, 124, 130, 132–134
  regional h., 11
helplessness of prisoners, 57
Hemphill, Essex, 39, 40, 47, 50
  "Heavy Breathing," 39
  "The Tomb of Sorrow," 39
Hernandez, Ezequiel
Hersh, Seymour, 3, 4, 52, 53, 5, 60, 61, 63
  "The Gray Zone," 3, 52
heterosex(ism)(uality), 10, 12, 17, 18, 46, 48, 49, 83

Hing, Bill Ong, 156, 163
Hisnanick, John J., 141
Hitler's hate speech against Jews, 81
HIV/AIDS, 10, 14–17, 25, 42, 45
Hoge, Warren, 98
  "Investigators for U.N. Urge U.S. to Close Guantánamo," 98
home building, 78
homeland security. See security, homeland
Homeland Security, Department of (Agency), 115, 117
Homer-Dixon, Thomas, 110
homosexuality, 1, 10–16, 24, 26, 30, 45, 46. See also gay(ness)(s)
hooks, bell, 105
Hoover, Herbert, 149
hope, 9, 37, 73, 85, 87
Horowitz, David, 68, 69
hostiles, 4, 65, 66
"House Rejects Proposal to Ban Gay Marriages" (Simon), 22
"House, 218 to 212, Votes to Set Date for Iraq Pullout" (Zeleny), 50
House Un-American Activities Committee (HUAC), 14
HR 4437, 7, 135
Huerta-Cruz, Albert, 145, 147
human rights, 2, 3, 17, 30–37, 94, 96, 100, 106, 107, 119, 125, 127, 130–132, 160
Human Rights Watch, 98–100
humiliation, sexual, 55, 57, 58, 60,
Humphreys, Mose, 83, 84
Hussein, Saddam, 9, 14–17, 25, 27, 99

identity, 77, 108
  American i., 107, 109, 113, 124, 127, 161
  drug-dealer i., 161
  i. fraud, 98
  national i., 103, 104, 109, 112
  political i., 101
  racial i., 40, 41, 46, 80, 87
  self-i., 81
  sexual i., 14
illegal aliens, 103, 140, 159

Illegal Immigration Reform and Immigrant Responsibility Act (IIRIRA), 112
Illegal Worker Free County, 164
"The Imam of Indigenism," (Paine), 67
immigra(nts)(tion), 31, 34, 47, 103, 143
  anti-i. sentiment, 6, 7, 104, 106, 109–112, 114, 116, 119, 125, 127, 130, 131, 147, 161
  Asian i., 137, 153
  Chinese i., 153
  color, i. of, 6, 104, 107, 119, 124, 132
  containment of i., 145
  Cuban i., 97
  i. debates, 7, 137
  i. enforcement, 115, 118, 122
  environmental destruction by i., 118, 128, 132
  European i., 108
  i. forefathers, 159
  green card i., 7, 135
  illegal/undocumented i., 1, 7, 103–106, 111, 114, 116, 119, 121, 125, 128–132, 135, 144, 145, 151, 155, 158, 160, 162, 164, 165
  i. Latina i., 109, 112, 113
  Japanese i., 153
  i. labor, 158
  i. legislation/policy, 6, 89, 97, 103, 107–109, 111, 112, 114, 117, 118, 133, 140, 147, 163, 165
  Latin American i., 142, 155
  Mexican i., 7, 8, 131, 132, 149–155, 157–166
  military, i. in, 7, 137–141, 145, 146
  non-refugee i., 112
  population growth, i.-induced, 117
  pro-i. rallies, 135, 137
  racialized i. group, 137
  i. scapegoating, 131
  threat, i. perceived as, 123
  white supremacists, i. targets of, 127
Immigration Act of 1990, 146
Immigration Act(s) of 1921/1924, 108
Immigration and Naturalization Service (INS) (also Citizenship and Immigration Services [USCIS]), 96, 115, 125, 146
Immigration and Reform Control Act (IRCA), 159, 160
immunity from prosecution, 99
imperial(ism), 4, 9, 42, 73
  i. assumptions, 72
  conformity, i. culture of, 82
  cultural i., 48
  i. idioms, 70, 71
  United States i., 65, 90, 101, 102, 164
  i. war in Iraq, 49
  i. notions of white supremecy, 73
Imperial Beach, California, 122
incarceration, 93, 101
incivility, 5, 70
inclusion, 5, 66, 87
  i.-exclusion, 78, 85
Indianness, 5, 65–67
indigenism, 65, 67
indigenous nations in southwestern United States, 104, 108, 119
indignation, moral, 82
individualism, 74, 87
infantili(sm)(zation), 76–78, 85
  politicized other, infantile negation of, 87
  i. regression, 76
innocence, American, 86
inquiry, 66, 68, 69, 73
insurgency, 4, 55, 60
intelligence, secret, 4, 53, 55, 56, 101, 118, 161
  Central I. Agency (CIA), 98
International Covenant on Civil and Political Rights, 98
International Criminal Court (ICC), 6, 90, 99
International Gay and Lesbian Human Rights Commission, 35
International Monetary Fund (IMF), 105, 152
International Relations (IR), 104, 109, 121
internment camps, 153
interrogation, 41, 48, 55, 60, 74, 90, 91, 98, 99, 101, 105, 107, 134

Index 197

Intersectional Feminism, 105, 106, 110, 112, 113, 132–134
"Investigators for U.N. Urge U.S. to Close Guantánamo" (Hoge), 98
Iranian airplane shot by U.S. troops, 95
Iraq, 4, 14–16, 51, 65, 99
   Abu Ghraib prison in I., 3, 19, 52
   democracy, I. transition to, 95
   enemy combatants apprehended in I., 93, 97
   insurgency in I., 59, 60
   interrogation of I. prisoners, 55, 98
   occupation of I., 25, 73
   I. wars, 4, 7, 9, 18, 24, 31, 32, 49, 61, 94, 135–137, 142, 144, 163
   funding for I. w., 50
Islam(ists), 33, 93
   Christian-I. tradition, 36
   I. countries, 33
   destabilized I. regions, 65
   radical I., 68
   terrorism synonymous with I., 107
   I. terrorists, 66
"It's a White Man's World" (McBride), 45

Japanese immigration, 153, 159
Japanese Imperial Army, 55
   J. I. A. occupation of Philippine Islands, 146
Japanese imported labor, 152, 153
Jews, 47, 81
Jim Crow South, 93
jingoistic fervor, 43
Johnson, Lyndon Baines, 95
Joint Task Force-Six (JTF-6), 115, 119
Judeo-Christian-Islamic tradition, 36
"Judge Says Gays May Wed" (DeLeon), 22
justice, 7, 30, 31, 33, 37, 50, 52, 58, 62, 63, 67, 85, 99, 106, 108, 120, 126, 133, 135, 165
   j. vs. law, 92
Justice on the Line (Border Action Network), 120
"Justice Served" (Bull), 18

Kant, Immanuel, 37, 76

"An Answer to the Question: What is Enlightenment?" 76
Kaplan, Robert D., 65
Kennedy, Anthony M., 15
Kerry, John, 23
Khalilzad, Zalmay, 11, 12
King, C. Richard, 4, 5, 65
Kipling, Rudyard, 90, 95
knowledge, 131
   anti-i. groups, k. produced by, 106
   dispassionate, instrumental k., 74
   hegemony, k. produced in service of, 113, 134
   politic(ization)(s) of k., 66, 134
   privileged actors, k. produced by, 106
Ku Klux Klan (KKK), 47, 71, 163
Kuznick, Peter, 12

LaBarbera, Pete, 15
labor(ers). *See also* workers
   l. agreements between United States and Mexico, 7, 149
   agricultural l., 159
   Asian l., 152
   capital-l., relationship between, 157
   cheap l., 150, 159, 160
   containment of l., 162
   exploitation of l., 156
   international l., 165
   Japanese l, 153
   l. law, 123, 160
   l. markets, 128
   Mexican l., 7, 8, 129–131, 149–158, 162, 164, 165
   l. pool, 139, 145
   l. rights, 165
   undocumented l., 160
Latin A., 105, 157, 158, 163
   L. A. migration, 142, 155
   Latinos/as, 127, 140, 142, 143, 159
   United States-driven proxy wars in L. A., 114
Latour, Bruno, 102
Lautenberg, Frank, 21
Le Corbusier, 58, 59
leadership, 11, 27, 60, 77

Leahy, Patrick, 98
Lee, Kyoo, 5, 75
legislation (immigration and security), 7, 50, 68, 89, 113, 139, 140, 143, 149–151, 153, 155, 157, 158, 162, 163, 166
Lesbian, Gay, Bisexual, and Transgender (LGBT) community, 2, 29–35, 37
lesbians, 2, 10, 16–19, 25–27, 29, 32, 35, 39, 47, 49, 50, 136
Lesher, Michael, 15
"Let Illegal Immigrants Earn Citizenship in Military" (The PatriotLedger), 145
LGBT Peace Work Project, 37
"Lifeboat Ethics" (Hardin), 116
Lindsley, Syd, 112
litany statements, 111
literature
　children's comfort l., 5, 77, 78
　environmental security l., 121
　maquiladora l., 157
Living Dangerously (After Stonewall Productions), 29
Lord, Leslie B., 146
Low Intensity Conflict (LIC) Doctrine, 103, 114, 115, 119, 120, 124, 126, 127, 132, 133
Low Intensity Warfare, 114, 120, 132
loyalty oath, 68

Mahdi Army, 51
"Make Friends not Fences" (Moran), 123
Malthusian logic, 111
maquila(dora)(dorizing)(s), 130, 156–158
marginalization, 35, 40, 51, 73, 93, 147, 158, 164
marijuana, 161
Mariscal, Jorge, 142, 143
marriage, same-sex, 1–3, 9–11, 13, 15–27, 33, 39–41, 45, 47–50, 140
　amendments banning same-sex m., 1, 19–23, 49
Marriage Protection Amendment, 17
"Marriage Protection Week Draws Reaction from Gays" (*The Spokesman Review*), 17

"Married Gay Couple Denied U.S. Entry as Family" (*The Spokesman Review*), 17
Marsalis, Wynton, 54, 56
masculinity, 45, 108
　black m., 3, 39, 40
　m. for black gay men, 46
Mayo, Wayne, 164
McBride, Dwight, 45–47
　"It's a White Man's World," 45
　Why I Hate Abercrombie and Fitch, 45
McCain, John S., 102
McCarran Internal Security Act, 155
McCarthy, Joseph, 13
　M. era, 12
McCarthy, Richard T., 144, 145
McVeigh, Timothy, 44
Means without End (Agamben), 91
media, 1, 4, 7, 17, 20, 23, 43, 56, 59, 66, 67, 69, 76, 106, 111, 124, 137, 139, 140, 149, 159, 163, 164
　digitalized m., 78
　international m., 34, 150
　legislation, relationship to m., 164
　neoconservative m., 70
Meissner, Doris, 115
memory, selective, 150
Mexico, 35, 109
　anti-M. legislation, 155
　anti-M. sentiment, 127, 163
　communities, M. transnational, 152
　M. constitution, 129
　drug smuggling from M., 161
　M. economy, 156
　M. government, 152, 157
　M. image, 150, 157
　M. immigra(nts)(tion), 7, 8, 108, 113, 130, 132, 149, 150–154, 157–166
　politics of M. i., 158
　injustice committed by United States against M., 165
　M. labor (workers), 150–160, 162, 164, 166
　M. labor agreements with United States, 7, 149, 153, 154
　labor law in M., 158

Mexico, *con't.*
  migration, domestic within M., 151
  M. people, 103, 108, 119, 129, 129, 132, 139, 140
  M. American people, 149, 153, 154
  illegal/undocumented M. nationals, undocumented, 151, 157, 158, 160, 162, 163
  illegal drugs, M. association with, 161
  organized crime, M. associated with, 161
  M. peasants, 152
  soldiers, M. immigrant, 138, 139
  M. Reparation, 149
  United States-M. border, 6, 8, 103–107, 111, 113–115, 117–120, 122, 124, 127, 129, 130, 132, 133, 150, 155, 156, 160–164
  militarization of U.S.-M. b., 6, 103, 105, 106, 113, 114, 117–120, 123, 124, 126, 127, 129–134, 150, 160
  United States, M. relations with, 105
  M. viseconsul, 154
Michaels, Walter Benn, 53
migraphobia, 8, 151, 158, 164
Migration Policy Institute, 143
military advertisement campaigns, 142
military-environmental-security complex, 110
Miller, Geoffrey, 60
minority myth, 136, 137
Minuteman Civil Defense Corps (Minute Man Project), 114, 125, 126, 128, 163
"Missouri Says No to Gay Marriage" (Thomma), 22
mob psychology, 82
mobility, 130, 141, 165
moral values, 2, 19, 23
Morales, Angelique, 126 127
Morales, Arturo, 126
Morales, Ronald, 126
Morales, Vanese, 126
morality, 49, 82, 104
Moran, Chris, 123

"Make Friends not Fences," 123
Mosher, Clayton, 161
Movimiento Estudiantil Chicano de Aztlan (MeCHA) separatists, 65
Mrozek, Donald, 13
Munley, James M., 165
Muslims, 44, 47, 57, 71, 80, 81, 82, 84, 93, 107

narrative(s), 5, 19, 77, 78, 83, 84, 86, 137, 140, 141
Nation, Immigration, and Environmental Security (Urban), 105
National Defense Authoritarian Act (NDAA), 138
National May Day for Marriage, 22
National Security/21st Century, United States Commission on (USCNS/21), 117
National Security Act, 117
National Strategy for Homeland Security (NSHS or NSS) (White House), 36, 95, 107, 110, 116–118, 121, 122, 129
  "Border and Transportation Security" section of NSHS, 118
nationali(m)(sts), 75, 82, 126
  American n., 82, 164
  n.conservatism, 78
  Mexican n., 154
"A Nation Apart" (Parker), 95
nationhood, 113
nativist groups, 149, 151
Naturalization Act of 1790, 108
negation, 3, 39, 41, 44, 87
neoconservative backlash, 66
neo-liberalism, 105
Neo-Malthusian, theory, 104, 110, 111
  N.-M. claims of overpopulation, 128
  N.-M. doomsday scenarios, 104, 123
Neuman, Bob, 67
"A New Kind of War" (Rumsfeld), 25
New York's Bravest (Osborne), 83, 84
Nicholls, Tracey, 5, 6, 89
nigger(ization)(s)
Nixon, Richard Milhous, 95

noncitizens, legal, 136–138
nonviolence, 31
normativity, 78
North American Free Trade Agreement (NAFTA), 113, 118, 122, 129–131, 152, 158, 160–162, 166
nuclear weapons, 36

Obama, Barack, 102
Oklahoma City Bomber, 44
On Painting (Alberti), 62
Ong, Aihwa, 139
"Open Letter to LGBTST Communities Opposing the War" (The Audre Lorde Project), 30
Operation Blockade, 162
Operation Gatekeeper, 6, 150, 162, 166
Operation Hold the Line, 115, 162
Operation Rio Grande, 115, 162
Operation Safeguard, 115, 162
oppositions, binary, 86, 159
oppression, 66, 99, 105, 107, 129, 131, 133, 134, 164
order, 5, 59, 66, 89, 102
   judicial o., 92
   moral o., 70
   new world o., 90, 95
O'Reilly, Bill, 67
organizations, 65, 147
   citizen-based o., 36
   environmental o., 110, 111, 122
   human rights o., 37
   non-governmental o. (NGOs), 106, 110
   political o., 68, 143
   private o., 163
   religious o., 34
   student o., 143
   terrorist o., 36
Other, the, 5, 89, 95, 108
   inferior O., 104
   intra-American O., 78
   self/Other, boundary between, 107
   threat, O. as, 109, 125
outcasting, 85
overpopulation, 6, 104, 110, 116, 128, 163
Owens, William Forrester "Bill," 67

Pacleb, Jocelyn, 7, 135
Padilla, José (aka Abdullah al-Mujahir), 90, 100, 101
Paine, Jim, 65, 66
pan-nationalizing, 85
paramilitar(ies)(y) groups, 6, 114, 119, 124–128, 131, 133, 163
paranoia, collective, 8, 87, 150, 152, 153, 155, 159, 162
Parker, John, 95
   "A Nation Apart," 95
past and present, blurring of, 65, 70, 96
"Pastors in Region Gather to Denounce Gay Marriage" (Zheng and DeLeon), 22
Patai, Raphael, 60
   The Arab Mind, 60
Patten, Wendy, 98
peace, 9, 11, 37, 95, 102
   p. crimes, 63
pentagon doctrine, 51
persecution, 34, 76, 83, 96, 100, 114, 154
Personal Responsibility and Work Opportunity Reconciliation Act (Welfare Reform), 105, 112
Pioneer Fund, 112
polic(ies)(y), United States, 1, 134
   asylum p., 96, 97
   border p., 103, 114–116, 120, 124, 125, 127
   Bush administration p., 30, 49, 76, 98, 105, 119
      habeas corpus, B. a. p. on, 98
      torture, B. a. p. on, 99
   p. debates, 36, 41
   deterence p., 104, 114, 115, 118–122, 124, 125, 129, 132, 133, 163
   domestic p., 31, 165
   economic p., 105
   federal Indian p., 62
   foreign p., 11, 19, 90, 95, 102, 165
   globalization p., 123, 133
   immigration p., 6, 8, 89, 107–109, 111–113, 128, 133, 157, 159, 163–165

polic(ies)(y), United States, *con't.*
  paternalistic p., 43
  post-2001 p., 3, 10, 29
  preemption p., 133
  repressive p., 31
  security p., 107, 117, 121
  welfare p., 112, 113
politicization of knowledge, 66
politics, 4, 52, 53, 55, 108
  affect and trauma, p. of, 78
  biop., 93
  color, p. of, 58, 59
  containment, p. of, 5
  genocide, p. of., 62
  high p., 110
  homosexuality, p. of, 26
  immigration, p. of, 158
  movement, p. of, 165
  representation, p. of, 113, 134
  respectability, p. of, 47
"The Politics of Homosexuality" (Sullivan), 26
poor, the, 31, 34, 50, 51, 63, 104, 111, 113, 136, 141, 160
population control, 13, 111, 113, 116, 128
Population-Environment Balance, 110–112
population growth, 104, 109, 111, 116, 117, 130
pornography, gay, 45, 47
Post Traumatic Stress Disorder, 126
poverty, 51, 52, 104, 109, 110, 129, 137, 157
power, 90, 91, 94, 105, 107, 121, 129, 131, 133, 134
  abuse of p., 120
  constructed p., 26, 27, 137
  containment of p., 90, 95, 100, 139
  executive/sovereign p., 5, 6, 89, 92, 96, 101
  Foucaultian technology of p., 93
  governmental p., 91, 92, 96
  institutional p., 103, 104
  marginalized people barred from centers of p., 51
  personal p., 92
  privileged few, power of, 137
  rule of law, relationship to p. of, 92
  self-conferred p., 102
  United States p., 5, 11, 30, 89, 91, 95, 97, 100, 153
  webs of p., 139, 140, 146, 147
  whiteness, p. of, 59
Power and Terror (Chomsky), 27
Precarious Life (Butler), 90
prevention, 43
prisoner of war status, 93
prisoner abuse, 1, 3, 6, 19, 51–53, 55–60, 63
prisoners of war, 6, 89, 97
Proposition 187, California, 112, 113
Proposition 200, Arizona, 112, 113
propriety, 66, 71
prosperity, 11
protagonist(s), 75, 80
protection, 10, 43, 81, 91, 92
  constitutional law, p. of, 100
  environmental p., 124, 133
  Geneva Convention p., 55, 98
  humanitarian law, p. of, 100
  human rights, p. of, 37
  labor, p. of, 165
  marriage, p. of, 16, 17, 20, 22, 23
  parental p., 85
  treaty p., outside, 99
Providing Appropriate Tools Required to Intercept and Obstruct Terrorism (PATRIOT) Act of 2001, 68, 163
psychic numbing, 35
psychological first aid, 86, 87
public opinion, 1, 9, 18, 20, 25, 103, 104, 107, 140
race, 1, 5, 37, 41, 43, 45–48, 66, 72, 81, 82, 85, 86, 89, 90, 94, 97, 111, 132, 136, 137, 139, 141, 145, 146
racial imaginary, 3, 39
racialization, 62, 71, 80
"Racial Profiling in Spotlight after 9/11" (Aubry), 45
racism, 1, 31, 37, 45, 47, 48, 52–54, 72, 77, 82, 85, 93–96, 104, 105, 108, 111, 126–128, 131, 133, 147, 152–154, 159, 162–164, 166
  r. rhetoric, 72, 73, 77
Ranch Rescue, 106, 111, 114, 124–126, 128

Reconstruction, 93
red line(s), 4, 53, 54, 57, 60, 61
reflex(ivity), 61, 77, 78, 80, 87
Refugee Convention, 1951, 96
  R. C. 1967 Protocol, 100
refugees, 34
  Cuban and Haitian r., 6, 89, 96, 97, 100
  differential treatment of r., 100
  economic r., 97
  international law on r., 97
regression, infantile, 96
religion, 41, 42, 52, 82
  religiously-identified populations, 93
Reparation, Mexican, 149
residency, permanent, 109, 143, 158, 160
restrictionist attitudes, 165
reunification, 150, 155, 158
Reyes, Sylvester, 161
Rice, Condoleezza, 99
Rios, Sandy, 17, 21, 25
Robinson, Gene, 16
Roloff, Betty, 21
  "Gays Want to Ruin Marriage," 21
Romantic writers, 75
Roosevelt, Franklin Delano, 97, 101, 146, 149
rule of law, 11, 91, 92, 98
Rumsfeld, Donald, 25, 55, 60
  "A New Kind of War," 25

Sadr City, 51, 63
Saito, Natsu, 72
same-sex couples, 1, 15, 16, 18, 20, 22, 23, 26, 50
same-sex marriage. *See* marriage, same-sex
Santorum, Rick, 21
Saudia Arabia, 33
  A.-Americans, 93
  A. codes, flouting, 57
  A.-"looking," 40, 44, 80
  A. people, 60, 81, 84, 107
  A. gay men, 34
  A. terrorist network, 81
    non-A. terrorists, 165
scapegoat(s)(ing), 40, 56, 107, 111, 1131, 128, 130–133, 152, 161

Scheper-Hughes, Nancy, 62, 63
Schiller, Friedrich, 75
Schmitt, Carl, 92
  Schmittian sovereign subjects, 80
schoolteachers, American, 86
Schwarzenegger, Arnold, 125, 128
Seager, Joni, 132
Secure Border Initiative (SBI), 115, 118–120
security, 50, 107, 108, 138
  border s., 1, 107, 117, 118, 125
  civilizational s., 6. 7. 103–109, 120, 121, 123, 132, 133
  s. discourse, 103, 104, 107, 109, 113, 118, 124, 125
  Egyptian national s., 33
  s. enemies, 113
  environmental s., 6, 103, 104, 109–111, 113, 116, 117, 119, 121, 123, 124, 128, 129, 132, 133
  government s. forces, 124, 125
  high tech s., 76
  homeland s., 14, 20, 21, 23, 107, 117, 121, 123
  home/o-land s., 45
  insecurity, 6, 103, 113, 116, 130–134, 165
  Internal S. Act, 155
  military-environmental-s.-complex, 110
  National S. Act, 117
  national s., United States, 1–3, 6, 7, 10, 11, 13, 19, 21, 27, 31, 34–36, 45, 86, 89, 91, 92, 95, 100, 101, 103, 106–110, 116–119, 121, 123–127, 146, 149, 150, 163, 165, 166
  s. paranoia, 87
  social s., 131, 132
  State Emergency S. Court, 33
  s. threats, 6
self-assessments, American, 94
self-contradiction, 61, 77
self-identity, 81
September 11, 2001: A Simple Account for Children (Poffenberger and Gottesman), 77

September 11, 2001: The Day that Changed America (Wheeler), 77
sexism, 48, 105, 111, 126, 128, 131, 133
  heteros., 48
sexual abuses, 52, 57, 58, 60, 157
sexual gratification/pleasure, deviant, 46
sexual relations, same-sex, 15, 16
shame, 45, 47, 56, 58, 60
Sierra Club, 110, 162
Signorille, Michelangelo, 32, 33
Simcox, Chris, 114, 125, 126, 128
Simon, Richard, 22
  "House Rejects Proposal to Ban Gay Marriages," 22
Simpson, David, 61
Sino-Soviet expansion, 12
slavery, 47, 93, 108
Sleeper Cell, 81
"Small Group Can't Redefine Marriage" (anonymous), 20
Smuggler's Gulch, 122, 123
social construction s., 103, 104, 149, 150
society, 22, 63, 102, 139, 146
  American s., 12, 13, 21, 23, 26, 27, 42, 49, 113, 121, 140, 144, 147, 149, 150, 158–165
  black s., 42
  discriminatory s., 94
  fragmentation of s., 93
  global s., 9
  raceless s., 71, 87
  superior s., 94
  white s., 48
sodomy laws, 18
solidarity, 43, 87
"Some People Push Back" (Churchill), 4, 66
Sontag, Susan, 56, 57, 76
Southern Poverty Law Center, 112, 126, 127
Southwest Border Strategy, 6, 114–116, 130
sovereignty, 6, 89–92, 96, 103, 108, 126
  Schmittian s., 80
Soviet Union, 12, 29, 95
Special Agricultural Workers (SAW), 160
Spencer, Glenn, 125, 127
squeegee men, 51

Stark, Michael, 15
State Emergency Security Court, 33
State of Exception (Agamben), 92
State of the Union Address 2003, 14, 15, 20, 21, 24
stereotyp(es)(ing), 41, 42, 113
  immigrant s., 130, 160, 161, 164
  racial s., 56
Strategic Environmental Research and Development Program (SERDP), 110
Streamas, John, 3, 4, 51
Structural Adjustment Policies (SAPs), 152
Students for Academic Freedom, 69
subjectivity, 46, 47
subtextualization, 78
Sullivan, Andrew, 26
  "The Politics of Homosexuality," 26
superiority, 54, 94
superpatriotism, 85
Supplemental Security Income (SSI), 112
Surviving Militarism, Racism, and Repression (American Friends Service Committee), 37
Swanson, Susan Marie, 84
  "Trouble, Fly," 84
Sze, Julie, 51, 63

terror(ism)(ists), 1–10, 14, 15, 17–21, 23–27, 29–37, 39–50, 54, 55, 59, 61, 65–73, 76–79, 81, 83, 85, 87, 89–91, 93, 95, 98–100, 102–106, 107, 117–119, 121–125, 128, 135, 137–140, 143–147, 149, 150, 160, 163, 165
Terrorism: The Only Way Is through a Child'e Story (Schnurr and Strachen), 77, 79
Third World, 51, 104, 111, 118, 131
Thomma, Steven, 22
  "Missouri Says No to Gay Marriage," 22
threat, 1–3, 6, 9, 11–14, 17–21, 24, 26, 27, 31–36, 39–50, 65, 71, 73, 79, 85, 89–93, 100–104, 106, 108–110, 112, 118, 119, 121–127, 131, 132, 150, 154, 159, 163, 165

Ting, Jan, 97
"The Tomb of Sorrow" (Hemphill), 39
torture, 30, 33, 51, 55–57, 59–61, 63, 91, 98, 99, 101
"The Tragedy of the Commons" (Hardin), 116
trash, 51–55, 62, 63, 73, 128
trauma, 5, 71, 77, 78, 85, 126
triumphantalism, 87
"Trouble, Fly" (Swanson), 84
Truman, Harry S., 13, 151
Turf, Luke, 125
Tusant, John, 22

unconscious, political, 87
United Arab Emirates (UAE), 33, 34
United States Commission on National Security for the 21st Century (USCNS/21 2001), 117
Urban, Jessica LeAnn, 6, 103
   Nation, Immigration, and Environmental Security, 105
us/them (with/against us), 1, 25, 48, 80, 90, 91, 94, 108, 121, 123, 140
"U.S. Sees HIV Cases Rise among Gay, Bisexual Men" (Wetzstein), 15

values, 67, 71, 78, 95, 98, 99, 163
   democratic v., 11, 94
   family v., 10, 13, 21, 25, 40, 49, 142
   Hispanic v., 142
   human rights v., 94
   moral v., 2, 19, 23
Vejar, Jesus Romo, 126
Vietnam War, 95
vigilante(s), 119, 124–127, 151, 163
violence, 3, 27, 30–32, 35, 36, 40, 42, 43, 47, 48, 52, 59, 62, 69, 90, 92, 99, 106, 107, 110, 113, 119, 120, 125–127, 131–134, 151
visas, 155, 157, 158
   H2A/H2B v., 159, 160
"Voters Citing 'Moral values' Win it for Bush" (D'arcy), 23

"Ward Churchill—Another Leftist Allowed to Promote Sedition and Treason" (Zieve), 67
War on Terror(ism), 1–7, 9–11, 13–15, 17, 19, 21, 23–27, 29–35, 37, 40–43, 45, 49, 50, 54, 55, 59, 61, 65, 66, 68–71, 73, 89–91, 93, 95, 99, 122, 124, 125, 135, 137–140, 143–145, 147, 165
waste, 51, 63, 123
We Are All the Same Inside (Bellavia), 84–86
Weaver, Robert, 98
Welfare Reform. *See* Personal Responsibility and Work Opportunity Reconciliation Act (Welfare Reform)
West, Cornel, 41, 42, 78, 113
   Democracy Matters, 42
Westernization, 90
wet foot, dry foot policy, 96
wetback, 7, 149, 160
Wetzstein, Cheryl, 15
   "U.S. Sees HIV Cases Rise among Gay, Bisexual Men," 15
white reflexivity, 77, 80
white supremacy(ists)(y), 47, 73, 105, 112, 127, 130, 166
whiteness, 44, 48, 49, 53–55, 57, 59, 85, 108, 109
"Whose Dream" (Boykin), 47
Why I Hate Abercrombie and Fitch (McBride), 45
Williams, Kristian, 51, 52, 59
"Will Iraq and Afghanistan Wars Produce a Thorny New Dilemma?" (Guerra), 144
Wilson, Pete, 161
   Border under Siege, 161
"With Congress's Blessing, a Border Fence May Finally Push Through to the Sea" (Broder), 122, 123

Wolfe, Alan, 16
 "Americans Don't Have Faith in Same-Sex Marriages, Poll Finds," 16
workers, 137. *See also* labor(ers)
 agricultural w., 149, 159
 American w., 152, 158
 Asian w., 152
 illegal/undocumented w., 107, 112, 130, 132, 151, 156, 157, 160
 maquila w., 157
 Mexican w., 149, 152, 154, 155, 157, 159, 160, 162, 166
 soldiers as w. for the state, 140
World Bank (WB), 105, 152
World War II, 9, 13, 98, 146, 149, 153

xenophobia, 27, 43, 66, 104–106, 109, 124–128, 131, 133, 134, 136, 145, 147, 153, 155, 160, 163–166

Zeleny, Jeff, 50
 "House, 218 to 212, Votes to Set Date for Iraq Pullout," 50

Zheng, Yuxing, 22
 "Pastors in Region Gather to Denounce Gay Marriage" (with DeLeon), 22

VIBS

The **Value Inquiry Book Series** is co-sponsored by:

Adler School of Professional Psychology
American Indian Philosophy Association
American Maritain Association
American Society for Value Inquiry
Association for Process Philosophy of Education
Canadian Society for Philosophical Practice
Center for Bioethics, University of Turku
Center for Professional and Applied Ethics, University of North Carolina at Charlotte
Central European Pragmatist Forum
Centre for Applied Ethics, Hong Kong Baptist University
Centre for Cultural Research, Aarhus University
Centre for Professional Ethics, University of Central Lancashire
Centre for the Study of Philosophy and Religion, University College of Cape Breton
Centro de Estudos em Filosofia Americana, Brazil
College of Education and Allied Professions, Bowling Green State University
College of Liberal Arts, Rochester Institute of Technology
Concerned Philosophers for Peace
Conference of Philosophical Societies
Department of Moral and Social Philosophy, University of Helsinki
Gannon University
Gilson Society
Haitian Studies Association
Ikeda University
Institute of Philosophy of the High Council of Scientific Research, Spain
International Academy of Philosophy of the Principality of Liechtenstein
International Association of Bioethics
International Center for the Arts, Humanities, and Value Inquiry
International Society for Universal Dialogue
Natural Law Society
Philosophical Society of Finland
Philosophy Born of Struggle Association
Philosophy Seminar, University of Mainz
Pragmatism Archive at The Oklahoma State University
R.S. Hartman Institute for Formal and Applied Axiology
Research Institute, Lakeridge Health Corporation
Russian Philosophical Society
Society for Existential Analysis
Society for Iberian and Latin-American Thought
Society for the Philosophic Study of Genocide and the Holocaust
Unit for Research in Cognitive Neuroscience, Autonomous University of Barcelona
Yves R. Simon Institute

Titles Published

Volumes 1 - 163 see www.rodopi.nl

164. Nancy Nyquist Potter, Editor, *Putting Peace into Practice: Evaluating Policy on Local and Global Levels.* A volume in **Philosophy of Peace**

165. Matti Häyry, Tuija Takala, and Peter Herissone-Kelly, Editors, *Bioethics and Social Reality.* A volume in **Values in Bioethics**

166. Maureen Sie, *Justifying Blame: Why Free Will Matters and Why it Does Not.* A volume in **Studies in Applied Ethics**

167. Leszek Koczanowicz and Beth J. Singer, Editors, *Democracy and the Post-Totalitarian Experience.* A volume in **Studies in Pragmatism and Values**

168. Michael W. Riley, *Plato's* Cratylus: *Argument, Form, and Structure.* A volume in **Studies in the History of Western Philosophy**

169. Leon Pomeroy, *The New Science of Axiological Psychology.* Edited by Rem B. Edwards. A volume in **Hartman Institute Axiology Studies**

170. Eric Wolf Fried, *Inwardness and Morality*

171. Sami Pihlstrom, *Pragmatic Moral Realism: A Transcendental Defense.* A volume in Studies in **Pragmatism and Values**

172. Charles C. Hinkley II, *Moral Conflicts of Organ Retrieval: A Case for Constructive Pluralism.* A volume in **Values in Bioethics**

173. Gábor Forrai and George Kampis, Editors, *Intentionality: Past and Future.* A volume in **Cognitive Science**

174. Dixie Lee Harris, *Encounters in My Travels: Thoughts Along the Way.* A volume in **Lived Values:Valued Lives**

175. Lynda Burns, Editor, *Feminist Alliances.* A volume in **Philosophy and Women**

176. George Allan and Malcolm D. Evans, *A Different Three Rs for Education.* A volume in **Philosophy of Education**

177. Robert A. Delfino, Editor, *What are We to Understand Gracia to Mean?: Realist Challenges to Metaphysical Neutralism*. A volume in **Gilson Studies**

178. Constantin V. Ponomareff and Kenneth A. Bryson, *The Curve of the Sacred: An Exploration of Human Spirituality*. A volume in **Philosophy and Religion**

179. John Ryder, Gert Rüdiger Wegmarshaus, Editors, *Education for a Democratic Society: Central European Pragmatist Forum, Volume Three*. A volume in **Studies in Pragmatism and Values**

180. Florencia Luna, *Bioethics and Vulnerability: A Latin American View*. A volume in **Values in Bioethics**

181. John Kultgen and Mary Lenzi, Editors, *Problems for Democracy*. A volume in **Philosophy of Peace**

182. David Boersema and Katy Gray Brown, Editors, *Spiritual and Political Dimensions of Nonviolence and Peace*. A volume in **Philosophy of Peace**

183. Daniel P. Thero, *Understanding Moral Weakness*. A volume in **Studies in the History of Western Philosophy**

184. Scott Gelfand and John R. Shook, Editors, *Ectogenesis: Artificial Womb Technology and the Future of Human Reproduction*. A volume in **Values in Bioethics**

185. Piotr Jaroszyński, *Science in Culture*. A volume in **Gilson Studies**

186. Matti Häyry, Tuija Takala, Peter Herissone-Kelly, Editors, *Ethics in Biomedical Research: International Perspectives*. A volume in **Values in Bioethics**

187. Michael Krausz, *Interpretation and Transformation: Explorations in Art and the Self*. A volume in **Interpretation and Translation**

188. Gail M. Presbey, Editor, *Philosophical Perspectives on the "War on Terrorism."* A volume in **Philosophy of Peace**

189. María Luisa Femenías, Amy A. Oliver, Editors, *Feminist Philosophy in Latin America and Spain*. A volume in **Philosophy in Latin America**

190. Oscar Vilarroya and Francesc Forn I Argimon, Editors, *Social Brain Matters: Stances on the Neurobiology of Social Cognition*. A volume in **Cognitive Science**

191. Eugenio Garin, *History of Italian Philosophy*. Translated from Italian and Edited by Giorgio Pinton. A volume in **Values in Italian Philosophy**

192. Michael Taylor, Helmut Schreier, and Paulo Ghiraldelli, Jr., Editors, *Pragmatism, Education, and Children: International Philosophical Perspectives*. A volume in **Pragmatism and Values**

193. Brendan Sweetman, *The Vision of Gabriel Marcel: Epistemology, Human Person, the Transcendent*. A volume in **Philosophy and Religion**

194. Danielle Poe and Eddy Souffrant, Editors, *Parceling the Globe: Philosophical Explorations in Globalization, Global Behavior, and Peace*. A volume in **Philosophy of Peace**

195. Josef Šmajs, *Evolutionary Ontology: Reclaiming the Value of Nature by Transforming Culture*. A volume in **Central-European Value Studies**

196. Giuseppe Vicari, *Beyond Conceptual Dualism: Ontology of Consciousness, Mental Causation, and Holism in John R. Searle's Philosophy of Mind*. A volume in **Cognitive Science**

197. Avi Sagi, *Tradition vs. Traditionalism: Contemporary Perspectives in Jewish Thought*. Translated from Hebrew by Batya Stein. A volume in **Philosophy and Religion**

198. Randall E. Osborne and Paul Kriese, Editors, *Global Community: Global Security*. A volume in **Studies in Jurisprudence**

199. Craig Clifford, *Learned Ignorance in the Medicine Bow Mountains: A Reflection on Intellectual Prejudice*. A volume in **Lived Values: Valued Lives**

200. Mark Letteri, *Heidegger and the Question of Psychology: Zollikon and Beyond*. A volume in **Philosophy and Psychology**

201. Carmen R. Lugo-Lugo and Mary K. Bloodsworth-Lugo, Editors, *A New Kind of Containment: "The War on Terror," Race, and Sexuality*. A volume in **Philosophy of Peace**